Misadventures in My High Heels

MISADVENTURES

in My *High Heels*

WALKING THROUGH LIFE'S UPS, DOWNS, AND SILVER LININGS

LISA RAMELOW

CONTENTS

FOREWORD

I have a friend named John Tillman.

I met him in a Rolling Stones fan club called the "Shidoobees." People in this group are avid fans of the Stones, and will travel to other cities to see them perform.

The group has a local get-together the night before each concert. That is where I met John, at one of these get-togethers, in Los Angeles before a concert.

He is an easy person to like and get along with, and interesting too. I have to say he is the very first Christmas tree farmer I have ever met (he lives in Washington state). He told me all about his travels for concerts and motor sports, and about his adoring wife, who doesn't mind his constant travels to see and do the things he loves. In fact, she acts as his travel agent and sets things up for him.

I invited him to become my Facebook friend, as I do to almost everyone I meet at these gatherings. That proved to be quite fortuitous, because through John's wonderful writings and sharing about his life, I have learned so much about him. His writing provides a window into his soul and I am excited every time he posts something new to share.

I was particularly moved by his post on his birthday. I read it, and then reread it several times. My God, it was perfect. He stated exactly how I felt and all I could think was, "I couldn't have written it any better myself." In fact, I was actually a bit jealous that I had NOT written it.

But no one could state it better.

Thank you to my friend John Tillman, for letting me make your brilliant writing the foreword in my new book.

Your friend, Lisa

BY JOHN TILLMAN

So today I turn 65 years old, and I couldn't be happier about it. Here's why:

The only way to get smarter is to get older. I don't mean smarter like it's really easy to figure out "how many shingles it will take to roof your house" kind of smarter.

I mean, smarter in how to be a good human. How to find the positive in almost any situation—that kind of smarter.

I have an appreciation for my family that can only come with age. They are truly my inspiration.

I have an appreciation for my friends that I could not have had when I was younger, because I've lost so many.

I have an appreciation for other people's success that I could not have had when I was younger, because I was solely focused on my own.

I have an appreciation for the opportunities that I have today, not everybody makes it to 65.

It seems that almost everything I thought that would make me happy when I was younger, is not what makes me happy now.

I now realize that all of my struggles in life were simply molding me to become the person that I wish I had always been, but I couldn't have been, without those struggles. It's kind of a conundrum.

So, anybody going through struggles, you're simply being molded to come out at a place, at some point, that is magical. Way down deep you're happy. You didn't know you could be this happy. But you are. Those struggles, the things that are weighing you down daily right now will be overcome, if you never quit trying.

When you get there, you will have one simple purpose. To tell others that their struggles can be overcome, that they are being molded, to continue the cycle, if they never quit trying. Now my happiness is found simply by making other people happy. To share my experience, To see them smile. To see them laugh.

So, I am super stoked to be 65 years old, still trying to figure out what I wanna be when I grow up. The adventure is far better than the destination.

I love you all. You truly make my world bigger than I ever thought it could be."

INTRODUCTION

Watching others survive difficulties, and seeing how they coped with challenges, may be the strongest motivator to create a meaningful life.

This book is a collection of stories that, in and of itself, illustrates an unspoken pathway from hardships, to fully celebrating life. I think stories provide more inspiration than a roadmap or steps. That feeling of, "if that person could do it, then so can I," is the most powerful inspiration of all.

We all have stories to tell, and those experiences shape us into who we become. I hope my stories will encourage and inspire people to live their very best lives. To see and understand that any person can move on from disappointment and tragedy. And to look for ways to find other directions in life in which to go, and to be part of adding to other people's lives.

A LITTLE ABOUT ME

I DID THINGS IN A DIFFERENT ORDER

In my life, I did things out of order; I somehow reordered the way in which most people experience the phases of their lives.

When I was in my 20's, I used to say I was a "40-year-old woman in a 20-year-old body." I didn't go to parties or clubs. I worked six days a week, and on my day off, I liked to sew and crochet. I didn't go out with friends; my coworkers were my friends. I was introverted and introspective, and didn't mind all the time to myself, or just being with my future-husband-at-the-time, Walt. It was all I wanted.

My mother was really worried about me. She found it strange that I rarely ventured from my apartment. She even had her friend's daughter call me up and ask if I wanted to go out and have a beer. A beer? I couldn't stand the stuff. No thank you.

In my 30's I was busy being a mother to my children, Ryan and Hannah; it was the only thing I always knew I wanted to be.

After 33, I was busy being a widow. And a year or so later, I was busy being a fledgling new business owner.

At some point in my 40's, I began to look for more "fun" in my life. My kids were now older and fairly self-sufficient.

3

In my 50's, I got even more "out there." I started walking in dog parades dressed as Gumby while my dog came along as Pokey, wearing crazy feather dresses, and rappelling off buildings dressed as Marilyn Monroe. The rappel adventure was my first fundraising experience; I did it to help the Special Olympics organization.

Also at some point, I finally discovered how beautiful shoes could be! Boy, was I late in figuring that out!! I was always a late bloomer I guess.

So . . . some of the things I do may not seem "age-appropriate."

I didn't think of myself as a boring person, exactly, but I began to realize it was OK to expand past my introverted nature, and take some chances. I tried many new opportunities that before I would have thought were "not me." Then I began to look for, and even search out, brand new challenges.

And I learned the difference between "normal" and "average."

"Average" is just how most people might do things. But, you are still "normal" even if you do things a bit differently. I'm good with that. Maybe what I do is just "Lisa normal." I'm just doing it all in a different order than most do.

MY FRIEND MICHELE (WITH ONE "L")

I spent my first ten years in Southern California, in what was called a "bedroom community," a new housing tract created on the outskirts of a big city. It was called Gardena.

I lived on Daphne Avenue. Almost every house had children, and every single house had a big front lawn. We rode our bikes and played outside after school. I was the number two child; so I have an older sister named Julie, and a younger sister named Teresa. And of course my brother, Fred.

My friend Michele (with one "l") lived across the street. We quickly became best friends. We were so proud that our birthdays were two days apart; she was Nov. 12th and I was Nov. 14th. I always said I knew her since we were "zero". We liked to do all the same things and we were very loyal to each other and our friendship.

We went to kindergarten together; Mrs. Bliss was our teacher. Michele was always so good in class. I wasn't. If you were "bad," you had to stay in during recess. I was bad on purpose, because I loved staying inside the classroom. I didn't want to go out and run around; I wanted to play quietly alone with the blocks . . . early signs of my true nature, because I still like to be indoors, and quietly solve problems and puzzles.

I am an introvert.

After school was out, all the kids on the block liked coming over to my house.

My mother was so creative, fun, and loud. She made up all kinds of games, and children were drawn to her. She let us make bread-and-butter sandwiches whenever we wanted, and we could watch as many cartoons as we liked. She was the mom who everyone loved to be around because she was full of love, extroverted, and hugged every person she came in contact with—there was never a dull moment, as she came up with one new game after another.

For me, the excitement was fun for a while, but as an introvert, I needed a lot of down time after so much craziness every day. Plus, our house was always cluttered and disorganized.

Michele's household across the street was very different from mine. I loved going there. It was very quiet and peaceful, and I felt very calm from the moment I entered. It was completely neat and tidy. Everything was perfectly put away. There was a grandfather clock that never stopped ticking, and it rang out every hour. It was so exact; I would stand there and wait for it to clang. I loved it.

Michele's mother, Liz, served us healthy snacks while we watched "Father Knows Best." I was fascinated with how much their home seemed just like the Andersons' home on TV.

And I just loved Liz. She was always working on dinner while we played and watched TV. Sometimes she would make salmon. My mother never made salmon, I wasn't even sure what it was, but it was so pretty that it didn't look like real food to me.

When Michele's father came home, Liz would say, "How was your day dear? Dinner will be ready soon." I found this fascinating and would stare every time. My parents never spoke calmly like that. They started fighting from the minute my father got home. That was just the way they communicated—they liked "hollering" at each other. It was too loud for me.

The wonderful thing about my mother was she never minded how much time I spent at Michele's house. She understood me and how I needed that quiet time.

When we were six years old, Michele's father got transferred. I was devastated. They moved only an hour's drive away, but to me, as a little girl, it seemed like she was moving across the country. However, in the years that followed, our mothers did a very special thing: they kept us close by having us go to each other's house for several weeks during the year over Christmas, Easter, and summer.

Michele and her family moved to Seattle, but we remain friends to this day. There is just something so very special about knowing someone since you were both "zero."

AUNTIE MIRIAM

I felt very loved by my mother, but for reasons I didn't understand at the time, I felt very drained after spending an entire day with her. As a child I did not know how to explain it, this need I had for quiet and solitude. My mother was the exact opposite—extroverted and gregarious.

But somehow she understood that I needed to spend some time in a different environment. That's why she never cared how much I went over to Michele's house, and she made such an effort in keeping our childhood friendship alive once they had moved.

There was another person on Daphne Avenue who offered me a quiet tranquil environment; her name was Miriam. She lived across the street and a few houses up towards the school. She was a very small woman, and had brightly dyed reddish-orange hair. She had wire-rimmed glasses, and was old enough to be my grandmother, but I called her "Auntie."

I loved going to her house; it was so quiet. She lived with her husband, Uncle Jim. He would nod at me when I came over, and not say very much. Miriam always welcomed me and seemed delighted to see me. It was as if I was an honored guest whenever I showed up. There was just something about her that made me feel so safe. I knew she understood me; I did not feel the need to explain myself or come up with reasons about why I was so quiet.

Miriam liked me just the way I was, even though I did not understand this concept at the time. She spoke to me quietly and she taught me things. She showed me how to dye Easter eggs by cutting out shapes from masking tape and putting them on the eggs before slipping them carefully into the dye. We would spend hours making the most beautiful eggs. It was so different from the kinetic easter-egg dying that would happen at my house—with four kids and my mother, the eggs were thrown from one color to the next while everyone was shouting—there was no time to slow down and make them pretty.

Miriam was also very proud of her garden, and would walk me through it while explaining different things about the flowers. She would even let me help her dig and plant; it was peaceful. We didn't have a garden at my house. We had the lawn, and I knew my dad did not like to mow it—he made that clear. And I don't remember my mother planting any flowers. Maybe she did, but she would have done it quickly and would never have walked slowly by the flowers with admiration the way Miriam did. She moved at a totally different pace.

One day it was Miriam's birthday; I think I was 8 years old. I had received a Betty Crocker baking set the previous Christmas; I decided I would make her a tiny little cake. I really thought the Betty Crocker baking set was so much better than the popular Easy-bake oven, because you baked things in the real oven, and not with a dumb light bulb. And it came with all these cute little pans and packets of cake mix and frostings.

I made a tiny vanilla cake and my mother helped me to safely bake it in our oven. I mixed up the frosting and covered the little cake. My mother helped me set it in the middle of a white paper plate.

I walked up the street to Miriam's house, carefully holding the cake on the white paper plate. Miriam opened her front door, and she greeted me as if I were the Queen of England. She was absolutely delighted I had made her a cake; first she carried it over to show Uncle Jim, and then she put it safely on her dining room table. I felt so treasured whenever I was at Miriam's house.

Years later, I went to visit Miriam in an assisted-living facility. She was as smiley as ever and still had her bright red hair and wire-rim glasses. She completely remembered all of the things we did together at her house.

I thanked her over and over, trying to explain what those experiences had meant to me. She said, "well, you would always come knock on my door, and say "Auntie, can I come in? It's too loud for me at my house.' And of course, you were always welcome."

My mother didn't really understand me, but she knew I needed time away from our frenetic household. She knew it was a respite for me and was always supportive of that. What a gift she gave to her introverted daughter.

I'M A HUMAN GPS

I was born with a great sense of direction. I didn't have to practice it or work at it, it just came as part of the package of "me," as much as my brown eyes and blond hair. I don't understand poetry and I am baffled by art and museums. And I have yet to understand even one quote from the bible (any sentence with "thee" or "thou" in it frightens me).

But you can blindfold me, and spin me around a half dozen times and I will still be able to tell you which direction is north.

I didn't know I was like this until I was 11 years old. We had been living in Gardena, a tract home neighborhood in Southern California. Almost every house on the block had a family with children, and they overflowed into the street after school to play.

In the summer my mother had a tradition. Every Wednesday she would pile as many kids as she could into her station wagon (no seat belts of course), and head to the beach. All you had to do was bring yourself and a towel; my mom brought the rest.

She would drive straight down Rosecrans Blvd., heading west until we got to Redondo Beach. We always set up our towels and blankets on the left side of the pier, and then we were let loose. We spent the day running in the water, eating grapes, and getting horrible sunburns (that would peel for days).

When my older sister was ready to start Junior High School in 1969, there was a lot of civil unrest in the country; kids were fighting with each other in schools in the Los Angeles area. Many families were leaving our neighborhood, with several relocating to the Palos Verdes area south of Los Angeles. But my parents did not want to leave their very first home, where they had lived more than a decade raising their young family.

My mom loved antiques and was drawn to a sale she had heard about at a house in Belmont Shore, an area of Long Beach. I remember her coming home excitedly and telling us that not only did she buy some stuff in the house, but that she wanted to buy the whole house itself! She had fallen in love with it, and with the community.

My parents spent some time checking out the area and the schools, and decided to purchase our home on the corner of Covina and Division. From our new home, you could look down the block and see the beach two blocks away.

For a couple of months, we went to the new house every weekend to fix it up. One day I was helping my father paint the upstairs bathroom. I sat down to rest. From where I sat, the ocean was behind me. It didn't feel right.

"Dad," I said. "The ocean is in the wrong place."

"What do you mean?' he asked me.

"Well, when I'm sitting down in our old house in a certain spot, the ocean is behind me. And it's behind me now, but it shouldn't be. It should be over there," I said as I pointed west. I somehow knew it should be 45 degrees to my left, and I could not figure out how it had "moved."

My dad looked at me incredulously (and with admiration) and explained that Long Beach has a south-facing beach, so that was why the water was now behind me. The coast had curved and Long Beach had a south-facing beach instead of a west-facing beach like most of the state.

I don't know how I knew that the ocean should be west of where I was sitting; I just did. I could "feel" it.

So . . . I can get anyone to wherever they need to go, but I still can't understand what is so great about the Mona Lisa. I will never understand art.

That summer we moved into our new home in Long Beach. And I got used to having a south-facing beach.

TEENAGE YEARS

A TIME THAT WAS NOT ALL JOYOUS

Not every story in this book will be joyful. My teenage years were quite tumultuous, and sprinkled with some incredible difficulties. I was not sure if I should include this part of my life, but it happened, and it explains quite a bit about the person I grew up to be.

We go through bumps in life that shape us into who we become, or maybe even who we were meant to be. Sometimes those bumps are significant, so much so that they can make or break us.

And as we mature, we learn how to make sense of those situations. We learn to give grace to those who may have hurt us. And to understand there are "gray areas" all around us—nothing is black and white.

And so, we learn to forgive. And most importantly, we finally see how all of these experiences added to who we became as we grew into adulthood.

There are some things that happen in our lives, which we probably believe at the time are the worst thing that could ever happen to us. And up to that time, they may be the worst thing.

Somehow we do whatever we need to do, and manage to go on. And then other things happen. And then more things.

But then as we get even older, it's quite a gift to realize that life was not meant to be easy. And once we have the maturity (and extra years!), we can look back and ponder about what happened in our past, and see how it contributed to who we became (as John Tillman explained in the Foreword).

I recently told a high school friend (one of my only friends back then) way more details about what had happened to me in my teen years. She knew some of it, but not all of it. I had probably been too afraid to tell her.

Marianne looked at me empathetically and said, "I didn't know." And then she asked, "How could you forgive your parents and get past that?" I'm not completely sure.

But I think one has to look at the overall picture of the people in our lives. What shaped them to act the way they did? And did they make up for what happened, even if they didn't say they were sorry for their actions? Did they do the best they could with what their own life experiences had been?

And also, with even more maturity: How did that experience shape who I became?

And how did it help me to help others?

MORE THAN STRICT

My parents were strict. My Mom could be very fun, and she was lively, but she still had strong expectations of us. That was OK. She was a wonderful mother to little kids.

The opposite applied to my dad—he was never fun. At least not that I could ever see. He was scary to me and my siblings, and as we grew up we knew that once he came home from work, we needed to stay out of whatever room he was in.

Dinner time was stressful as well. Our parents loved to argue and yell at each other; they seemed to enjoy it. My father would complain about the quality of the meat, and my mother would yell back at him that she had bought the best stuff. We ate as fast we could to get away from the table.

When I was 11 years old, we moved to a part of Long Beach called Belmont Shore. Many moms did not work and stayed home with the kids, but my mother was a residential realtor, and she loved her job. She adored finding the perfect home for new couples and families. My father was always very supportive of my mom working, which wasn't always the case in some families. They were quite a team in this way.

My father wanted to try investing in some property, and so by the time I was 12, my parents had saved enough money to put a down payment on a duplex. It was right up the street from our house on Covina Ave. in Long Beach, California. My parents were super proud they had accomplished this. Their plan was to fix up one place, rent it out and care for it, build on the equity and save money, and then buy another property. And, over time, that is what they did.

My father believed in hard work, plain and simple. He grew up on a farm and he helped his father every single day. Even if it was a school day, he got up when the sun came up and worked a few hours before school. Then after school, he headed straight out to the cornfields again.

So that is what my father expected of us. We were expected to help him with the apartments, and we did. Every weekend, both Saturday and Sunday, we went to whatever apartment was empty and we painted, swept, and cleaned toilets. We all had to be there, even if there was not enough for four kids to do; it was a requirement. Even my nine-year-old sister painted and swept, but her favorite job was to ride her bike to Jack-in-the-Box up the street to get our lunch.

Our father was a firm boss as well. He didn't like when we talked very much, or especially if we laughed. This was serious business. I remember painting with my older sister and we had laughed about something and he got mad. "When your mouth is open, your hand moves slower!" So, we painted quietly.

13

None of us really liked having to do this every single weekend. But in retrospect, all four of us grew up to be hard workers. And it is a credit to our father (and our mother) for instilling in us that work ethic. I don't think we understood this at the time.

I think it was easier for my parents when we were younger, but as we grew into teeagers, I believe they parented more in fear. It was very clear where they stood on dating, and especially on premarital sex. Mainly, don't ever do it or you will pay a heavy price. My mother had been brought up Catholic and my father often said, "I would never have married your mother if she had been 'used.'" He seemed to think that was funny, and she didn't seem to mind him saying it either. Sometimes he said it much more sternly though, as a strongly veiled threat.

It was just better to avoid these subjects at all costs. We wouldn't dare say out loud that we had a boyfriend or liked a boy. We all learned to hide almost everything we were doing, and we looked out for one another, mainly helping each other not "get into trouble" which was always our term for having our parents be mad at us.

I WAS NEVER A BRUIN

Lately I have run into someone who, every time he sees me, says, "Ahhh, you're a fellow Bruin!" in reference to the fact that we went to the same school, Woodrow Wilson High School in Long Beach, home of the Bruins.

For me, I will never be a Bruin. I never was a Bruin. I don't even know what that would feel like to look back fondly at high school and think, "I'm a Bruin." But honestly, I don't blame the school. Woodrow Wilson High School had nothing to do with how I feel about that. And I'm happy for anyone who has positive memories of going there.

I started at Wilson in the 10th grade when I was 15. My favorite class was trigonometry, where I sat next to a girl who had lots of freckles and the greatest laugh I had ever heard. She had a sort of ongoing, never-ending giggle, that was so completely authentic. I loved seeing her in class every day. Her name was Marianne, and we became good friends.

I then met some of her friends from childhood, but beyond that I remained very introverted and quiet. I didn't join clubs or sororities, or bake cookies for football players. I went to class and listened politely. Then I rode my blue Schwinn bicycle home, and once there, I did my homework, and then watched TV as I sewed or baked.

I loved sewing with a passion. I made all of my own clothes, almost all dresses, but also sometimes midi-length skirts with accompanying white eyelet crop tops to go with them.

But I didn't dare share my love of sewing with anyone. It was the early 70s, and the passing of the Equal Rights Amendment was supposedly imminent, and it was all everyone talked about. Back then, it was a new referendum, and women were excited to move forward and have equality, which I understood. But it was also clear, in an underlying and unspoken way, that it was not cool (or hip!), to enjoy traditionally girl-like projects, like sewing, or baking, which were my two favorite things.

My older sister was a real activist. She formed a club at the school, called S.E.R.A., which stood for "Support of the Equal Rights Amendment." I was always in awe of her—I would never even know how to form a club at the school, or how to even "fight" for anything.

She was dating a guy who was the eldest of 10 kids in a Catholic family. He was wildly funny, and wickedly smart, just like my sister. They seemed like a perfect match.

My sister's boyfriend had a good friend who was one year younger than him. His name was Danny; he came from an Orthodox Greek family and had four sisters. He was very quiet and soft-spoken.

Sometimes after school, my sister's boyfriend would stop over to our house, and often Danny was with him. I was always drawn to Danny's energy—it matched mine completely. He explained he had learned how to listen after growing up as the only brother to all of his sisters.

He was extremely humble as well, which made him even more attractive. There was an annual swimming contest put on by the local Greek church, and he had quietly won it the last three years in a row. I use the word "quietly," because he never even mentioned it. I only knew about it because his friend bragged about it on his behalf.

I liked this about him so much. He was super handsome with his Greek chiseled face and muscles, his dark brown hair and eyes. But he didn't even seem to know he was so attractive. I don't think he even realized how many girls had been flirting with him and trying to connect with him.

Danny and I had a mind meld of sorts. We were instantly kindred spirits, both quiet, both pensive and thoughtful, and both kind. We didn't want the attention to be on us, and we were good kids, and, dare I say it, even obedient—we got good grades and cared about what our parents thought of us.

Danny and I fell in love.

Neither of us had ever had a serious girlfriend/boyfriend before. We understood each other and felt safe together.

In January of 1974, we had been together as a couple for a few months, I was a junior and he was a senior. But we both remained our introverted selves and did not usually express our feelings about each other around anyone else. It was our private special connection.

That year, "streaking" was a big thing—a guy even streaked across the stage at the Oscars ceremony on TV.

Someone challenged Danny to streak across the quad at lunchtime. This was so out of his comfort zone. But he agreed to do it, wearing a brown bag over his head (with the eyes cut out) to hide his identity. On the designated day, I brought a camera to school, and was sitting under a tree waiting to see him do it. The quad was especially crowded that day, as everyone seemed to know what was about to happen.

This was WAY before any type of social media! But even then, teenagers knew how to talk and quickly spread the word.

All eyes were on the entrance at Park Ave. and 10th St., where he was slated to begin. And then, there he was!

Barefoot and completely naked! Looking like a Greek god and running from the entrance between the 200 and 300 buildings, straight through the quad, and quickly to Ximeno Ave., where he had friends waiting for him with his clothes. I was so proud of him.

This was the closest I came to ever feeling like "a Bruin." Maybe because I was in the quad experiencing something with other students.

But even then, it was really just me and Danny.

OUR SPECIAL TIME IN THE SNOW

Danny and I always enjoyed every second we were together. Neither of us were big talkers, we just needed to look at each other and we would start giggling; we just had this knowing of each other's soul.

We both loved music, and would ride around in his little silver car after school, listening to the radio and singing together. Well, mostly I was the one singing, but he would look over at me constantly, with a shy smile and his eyes filled with so much love.

By December of 1973, we had been together a few months and we decided to take a road trip up to Big Bear, about a two-hour drive from Long Beach. Being 16 and 17, we didn't think too far ahead about where we would be staying. We figured we would just sleep in the car. We brought along sleeping bags, blankets, and pillows, and a bagful of snacks.

I probably told my parents I was spending the night at a girl-friend's house.

I had only been in the snow once before, so I had almost zero experience with being anywhere that cold. But I wasn't worried at all. I always felt safe with Danny; he always looked out for me and took care of me.

Neither of us had ever skied, but we knew there were a couple ski areas up the mountain. We decided to rent our skis locally at a sporting goods store before heading up the mountain—I used my babysitting money to pay for the rental.

We left early one afternoon and drove the two hours up into the mountains. It had started to lightly snow as we had headed up the hill. There was a storm coming in, which we didn't know about because there were no weather apps back then, and neither one of us watched the news to see a weather report.

Once we got to Big Bear, we parked in a big parking lot that surrounded a large lodging area near the ski slopes.

I think we got out and checked out the lodge, and walked around a bit until the snow was just blowing absolutely everywhere and it was no longer fun to be out walking in it. We decided to head back to the car to take shelter at about 6PM. A man saw us getting in the car and laying out our sleeping bags inside, and he told us (very nicely) that there was no way we would stay warm enough in a car during a blizzard.

We didn't believe him, nor listen to him. We just got all cozy and watched the snow around us. But it was quickly piling up on the roof of the car and around all the wheels. Danny got out many times and cleared as much snow as he could off of the car. He would then get back in and turn the heat on for a little bit, and then turn off the car so we wouldn't get carbon-monoxide poisoning.

But, eventually, no matter how tightly we held on to each other, and even with using all the sleeping bags and blankets, that man's advice turned out to be right. We were never going to stay warm enough in that little car with no insulation, especially with a blizzard happening all around us.

We decided to head into the lodge; we walked over and huddled near the fire in the reception area. We didn't bring enough money to get a room, and neither of us had a credit card, so we made the (ignorant) decision that we would just stay in the lobby all night.

At some point, the hotel personnel told us that we definitely could not do that. They didn't allow people to just hang out in their lobby all night, for free.

We didn't know what to do. It would be really risky to try to drive back down the mountain late at night in the storm. There happened to be a few other couples hanging out in the lobby—they were in their early 20's, and they were all staying together in one room. They were quite friendly, and when we shared our predicament, they said we could come with them to their room and sleep on the floor.

I was a little nervous, but they were really nice, and I knew Danny would protect me. So that is exactly what we did. We brought our blankets and pillows along with us, and slept on the carpeted floor of their double room in the lodge. Thank goodness they had offered, because I doubt we would have been safe staying in the car all night, or even worse on an attempt to drive down the mountain in the dark night of the storm.

In the morning, the storm was suddenly completely over, and the sun was shining brightly over all the powdery snow, which seemed to already be quickly melting. We decided to skip paying for the ski slopes, and headed on home down the mountain.

Part way down we spotted a parking area near a field with freshly fallen snow; we decided to stop there and park. We got out of the car and carried our skis over to the edge of what seemed like a large meadow. We both put on our skis and attempted to propel ourselves around in the snow. Neither of us knew what we were doing, so we didn't get very far. But still, we laughed and were just happy to be together.

I don't remember that I carried a camera with me very often as a teenager. But somehow, I had brought one with me on our little excursion. And I captured those moments of the two of us playing in the snow. Danny was even able to hold the camera way out, and take a couple "selfies" of the two of us, which was not something done way back then!

I always loved those pictures of the two of us together in the snow. And I'm not sure why, but I always kept those photos.

INTROVERTS CAN BE RISK TAKERS

There came a time when we knew we wanted to be intimate. We were both virgins.

Because my sister was involved with every kind of women's rights movement that was happening, she knew all about Planned Parenthood, and she gave me the big-sister advice to go there if I needed birth control. And that's what I did. I was a straight-A student who was meticulous and responsible.

Danny had his little car with the surf racks on top; he was an avid surfer. Sometimes he would sneak over to my house after school when I knew my parents would not yet be home.

One afternoon we were upstairs in my bedroom and we heard someone coming into the house way earlier than normal. Thank goodness we were already dressed and just hanging out. I could tell it was my father. Oh no! I wasn't really allowed to have boys hanging around upstairs, much less to be doing what we had been doing. I wasn't sure how I would be able to distract my father in order to get Danny back down the stairs and safely out the door.

I panicked. And then it got worse. Suddenly, I could hear the plod, plod, plod of my father coming slowly up the stairs.

My parents' bedroom was on the first floor, and all of us kids were upstairs. Neither of my parents hardly ever came upstairs, and especially not my father. He never did. But now I could hear him coming up. I told Danny to go out on the upper deck area that was located off of my bedroom, and to hide in the little storage shed out there.

My dad came up to my doorway and stood there. I acted like everything was normal, even though we both knew this was not the least bit normal, and not something he ever did. He sat down in the antique rocking chair my mother had given me, and asked me how my day had been.

This was something he never did either. It was starting to seem like a game of cat and mouse as we made small talk. He rocked back and forth for about 10 minutes, and then he finally got up and went back downstairs. He probably decided he would just wait down there, because "that boy" would have to come down at some point, right?

Wrong.

Once I could hear my father safely downstairs, I rushed out to the deck where Danny was hiding. We thought about another way to get him out of the house without my father seeing him. It was easy to climb down the front of our house from the small balcony in front because of the decorative black irons on some of the windows—I had done it many times. But if my father was in the living room, he would be able to see him.

On the back deck, there was an old clothesline that we never used. Danny untied it from the posts and decided he would use it to climb down the back side of the garage where there were no windows where he could be seen. He tied the clothesline around one of the posts and made sure it was knotted tightly. Then he hoisted himself up and over the wall, and while still holding onto the wall with one hand, he grabbed the clothesline with the other.

"Are you sure you can do it?" I asked.

"Yeah," he answered as he smiled back at me.

The plan was for him to go slowly down the rope until he got to the bottom. But as soon as he took his hand off the wall, and grabbed onto the clothesline with both hands, it snapped. It was too old and frayed to hold his weight. He fell all the way down from the second floor to the ground behind the garage.

My heart stopped. But then he looked up at me and smiled. He whispered that he was OK, and I was so relieved. But when he stood

MISADVENTURES IN MY HIGH HEELS

up to walk, he was really limping, and mostly hopping on his other foot. But he headed off anyway, limping away, and looking back at me, reassuring me with gestures that he was fine.

I'm sure that evening my father was very perplexed. He had obviously seen the little silver car with the surf racks parked out front, so he knew he had been up there. But he never saw anyone come down the stairs. I acted like nothing had happened.

The next day Danny's mother took him to their family doctor because he was limping so much. He had told her he was walking on a high curb and not paying attention, and he had slipped off of the curb and twisted his ankle.

At the doctor's office, he and his mom were both called into the examining room. He repeated this story to the doctor. The doctor looked over at his mother, and asked her to please go wait out in the waiting room while he examined him. Once she was gone, he turned back to Danny and said, "OK, Dan, now what really happened?"

And Danny told him he was escaping out of a girl's bedroom, so her father wouldn't find him up there. His doctor shook his head and chuckled; he was not surprised. And luckily it was just a sprain and nothing was broken.

CLAREMONT AVENUE

We didn't dare go back to my house after school anymore. It was just too risky. Usually, we just drove around and hung out. But one day we were trying to find a place where we could park and have sex.

He suggested we park in the beach parking lots on Ocean Blvd. But I said no, I was too nervous. Even though I couldn't think of any reason my father might drive down Ocean Blvd., it made me too scared. What if he saw the car and came over?

So instead, we turned up from Ocean onto Claremont Ave., one of the small one-way streets in Belmont Shore. We parked on that very

22

first block. It was a cold overcast January day, and there was no one around. It felt about as safe as we could get.

We were very passionate, and it wasn't long before the windows were completely fogged up, so who could see in anyway? Right? But suddenly, there was a sharp knock on the window. We both stopped what we were doing and gasped, and quickly sat up. Danny peeked out the window, and said, "Don't worry, but it's a cop."

We were both already quickly getting dressed. I was wearing my favorite turquoise sweater with the big butterfly applique on the front, and some light-colored blue jeans. I got dressed so fast that I didn't bother putting on my bra.

At some point Danny rolled down the window to talk to the officer. I'll never forget his name: Officer Richardson. The reason I will never forget is because he lied to us. Officer Richardson said he needed to take us down to the station so they could just "talk" to us. And then they would "let us go," he said. We believed him.

He put us in the back of his patrol car and took us to the police station. Once we were there, they separated us and then they immediately put me in a jail cell with some other girl, and told me they were calling my parents. I felt so betrayed.

I knew my life was going to change forever.

The walls of the jail cell were this ugly mint-green color, and I paced back and forth, over and over again. I don't remember much about the other girl except that she kept asking me why I was so worried. I tried to answer her, but there was no way to explain the amount of trouble I knew I was about to be in. "You don't understand!" I kept repeating over and over to her as I paced. "My father is going to kill me."

She thought I was crazy. "Oh, I'm sure he'll understand."

"No, no, no, he won't. He will hate me, and I'm afraid he might hurt me." I could barely breathe; I was consumed with fear, and it was mounting.

At some point they unlocked the cell and slid the bars to the side. They told me my father was there to pick me up. Because I had left my bra behind in Danny's car as I hurried to get dressed, I shyly walked down the hall of the police station crossing my arms over my chest as I followed the officer. They led me to a room where a chief (or someone) sat behind a desk. My father was sitting in a wooden chair across from the desk and against the wall to my left. I glanced at him.

I knew.

I already knew, but when I saw his face, I knew even more. I was in so much trouble. My father could barely contain himself as he looked up at me and glared. He was seething. His anger was like a bubbling volcano, but he knew he had to contain it in front of these police officers.

They made me stand there in front of the desk facing the chief guy. I don't remember exactly what he said, but the officer reiterated something about how awful we were, and about what we had done and how disrespectful we were and what bad kids we were. I had to stand there and just nod my head, and blindly agree with him that I was a terrible person. Just a horrible human being. I looked as repentant as I could.

We were then excused from the small office, and told we could go. My father walked out ahead of me. I followed with my arms modestly crossed again over my chest, and my head down. My father reached the elevator ahead of me and pushed the button. I knew his fury was ready to erupt.

There was a police woman behind a desk near the elevator. I took a chance, and leaned in and whispered to her, "I'm really scared of what my father is going to do to me." She shrugged her shoulders and said, "If you have any problems with your father then just give us a call."

That's when I knew it was hopeless. My father would always know how to act in front of authorities; no one would ever believe me.

The elevator door opened. My father went in and I followed. I was terrified. He pushed the button and the doors closed. Out of sight of anyone, he turned to me and started screaming at me while he punched me over and over again in my upper arm.

"How could you be so goddamn stupid?!?"

"How could you be such a goddamn whore??"

He just kept punching me over and over again on my arm until the elevator doors opened, and then we headed to his car and got in. He had a red Volkswagen beetle, with a stick shift.

As we drove home, he continued to scream and yell at me and make sure I knew I was a total disappointment as a daughter. And every time he moved the stick shift to the next position, he raised his fist and pounded it into my left thigh. Over and over and over again.

"I can't believe you're a goddamn whore!!"

He made some other comment about how I was probably sleeping with the entire football team. I wanted to tell him I didn't even know anyone on the football team, and I loved Danny, and he was the only boy I had ever been with. But I knew to stay quiet. And just take it.

When we got to our house he had us hurry inside. He told me to go up to my room. I ran up as fast as I could. But he followed. Slowly and methodically up the stairs, I heard that slow plodding sound. I knew I was doomed.

When he got to my room, he told me to lay face down on my bed. I did. Then I could hear him taking off his belt. And then, he took the belt and he began whipping me over and over again with it. Over and over and over. And while he was whipping me he kept telling me how horrible I was. That I was such a disappointment. That I was a failure. That I completely disappointed him and my mother.

He said I was a goddamn whore. And he hadn't raised me to be a goddamn whore.

The belt lashes stung and were painful, but his words were just horrific and humiliating. It cut me deeply to be told I was a disappointment, that I was worthless, that I was now worth nothing to him. He was breaking my spirit.

I don't know how long it went on. At some point during the beating, my mother had come home. She ran upstairs screaming, asking what was wrong, what had happened. When she got to my room, he stopped hitting me with the belt and said to my mother, "Let's go downstairs so I can tell you what your whore of a daughter has done!" They left my room and went downstairs and there was a slight pause. And then I heard my mother wailing. Absolutely wailing like an injured animal, as if someone had just died.

I was already beaten down both physically and mentally, but hearing my mother wail like that just cemented for me what a disappointment I suddenly was. I was in a mindset that is hard to describe. Every part of my body was shaking; I was trembling so much that I could barely stand. It is hard to describe the absolute terror that I felt. The shaking was overwhelming; I felt like my world was ending.

Here I was, a 16-year-old girl, and a good girl. I was a good student; I did whatever my parents wanted me to do. I worked on the apartments. I babysat. I worked at Woodies Goodies. I was a good girl. I was a good daughter.

But suddenly none of that mattered. I was now a complete failure.

My mind raced to find a way to alleviate how my parents now felt about me. How could I fix it? What should I do? I looked at my bedroom windows on the second floor that looked out over Division Street. I wondered if I should jump out the window. I didn't want to die. But I remember distinctly thinking, "Maybe If I break my legs they won't be so mad at me." It was the only solution I could think of—to jump out the window and break my legs.

I didn't realize exactly how bad of shape I was in, until my younger sister, who was just 13, came quietly to my door. I looked at her and immediately began backing away. I was terrified of her. I didn't know who she was at first. I couldn't stop shaking. I held up my shaking arms as if to say, "Don't come near me!" as I kept backing away.

I was so frightened. As she slowly walked toward me, I cowered in the corner. I looked at her, and I knew that I knew her, but I was just so terrified that I huddled into a little ball. I peered up at her. She just kept reassuring me. "It's me. It's me. I'm not going to hurt you. It's me, your sister."

I finally let her come over to console me. But I cried very quietly. I thought if they heard me crying they would come back upstairs. I did not dare leave my room, not even to go to the bathroom. Everything frightened me. And I felt like such a weak person. Why didn't I stand up for myself? Why did I lie down on the bed like that and let him whip me?

After some time, I could hear my mother making dinner. Then we were all called down to the table. No one spoke. We passed dishes around to each other, and I remember my mother saying to one of my siblings, "Pass the mashed potatoes to the whore." It was clear my parents were on the same team, and my mother thought I was just as disgusting and disappointing as my father did.

Later that evening I heard the dreaded slow plod, plod, plod of my father's footsteps coming once again up the stairs. I braced myself. Now what??

He came into my room, and over to me where I sat on the edge of my bed. He seemed calmer, and almost pensive and thoughtful. He sat down next to me. "I just want to know why you did it. Why?"

This was new. He didn't sound mad. I was amazed. I felt like he might be able to hear me, maybe he would even understand me. He had asked with seemingly no judgment. This was my chance, my chance to be like my older sister and stand up for myself. Surely he would understand. My father had been 18 when he met my mother, and she had been 17. He would understand being in love.

I took a deep breath and said simply, "I really love him."

There was a silent pause. Then my father slowly raised his fist all the way up near his head, and then quickly slammed it down into my thigh. "What do you know about love at your age?! Don't you ever talk about love like that to me again!! You're so goddamn stupid!!"

I remained silent. There was no grace. There was no hope. I would never get through to him.

I never forgot that moment. As his fist slammed into my thigh, I went into survival mode. At that instant, I knew I had to become two different people—the perfect daughter that was everything he wanted me to be, and the real me that I would keep very hidden. I was not strong enough to stand up to him. He was too powerful; he would crush me. I was smart enough to know I couldn't do it.

I split my personality in two at that very moment, and I knew that hiding myself was the only way to survive. I turned to him and said, "I don't know why I did it! I'm so sorry! I'm so sorry I disappointed you! I made a terrible mistake."

Believe me, I wasn't sorry. I loved Danny. But I needed to survive. And I didn't know what he would do unless I acquiesced.

This was the beginning of a new way of life for me.

HOUSE ARREST

The physical part was done. Now came the mental part.

My father warned me over and over again if I ever saw that boy again, he would "have him arrested for statutory rape!" I believed he could do it.

And my parents decided the only way to control me was to basically imprison me. The next day I was allowed to go to school, but I was to come home immediately afterwards, whereupon my mother would be waiting for me. Once I was home, I was to go straight to my room. My older sister Julie had gone off to college, and I had moved into her room. I so wished that she was still home. I could only leave my room to go to the bathroom or come downstairs for dinner. But I was not allowed to go to my younger sister's room to watch TV. And I could not talk to anyone on the phone.

My younger sister and brother were not allowed to speak to me at dinner. I was even forbidden to talk to my siblings at all, so as not to taint them with my horrible behavior. Or to give them any "ideas."

Up in my room, I could play my records though, so that's what I did all night, every night, until it was time to fall asleep. Every day, it was like that.

And I was never shown any love. I was shown only disdain and disgust. I was basically disowned and shunned, but my parents knew they had to provide me food and shelter, and of course, they didn't want anyone outside of the family to know of my evilness. Neither of them ever hugged me, asked me how I was, or told me they loved me. I was treated like a piece of furniture, only worse, because every day I was shown that I was unworthy of even being spoken to.

There were some times when my mom had her real estate friends over. She would cheerfully call me downstairs to play the piano for them. In front of them, she would act fun and treat me like she used to, and she would act so proud of me after each song I played. She would smile and pat me on the back and act so loving in front of her friends.

And then I would go back up to the solace of my room, and my records, and close the door. "The Who's" album, Quadrophenia, was my best friend. So were albums by the Rolling Stones, the Moody Blues, and Led Zeppelin.

For weeks and months, both of my parents kept up the looks on their faces that said, "I hate you. You're a disappointment and the worst daughter that ever lived." I was always allowed to come down to eat dinner, but rarely did anyone speak. Sometimes my parents would talk to each other about their day, but I was never to comment. I had to remain mute. After cleaning up the dishes, I was relegated back to my room.

It was basically house arrest, or maybe it could be called "room arrest." On the weekends, I never bothered to get dressed—there was no point. I stayed in my pajamas and in my room the whole time, every weekend. And listened to my records.

One Saturday, my father needed a letter mailed. He called me to come downstairs, and he told me he wanted me to go up the street and mail the letter for him. I couldn't believe it! He was going to let me out of the house on a Saturday?

I ran back up, quickly got dressed, and then went downstairs. He handed me the letter and stared at me like he wanted to kill me. It was the same look he had given me at the police station. He wanted to make sure I "stayed in line."

"Come right back after you mail the letter!"

I went out the door and headed up Covina Ave. toward the post office on 2nd St., which was one block over on the corner of Corona Ave. It seemed like such a pretty day; I remember I even started skipping with happiness! I was out of the house and not just to go to school, I was going to go to 2nd Street! And on a Saturday! I was so excited as I reached the mailbox. I pulled open the lid, and I put in the letter.

Oh. Then I realized it was over. I had to go straight back.

My shoulders slumped, and I dropped my head as I slowly headed back the one block over on 2nd Street, and then the one block down to my house on Covina Ave. When I got there, my father was waiting and opened the door. "Did you mail the letter?!," he demanded. "Yes," I said dejectedly. It was more demeaning than I even realized at this point, because how hard was it to mail a letter? He didn't think I was even capable of that?

I went back upstairs to my room and stayed there for the rest of the weekend.

I STILL LOVED HIM

I still loved Danny. And he loved me.

We spoke at school the day after it happened. He felt just terrible about how my parents were treating me. His mother had come to pick him up at the police station and she barely shrugged her shoulders as they headed out and on home. He felt terrible that he had believed Officer Richardson (#asshole). He said, "I should have blocked him in some way and told you to run." But it was all hindsight at this point.

Danny said we should immediately stop seeing each other. But I didn't want to do that. We loved each other. We understood each other.

We saw each other as much as we could on passing breaks at school, and for just a little while after school. I would meet Danny after my last class, and we would have 30-40 minutes to be together, mostly just in his car. There was nowhere else for us to go. I was terrified that my father had spies watching from everywhere and I didn't want anyone to report back to him that I was with Danny.

I was so afraid that as soon as I got in Danny's car, I automatically put the seat back so I was riding in a prone position. I would never sit up in the seat and take the chance that anyone would see me and tell my parents. And then before the bewitching hour of 4PM, Danny dropped me off in one of Belmont Shore's many alleys, and I would walk home.

After a few weeks, my parents were not always home at a strict time like they had been initially to stand guard over me. Instead, they would call the house by 4PM, and if I answered the phone, they trusted that I was obeying and being a "good girl." Then they could convince themselves that the house arrest and limitations were working, and that I was capitulating to how they felt.

And they had every reason to feel that their actions were working, because I became a total actress whenever I was around them. I was absolutely perfect in front of them. I was the best and nicest daughter they could ever have wanted. Of course, before all this, I had already been a good daughter, but my "big giant sin" had completely wiped that away. I now had to regain that position by majorly sucking up, being inauthentic, running scared, and never, ever showing my real self. That was to be kept hidden away. This was the only way I could protect myself.

A few times Danny and I took chances and would go to his house at lunchtime, or for an hour after school so we could be together. But I made sure he dropped me in the alley a few minutes before 4PM.

And every time when I opened my front door, I was not only filled with dread, I was filled with fear. My stomach hurt, and my heart raced.

What if my father had found out? What if he saw us? What if some-one told him?

I couldn't relax until one of them called to check up on me at 4PM, and I could cheerfully report that I was home and doing my homework. Whew! They hadn't found out; I would take a deep breath.

But the lying and sneaking around was wearing me out. I loved and needed Danny, but the terror that followed after being with him was really difficult for me.

"GETTING STONED"—THAT'S WHAT WE CALLED IT

I had tried marijuana a few times before all this happened. But I rarely used it, and I did not drink at all. (See? I was a good daughter).

I now needed something to calm me down after I got back into the house each day. Not only to help me with the fear, but to be able to tolerate being alone in my room for the whole evening by myself. I bought some marijuana, and I learned how to roll a joint.

In the afternoons, once I was home at the appropriate time, and my parents had checked on me that I was there, I would go into my closet and smoke a joint. I had to—it was the only way to cope with being alone in my room all night, every night, just listening to my records.

It was a blessing that my parents' bedroom was downstairs, and all of us kids' bedrooms were upstairs. Sometimes, if it felt safe, my brother and sister would sneak me in to watch TV with them in my sister's room, but we were always alert for my father's footsteps, and we had a back-up plan where we would say I was just using the bathroom on their side, across the hall. But when my father was in a foul mood, which was often, we couldn't chance it. My siblings always felt bad that I was over on my side with the door closed, while they watched TV.

My parents had splurged and put in a second phone line because they were sick of how much we, as teenagers, were always on the phone.

There were so many nights I wanted to call Danny but I didn't dare—it was too risky. Sometimes he would have one of his sisters call and ask for me. If my younger sister answered, she would come get me. And his sister would give the phone to him. But we only talked for about five minutes though, just in case. I was just too scared.

Because the phone was located right outside the bathroom, I always had that contingency plan to explain why I was out of my room. I could always say that was where I had been, in case I heard the slow plodding footsteps coming up the stairs. I always had to be aware and have a plan.

This "incident" had happened in January of my Junior year of high school. I spent the remainder of 11th grade locked away like that, for six months, becoming more introverted than I ever had even been. The few friends I had mostly fell away, which was quite understandable. They were busy being teenagers in Long Beach, participating in school activities, sports, and other things they were interested in. I couldn't really talk about what had happened.

Everything in my psyche changed dramatically after that. Suddenly, being at high school became totally different. If I heard someone say to a friend, "let's do something this weekend!" I would be grateful no one had asked me because how could I explain that I wasn't allowed out, that I just stayed in my pajamas. I mostly kept my head down and didn't interact with anyone.

And I suddenly felt so much "older" than everyone else my age. I couldn't relate to anything that my peers were talking about, like football games and dances, or other high school type things. I never even went to even one football game. It all seemed so superficial and trivial compared to what I was experiencing. It wasn't that I wasn't happy for my friends, I was, I just could not relate. I felt like I had been through something (and was still experiencing) that I could never tell anyone about. No one would understand.

I didn't feel like a "high school girl." Ever. And that's why, to me, I've never been a "Bruin."

"I'M TAKING YOU TO A DOCTOR"

A month or two after the police station experience, my mother informed me that she was taking me to a gynecologist. I did not need to go to a doctor; I was on birth control pills so I knew I wasn't pregnant. And Danny and I had both been virgins, so I didn't have to worry about sexually transmitted diseases. But I knew I was not allowed to question this. When she told me, I just said, "OK."

I knew I could never tell my mother I had already gone to Planned Parenthood. There was this theory my parents were going with that I was "swept up in the moment" or that maybe "that boy" had "given me beer" and I lost control. It was all so stupid. I had been completely responsible. And I would never drink a beer anyway. I didn't drink at all. Ever. I couldn't believe how little my parents actually knew about me.

But I was filled with fear at my mother taking me to a doctor. I was scared. Would the doctor give me some kind of blood test? Would the doctor be able to tell I was taking birth control pills? If the doctor could figure that out, she would surely tell my mother, right? I was so terrified that this could happen. So, I decided to stop taking birth control pills before the doctor visit.

A few weeks later, we were at the doctor's office. It was so uncomfortable. My mother looked at the pictures of newborn babies on the walls, and kept commenting on how cute the babies in the pictures were. She had a big smile on her face when we were out in the open around other people. She pretended that everything was normal and we were this happy mother-and-daughter.

I was led into an office alone, without my mother. That surprised me. The doctor came in and was smiling. "What's going on?" she said. "Your mother said you are having trouble with your periods." What? No, I wasn't.

I looked at the doctor and told her I wasn't having any trouble at all with my periods. "Then why are you here?" she asked quizzically. I began to blurt out a few things. "Well, I got caught having sex in a car by the police, and my parents are really mad at me."

That was really the understatement of the world to me. It eliminated the beautiful relationship I had with Danny, and made it sound like I might get grounded for an hour or two, instead of my nightly lock-up in my room.

The minute I said it out loud, my fear kicked into high gear. I suddenly felt like I was in "fight or flight" mode. What if this doctor told my mom what I had said? What if she felt the same way as my parents about teenagers having sex? What if she told my mother I had told her the truth about what happened, and that I didn't have any problems with my period? After all, Officer Richardson had betrayed me, this doctor might too.

I think the doctor saw my terror, and she softened somewhat, and I felt less scared. She asked me if I wanted birth control. What? Was this a trick? I didn't trust her. What if I said yes? I was now certain she was a spy for my mother. I told her I didn't need birth control because "I had broken up with the guy."

My mother and I rode home and I said absolutely nothing. She made small talk and didn't ask me anything about what had happened when I was alone with the doctor. It was always so surreal to me to live in this pretend environment where we acted like everything was normal and happy. I was now used to living as two different people. And I always knew it was risky to show any of my real self.

I was so relieved to get home, and go back to the safety of my room. The minute I closed the door, I put on "Quadrophenia" by the Who. When my mother left for work, I smoked a joint in my closet, and I lay on my bed and listened to "Love Reign O'er Me," over and over again.

I felt safe. Back in my room.

WHY DID I PUT UP WITH THIS?

Why didn't I run away? I berated myself over and over again for not standing up for myself. I was never strong like my older sister. She stood up to everything. I just didn't have her moxie. She would never have laid down on a bed like that at age 16, waiting for her father to take off his belt and whip her.

I knew I had tried on that first evening to stand up for myself—I had told my father the truth. That I loved Danny. But that's when he had slammed me in the leg and I knew I wasn't safe. I would accept the punishment. And where else could I have gone anyway?

Danny and I started to see each other less and less. It was just too stressful. I could never stop being nervous. His mother had gotten a full-time job so no one was home in the afternoons at his house and we could steal away there for an hour. Any time more than that and I was convinced there were spies outside of every window.

My junior year ended and summer started. It didn't really matter to me. I still wasn't allowed to go anywhere anyway. It had been more than six months of being confined in my room every night, of being left alone with no one to talk to, of becoming incredibly paranoid that I was being watched from everywhere and I was never safe.

In July of 1974, all that changed.

My older sister came home from her first year in college. She was 18. While she was out of the house one day, my mother was unpacking some of her things, and she found my sister's birth control pills. When my sister came home, my mother was waiting. She confronted her about what she had found. She lay down the law to her, and threatened to tell my father once he came home from work about what she had found, unless she agreed to what would now be expected of her:

1. She had to move back home
2. She had to give up her boyfriend.
3. She had to give up her pre-med studies at UC San Diego and now go to Cal State Long Beach

If she did all those things, my mother said she would not tell my father.

My sister went upstairs and packed up everything she owned and moved out that afternoon, before my father even got home from work. She would have none of that. I was in awe of her strength. I wished I could have been strong enough to do what she did.

I felt really sorry for my sister, but somehow with this new development, my whole world changed. For my parents, it became a huge "a-ha!" moment. Suddenly, they decided that I wasn't that bad of a daughter after all—it had been my sister all along, encouraging me. Of course, that wasn't true, but I was suddenly seen in a better light. I was not the worst daughter anymore.

I really admired my sister—I could never do what she did. She walked right out. She knew she would have to give up college at that point without any money to pay for it. She found a waitress job and started working. She got a tiny apartment on Redondo Ave. at 2nd St. True to form, my parents forbid the other three of us from having anything to do with her. But I snuck over to see her all the time.

My life changed overnight. I had been in my room every night from January 16th until that day in July, for six whole months, but I was now suddenly trusted. I was suddenly good again. I was given more freedom.

I WAS LATE

I had gone off the pill when I knew I was going to be forced by my mother to go to the gynecologist. I was still seeing Danny for an hour here or there, but I wasn't yet worried about getting back on birth control. I had heard this rumor. Someone had told me that if you had been on the pill, and then went off of it, that its effects would continue to work for about three months. So, you didn't have to worry about getting pregnant for three months or more.

I don't know why I believed this and accepted it as fact. But I was too afraid to go back to Planned Parenthood to get more birth control pills. What if someone saw me there? What if they told my father? I lived in constant fear.

And then . . . my period was late.

Back then, the only way to know if you were pregnant was to go to a doctor or Planned Parenthood and give a urine sample. Danny went with me to the facility in North Long Beach. After I took the test, this lady came out and led us into a small room. She told us the test was positive. OK, now I was 16, and pregnant. And I wouldn't have been if my fear of my parents hadn't made me go off the pill.

I asked the lady what I needed to do to get an abortion. She asked if I wanted any other kind of counseling or to consider other options. No. There were no other options for me. The thought of my father finding out I was pregnant, and realizing I had still secretly been seeing Danny for months after, was too terrifying for me to hear about any other options.

Abortion had become legal the year before, in 1973. My parents subscribed to Time magazine and it came in the mail every week. There were lots of articles about abortion. I remember seeing one very graphic cover of a drawing of a woman with a coat hanger near her, and she was slumped over and seemed to be dead. Inside the magazine was an article that told of botched abortions, with women using coat hangers, and women ending up dead after going to Tijuana to get the procedure.

Once I found out I was pregnant, I knew if I couldn't do it legally, I would try all of those things. I would do anything and everything to make sure my father wouldn't find out. The coat hanger, Tijuana, all of it.

I couldn't believe it—I had finally just been released from being in my room/prison for so much of each day for six whole months. I was finally thought of as a "good daughter" again. But if my father ever knew I was pregnant, it would be over. I feared he would punch my stomach in, over and over until "it" was gone.

We scheduled the procedure at a place in Los Angeles five days later. Those five days were excruciating for me. All I could think about was how I didn't want to miscarry before I got the abortion. I didn't know what a miscarriage was like, and I was worried that I would not be able to hide something like that from my parents. What a weird prayer I was saying, over and over again, "Please God, don't let me miscarry before I get the abortion." The fear of my father controlled me.

The day finally came. It was a Saturday and I was allowed to go out for longer on the weekend now that I was suddenly "good" again. I don't remember where I said I was going for the day as I rode away on my bike. I locked my bike somewhere and Danny picked me up in our usual alley between Covina and Corona Avenues, just north of 2nd St. We drove silently to Los Angeles. He offered to go in with me, but I made him stay in the car while I went inside alone. I was too scared to be seen with him. Any of these people could (and would) call my parents, was what I was thinking. I could not be too careful.

There were women of all ages in the waiting room. It looked nothing like what I expected from things I had seen on the news. I think at that time, women getting the procedure were depicted as uncaring, and just using it as their form of birth control if they got pregnant. But this was a room of sadness and seriousness, and there was no one in the room who was taking it lightly.

A nurse came out and gave me two Valium to relax me, and I sat down and waited for my turn. I had never had any medication like that before. When they did finally call me to go in, I stood up, and then I fell against the wall, in fact, I almost fell completely over and could barely walk. The nurse grabbed me and guided me to the procedure room.

Under the effects of the Valium, I was more than relaxed, I was totally loopy and almost weirdly giddy. I had never felt like that before. The room seemed to be spinning, but not in a bad way. I actually felt very euphoric, but I did remember hearing the sound of the vacuum-type machine being turned on. It was eerie and hit me like a punch in the gut.

When it was done, I made it back to Danny's car, and he was a nervous wreck. It had taken far longer than either of us thought it would, and he was fearful that something had gone wrong. He wanted to go in and check on me, but he did not want to violate my request that he not come in. He was so relieved to see me. We drove back to Long Beach, and Danny dropped me off in our alley.

I was too nervous to ride my bike home, so I left it locked where it was and walked slowly home, and in the front door. My mother was overly cheerful and talking about something that seemed so inconsequential to me. I remember how much disdain I had for her cheerfulness—it made me sick. She had absolutely no idea what her daughter was going through. I was her little girl and she knew nothing about me. And I couldn't tell her, I couldn't tell her anything. I knew she would turn on me and disown me again.

I had to hide the physical discomfort, the cramping and bleeding, and the emotional pain I was in, and put an equally cheerful smile on my face as I headed up the stairs to my room. I wondered what it was like to have a mother to share with, to confide in, to cry with. A mother who would dry your tears and console you.

My mother had been that type of mother when I was a little girl—she was wonderful. She was fun and kind, and was nice and soothing if we fell down or hurt ourselves. She protected us in her own way by reminding us not to go into the living room when our dad was resting after work. She always made things better and dried our tears.

But I think with her strict Catholic upbringing, she just had zero acceptance of anything that did not fit in with what she believed was right. She just couldn't provide kindness and understanding to me as a teenager, because for her, I was violating a sacred covenant, and nothing else mattered.

And I can only guess that she was convinced she was doing the right thing, that by making me feel guilty and horrible I would turn into a better person somehow. And I don't think she wanted to go against my father either.

REFLECTIONS

It was weird that for someone who wanted to be a mother her whole life, I never once thought of that pregnancy as a baby, as a soul. To me, it was just a problem to be gotten rid of. And for me, getting rid of it was paramount to my actual survival.

Years and years later, I thought about this baby many times. I told it I was sorry I had not even said goodbye or anything like that. Or had even considered it at all. And how bad I felt that I actually just thought of this baby, this soul, as an "it." I had been too terrified to get to any place of depth or thought. Fear had controlled me. I had a lot of guilt.

In some way I always imagined it had been a boy. I don't know why. Many years later, after I was married and had had my son, I got pregnant again, but had a miscarriage very early in the pregnancy. I was sad and distraught, but in the days that followed I always felt that the "miscarried baby" was now with the "aborted baby." These two souls were now together. It gave me closure for both losses.

Back to 1974 . . . after the pregnancy and abortion, my fear level was so high there was no way that I could keep seeing Danny anymore. I didn't trust anyone, and I was consumed with paranoid thoughts. I now thought my father was around every corner watching me. I could no longer live with the sneaking around, and riding on the floor of the car, and being dropped off in alleys. I couldn't live with opening the front door and wondering, "Do they know? Did they see me with him?" Danny didn't want us to break up, but he understood my decision and respected it.

My senior year of high school is basically a blur. Danny had graduated and was in his first year at our local college, so I didn't see him at school anymore. I was allowed to go to school and do other things. My parents began to speak normally to me again. I missed Danny, but

I could now come home each day and not be terrified anymore as I opened the front door. I had to give him up in order to alleviate the fear.

I spent much of my time in Recreation Park across the street from the high school, getting stoned. I still got good grades though. I had almost no friends, and I didn't get involved in many things. I did go to some concerts now and then, but I had become quite a loner.

There was no one I could really talk to. I still felt so much older than everyone else my age—like I was a 40-year-old woman in a 17-year-old's body. I found it difficult to carry on a conversation about "teen-age-type" things or anything that seemed superficial or trivial, like what should I wear to the football game on Friday night? I never even went to a football game. I didn't have a bunch of close girl friends who talked about makeup and clothes. I kept mostly to myself.

And, in front of my parents, I continued to be my good-daughter-self at all times, and was only my real self in other places. And actually, almost nowhere was I my real self, because I no longer opened up to anyone.

My parents and I never spoke about what had happened. We all pretended that it had never happened at all. In some ways I hated my parents. How could they treat me that way? How could they do that to me? But on another level, I thought maybe I had deserved it. I had disappointed them after all—maybe it really was my fault, maybe that's why I could not stand up for myself. Maybe I deserved what I got.

But I could never get past how someone could turn on their child so completely. How could they love them one day, and then after one "misstep" completely take away all their love, and deliberately cause their child so much pain and angst? And so much fear and terror. And why would anyone want to make their child feel so low and so bad and so defeated?

I knew I would never treat another human being like that, ever. I vowed if I ever did become a mother one day, my children would always know I would be there for them. No matter what.

A PROFOUND EFFECT

This experience shaped so much of me and who I became. It explains why I married my husband, Walt, who was 22 years older than me. He had once asked me, "Something once deeply hurt you, didn't it?" How did he know that???

I never felt the crazy kind of love for Walt that I had with Danny. But that was OK with me. I decided that wasn't important. Here was someone who loved me for who I was. I didn't have to pretend with him. I didn't have to be two different people with him. He knew me. He got me. He understood me. I was safe with him. And, as I always liked to say, he didn't just love me, he liked me too. I knew he would never pull away his love if I made a mistake.

My parents' treatment of me when I was a teenager shaped the kind of mother I became. I wanted my children to feel loved no matter what. I was determined that I would never turn on them, nor make them feel bad or disgusting for something they said or did. I wanted them to know I loved them no matter what. And no matter how difficult some experiences were, I never took away my love. I never shunned them or made them feel bad for who they were as people.

My teenage years also completely shaped the type of boss I became at my restaurant, La Strada. I was blessed to provide an environment where I got to watch so many young people grow into competent adults. Most of my employees were in their teens or early 20s. I made sure they felt welcome. If they did something wrong or incorrectly and were nervous, I just gently corrected them and reassured them it was OK. I let them know I appreciated them and they were still part of the team. No one would be disowned.

There were many evenings when a young staff member would stay late after we closed to sit and talk with me. Sometimes they just needed someone to listen. Sometimes they had problems with school or their home life, or with a boyfriend or girlfriend. Sometimes they had a problem and were afraid to tell their parents about it. They knew there would be no judgment from me ever. I only gave out love and encouragement. And total acceptance. And they knew that.

The deep love I felt towards my employees did make one part of my job way more difficult—when I found the need to fire someone. There will always be a time when an employee will not not work out for one reason or another, and it's never easy for any boss to fire someone. But for me it was especially rough.

Even if someone had wronged me, such as being caught stealing, or being too unreliable, I still found firing someone so very difficult. It activated something so deep within me. It felt like I was ostracizing them and turning my back on them, like I was telling them they weren't good enough anymore, and that they were no longer worthy or needed. I never wanted anyone to feel discounted the way I had been.

We cannot change our past. "It is what it is" sounds like such a trite phrase, but it is so very true. Instead, we can look at what happened and see how those events shaped us and our lives. We can see how our past affects our reactions, and shapes the decisions we make. And we can be more forgiving of ourselves when at times we may not act, or react, in a positive way.

My experiences during these teenage years were thoroughly life-changing for me; they affected every part of my life afterward. But acknowledging my past, learning from it, and accepting that it made me, "me," is what makes life, "life."

And after that, life can be an adventure.

FORGIVENESS

Remember how my friend, Marianne, asked me how I could ever forgive my parents? There are many reasons.

Probably number one on the list was how wonderful they were as grandparents.

My husband died when my children were very young. I felt sorry for my children that they would be missing the precious love of their father.

And for me, there was now no one to turn to daily, to talk together about how wonderful we thought our children were. I was now the only person in the world who would love my children the way he and I had.

I would now be alone in my wonderment towards them. When they reached a milestone or said something funny, if they just walked or talked or laughed . . . there was no one there to glance at knowingly, and smile and feel so much pride. This made me incredibly sad. It was one of the most difficult parts of losing him.

But when I started helping out at the restaurant, something magical slowly began to happen. My kids were with my parents every evening. They loved going to their house and being with them. My mother was fun and loving; she read to them every night, and had them bathed and asleep in their pajamas by the time I returned each evening. And my father was just crazy about them, and he made them feel safe and protected.

Over time, as I returned each evening to pick them up, both of my parents were full of stories about what my kids had done that evening. Their faces would light up as they told me every funny thing they said or did. They would marvel at how special and smart they were. They were completely opposite of what they had been like as parents—there was no harshness, only kindness and love.

At some point, it became so obvious. My parents now looked at my kids in the same way that I did, in the same way that Walt had. This eased the angst I had about my children having only one person in the world who would love them completely. Because they now had three.

For my father, being strict was all he knew. He had grown up with a father who expected him to work many hours on the family farm, to follow rules, and to honor his parents. I later learned from my aunt (my father's sister) that his father had whipped him with a switch almost every day, even though he had worked on the farm from sunup to sundown.

For my father, there was a right way to do things, and a wrong way. Everything was black and white. There was no gray area. There was no grace—that was for weaklings. He always said, "I don't want excuses, I want results!" He believed you were either good, or you were bad. That's all he knew.

The other reason I could forgive them was because of my dear Walt, because of all he taught me in the 11 years we were together. Walt saw nothing in black and white; for him, there was nothing but gray area. No matter what anyone did or had done, he would say, "Honey, you don't know what that person has been through in their life." And he never even thought badly of my parents. He thought their actions were stupid and even horrific, but still, he didn't fault them for anything.

But after Walt died, something so strange happened. My father's grief for me was overwhelming and palpable. He came to my house afterwards and wept in my arms. And from that day forward, my father treated me like a saint, like an angel. He never said one unkind thing to me ever again. He never gave me those stern looks anymore. Instead, he looked at me with reverence.

And if it wasn't for my father, Caffe La Strada would never have existed. He had noticed I was spiraling downward in my grief at the loss of my husband, and he had asked me to come help him, so I could focus on something else. It was the light I needed to recover. I knew I had to let it all go and move on. I had kids to raise alone, and my parents became my biggest champions. I knew how much they loved me. They were always so proud of me, and would beam with pride at anything I accomplished.

To me it was all now "in the past."

And it was basically the same with my mother. She didn't have the best upbringing either. Her father used his belt on her two brothers all the time, so that was normal to her. And she went to Catholic school all the way through high school, and it was drilled into her that you honor your mother and your father. Any sign of disrespect or disobedience warranted strict punishment. I think she actually believed that all those hours up in my room made me become a "good girl." We never talked about it again.

And her love for my children was pure adoration. Every time I saw her look at my children, with so much love in her eyes, and when she hugged them so tightly, I knew she was hugging and loving me at the same time. My mother died peacefully in 2010, after suffering from dementia for more than 10 years. It was a blessing for her to finally be released from her illness.

In 2013, my father suffered from Parkinson's disease and was fairly crippled—it was hard for him to move. And it wasn't always easy to understand what he was saying either.

Just a few months before he died, his caregiver, Martha, called and said he was terribly upset and wanted to speak with me right away. "Your father is crying and crying. He said he wants to talk to you."

I left work at the restaurant and walked the couple blocks to my parents' house. My father stood in what my mother called "the Galleria," a very wide-open hallway with glass doors that looked out onto her patio. The walled side of the Galleria was covered with family photographs.

I walked toward him and he was overcome, and pointed at the wall, at some of the pictures of us as children. He could barely get the words out because of his now not-working voice, and the tears flowing down his face.

He was leaning on Martha for support, and then he took a few steps forward and held onto me. He looked directly at me, and then he said, "I think maybe I was too hard on you kids." He could barely get the words out, and then he really started crying.

I couldn't believe it. This was not like the father I knew. The stern man who was all powerful and could hold it together in any situation. Getting older and being sick had really softened him. For him to cry like that, openly in front of me, and for him to say those words to me . . . well, I just couldn't believe it was happening.

I had always rehearsed in my mind for the day when I would be strong enough to say to him, "You were so mean to me! Why did you do that to me when I was 16? Why did you hurt me so badly? I loved Danny. I was a good daughter. Why did you take away all your love, just because of something I did that you didn't like?"

But now, I was a woman in my mid-50s. That had been so very long ago, so far away in the past. In that moment, standing there with him, I realized that maybe he had never forgotten what had happened, way back on January 16, 1974, even though we all pretended it hadn't. I wondered if he had thought about it, and questioned if he had done the wrong thing that day, and for the months following.

He continued to stare at me, waiting, with tears running down his face. I thought of maybe just saying, "Yes, you were too hard on us."

But I didn't. I looked him straight in the eye and said, "You were a wonderful father. Everything you did is OK now." I smiled and leaned in, and hugged him. He put his head on my shoulder and started sobbing.

I could tell they were tears of relief. I knew he loved me, he always had. I don't think he meant to be so hard on me, and on my siblings. It was all he knew how to be as a parent, it was the way he had grown up.

We stood there for a long time together before he let go of me. I kissed him on the cheek goodbye, and headed back to work.

I couldn't believe it. He had known. He had realized it. And I knew then that was all I ever wanted. His acknowledgement and tears were all I had needed. And he needed forgiveness. And he did deserve that forgiveness for being the most wonderful grandfather, and for the decades he had treated me like a saint, and looked at me with deep love and reverence. That was his way of making it up to me.

A few months later on the morning he died, very early, I was the only family member the hospital could reach and I raced over there.

His heart had stopped twice and they had revived him both times. He was no longer conscious, but I held tightly to his hand and whispered over and over to him that I loved him and everything was OK. His heart stopped again, and as they tried to resuscitate him, I prayed to my mother to take him, and for him to let go. And he did.

I felt so blessed that I was the one there with him when he died. I felt so much peace. I was so glad I had given him the grace he had needed.

He was a wonderful father.

THE NOT SO ROARING 20'S

I ALWAYS WANTED TO BE A MOTHER

When I was young, my most fervent desire was to become a mother one day. I loved little children; their enthusiasm and joy inspired me, and it came naturally to me to care for others.

When I was twelve, I began babysitting every kid in the neighborhood. I started at 50 cents an hour but that quickly moved up to $1/hour—inflation, you know. I used to stack my dollar bills in a pile and hide them in the top drawer of my dresser; I suppose I was a budding entrepreneur of sorts. But mostly, I loved the kids. I came up with many creative and fun things for them to do—my mother had been a great example for me. The mathematical side of me came into play as I kept track of just how often I had babysitting jobs, and I remember my record was 37 nights in a row.

After my difficult teen years with my parents, I went on to college and got a degree in Nutrition/Biochemistry from the University of California at Davis. Away at school, I got very involved in Transcendental Meditation, which suited my solitary personality. I was never in a sorority; I didn't go out to drink or go to any parties. I only dated one man in college, and it wasn't difficult to say goodbye to him when I decided to move back to Long Beach after getting my degree.

Once I was back, I wasn't exactly sure what I wanted to do. Most people with my degree went on to get a master's degree and became registered dietitians. I had absolutely no desire to do this; I hadn't really thought through my career choice when I chose my school.

My father had been an engineer who worked on the Apollo missions, and he suggested I apply at Rockwell International, an aerospace company. I was skeptical because I did not have an engineering degree. But he dropped my resume off to a few old friends still working at the Rockwell facility in Seal Beach, CA. Through some kind of meeting, my resume got handed off to a few people who worked at the Downey facility, but who happened to be in Seal Beach for a meeting.

I got a call to come in for an interview.

I arrived at the Rockwell facility in Downey, and a very nice secretary directed me to a seat to wait for my interview with a man named Walt Ramelow.

She gestured that he was the one standing in an open office talking on the phone about ten feet away. I sat down and looked over at him. I was not impressed. He seemed to be fairly annoyed at whoever he was speaking to on the phone, and that was such a turnoff to me. Even worse, he was smoking, and I couldn't stand cigarettes. I really wanted to leave and not have the interview.

I think the secretary could read the look on my face, and she said something like, "it won't be long, and don't worry." He hung up the phone and came over to introduce himself, and gestured for me to come into his office and take a seat. He smiled warmly and acted very kind, and nothing like he had been when he was on the phone.

I can't remember very much about the interview except he asked me to tell him all about myself, and I did. I remember looking at him while I spoke, and I could just tell he was listening to every word I said. He never interrupted me. When I was finished, he explained he was looking for someone for an introductory position as a software engineer. A degree was necessary, and an engineering degree was preferred. But then he just waved his hand and said it wasn't that important that my degree was not in engineering. I remember him saying, "if you can analyze chemicals and molecules, then you can analyze data too."

I was actually surprised at how well he already seemed to understand me, and even more so that he already had my brain figured out. Because, yes, I could certainly analyze and quantify things—I did that all the time. He walked me to his manager's office and introduced me to him, and vouched for me as a good candidate for the position.

The next day he called to give me a formal job offer. I was stunned, and even more so at the amount of money that came with the position. But I told him I needed to think about it over the weekend, which was actually completely ridiculous. I didn't need to think about it at all, but every book I had read on getting a job said not to accept any offer right away. I called the next day and said yes. He seemed very nice, and pleased I was accepting the job offer.

I was now a software engineer, and would be trained in how to write computer programs that would access large data bases. Rockwell was working on the Space Shuttle program, and this was six months before the first launch. I liked my job right away. I sat directly across from the nice secretary I had met on the day of the interview. I told her I was worried on that first day because the boss seemed mad on the phone; I didn't want to work for anyone that yelled at anyone.

She laughed and said, "he's the best boss I've ever had. The kindest, most sensitive, most caring. Don't worry, when you saw him talking on the phone that day, it was to the boss of the 'user group,' and they always banter like that. It's nothing." She was right. He always seemed to be checking in on everyone who was working for him. And he never yelled at anyone.

I was trained in computer programming by a lady named Erica. And I absolutely loved the actual task of programming. It was so exact:

"if this is like this, and that is like that, then this is what will happen." I was drawn to anything that involved logic, was logical, or could be accurately explained with quantifiable details.

My job was really all I had going on in my life, besides my hobbies of crocheting and sewing. I was quite a "plain Jane"—I never wore makeup, or got dressed up on the weekends to go out to parties or dancing like most 20-somethings did. I didn't hang out at girlfriends' houses to gossip and have fun. I didn't drink at all, and I had given up my "getting stoned" days. I still felt older than everyone else my age, and it was difficult for me to participate in discussions about things that seemed trivial, like makeup and what to do on Saturday night. I couldn't relate at all.

I loved my job so much that when given the option of working overtime every Saturday, I happily accepted. I showed up every single Saturday to work more. It was exciting to be 23 years old, and working on something that was talked about on the news every night. The very first space shuttle would be launched in just a few months, and the whole country buzzed with excitement about it. That was enough for me.

But something else made me love my job so much. I felt safe there. I felt understood. My boss, Walt, seemed to "get" me on a deep, contemplative level; it felt very fulfilling to me—to be understood and accepted. He seemed to know me right away. During my first week at work, he had even once said, "something hurt you very deeply once, didn't it?" I don't remember how I answered his question. But my mind raced as to how he could possibly know about that? How did he know something had deeply hurt me?

How could he know how my parents had treated me when I was a teenager? How could he know about Danny and how I loved him, and how my parents kept us apart? And how they kept me locked away, and took away all their love? And how I never said goodbye to our baby? And how no one ever talked about it ever again as if it never happened.

But, of course, he didn't really know any of that; he was just such a deeply sensitive person, and he could somehow read my soul.

Not once did I think I was actually "attracted" to him, not like THAT. After all, he was 22 years older than me, and that was unthinkable to me. Plus, he smoked, and that was a huge turnoff. I wondered what was wrong with me for being so drawn to him. But whenever he took a day off from work, the entire day felt different to me. It was sort of empty, like something was really missing.

I never really even considered that I was falling in love with him—there wasn't really any of the usual flirting or any of the other signals one would experience with a potential partner. And I was sure it was only on my side, so I just tried to ignore it.

One day though, he asked me to go have a drink with him after work to discuss something with me. I didn't drink and he knew that, and I reiterated that. But he said, "I'll buy you some tomato juice." I didn't like tomato juice either, and I felt unsure about this meeting. But I went. And he ordered me a tomato juice, which I just stared at.

After just a few minutes, he turned towards me and looked very directly at me. He seemed completely vulnerable and almost nervous as he told me that he was completely 100% in love with me. He loved how sensitive I was, how kind. He understood me, and knew I was an introvert, but smart like he was, and that I had a keen sense of humor that only came to the surface when I felt safe.

My head was spinning. I knew how much I always wanted to be in his presence, but I had never felt like I could say the words, "I am falling in love with this man." And the obstacles were huge. He was 22 years older than me. He was my boss. He had been divorced for many years, and had three teenage daughters. I think I said all of that, but none of it mattered to him.

Because of the harshness of my parents, I had developed a way to split my personality in two, and I only showed the one "acceptable" side of me to my parents. I hid all the rest.

But Walt loved all the rest. For the first time I did not feel I was "too much like my father" or a big disappointment in some way. Walt loved me for who I was. He liked me too. He didn't want to change me; my essence was what drew him to me.

I looked past all of the obstacles so I could finally be myself. I could be me. We were together six years before we got married. My parents never approved of us, and would never meet him during all that time. They said awful things and basically believed he was "using me."

I knew that marrying Walt would also be unacceptable to my parents, and it was. My parents tried everything to keep me from marrying him. When that didn't work, they showed their disapproval by not coming to our wedding in May of 1987. They were good at emotional punishment.

My frustrated and angry father had asked more than once, "What happens if you have kids with him, and he dies before you?!?" Believe me, I had thought of that. But it still made me mad whenever he said that to me.

A year after we got married, in 1988, my most precious dream of becoming a "real" mom came true when our son Ryan was born. And in 1990, we welcomed our daughter, Hannah. Walt was a fantastic father and adored our children. And I was in my happiest element ever—I was finally a mother.

MY MOST DIFFICULT TRAGEDY

Around Christmas time in 1990, Hannah was three months old and Ryan was 2½. I distinctly remember one afternoon I decided to finally give up my fear, my fear about our age difference and about how Walt could possibly die suddenly. I was tired of replaying my father's words in my head, and somehow with the Christmas spirit all around me, I vowed to let go of my fear. I felt very free, and actually proud of myself. It was not easy for me to give up fears, and to stop worrying.

But then, at the very beginning of 1991, on January 3rd, the prediction that my father had angrily shouted at me, did come true. My husband, Walt, died of a heart attack just eight days after Christmas. I had finally let go of my longstanding fear that this might actually happen. And then it did happen. I knew I hadn't caused his death by letting go of my fear, but it haunted me for a very long time.

I struggled for months and months trying to cope with this loss. Losing him was hard enough, but having such little kids compounded the challenges. I chronicled this experience, and the many difficulties I encountered, in my first book, "A Kindness I Will Never Forget." It details my journey through grief, and finding hope and beauty in so many of life's moments.

I had lost my husband, but I still had two children to raise, and I was now their mother, and also their father. I had to find a way to move on and create a good life for myself. I found that path back by putting all of my energy into being the best mother I could be. Even through my sadness, I relished being a mom.

And eventually, life came full circle for me; I found myself in a profession (owning a restaurant) where I got to be a mother to many—all of my young employees, some teenagers, some in their 20's. This environment allowed me to care for others, which suited me perfectly.

And as difficult as it was to lose my husband, I could, after many years of reflection, view it with a deeper level of understanding and reverence. It was not that I ever was happy he had died, but I could see all the gifts it somehow had brought into my life. And I reflected how different it would have been if he had lived.

One of the strangest things for me to think about, was that my restaurant, La Strada, would never have existed. To think those 27 years of history at my business would never have happened, always made it seem somehow like things happened in the way they were supposed to happen.

To think of all the people who developed relationships by working there, or dining there, would never have existed. And the marriages and many children conceived through those friendships would not be here today.

And mostly, I would not have been a second mother to so many young people; I would not have been there to provide them a safe space for them to learn to be adults, to have someone to whom they could tell their secrets, to have someone who would love them no matter what, and for just who they were. I always wanted to be a mother, and I was, in so many different ways.

I was never happy, and could never be happy, that Walt had died and had missed out on seeing our children grow up into the beautiful people they were meant to be. I could never be totally at peace wondering about all the things my children had missed about having a father.

But I learned over time, that focusing on the good things that have come out of sorrow, is the best way to grow and learn, and have gratitude.

This book is not about loss; it's about hope and reflection, and finding a way back after the tragedies that happen to all of us in life.

And to inspire others to keep moving forward, and to make their own lives into an adventure.

WRITING STORIES

THE INSOMNIA REPORT

I had what I called a flip-flop schedule. Because I owned and operated a restaurant, I did not need to set an alarm clock in the morning, because I usually headed off to work each day at 5PM, precisely when other people were ending their work day.

I got home before midnight, but after doing a little of this and a little of that, I rarely got to sleep before 1AM. And then, for some reason, I woke up almost every night around 4AM, unable to fall quickly back to sleep. Having insomnia was incredibly frustrating, but even more so because it felt like a giant waste of time lying there trying to fall asleep again. Often, I would reach for my computer.

And so began my nightly "Insomnia Report," posted on my Facebook profile. This was not a time when I could write a long creative story. My mind was always cloudy. Mostly, this was just my time for complaining, or for making random comments on various subjects.

These were short informational reports such as, "It is so quiet and still at 4AM." Or rhetorical questions like, "Why can't I fall back to sleep???"

Then I started saying whatever was on my mind. I would let everyone know there was too much salt in my bed (because of whatever I had eaten the night before). My readers would share about what they were eating, or would also lament about not being able to fall asleep themselves.

Sometimes I would comment on products in infomercials on late night TV. They were all so dumb, but I always had to admit that my daughter would have ordered most of them. She LOVED all those gadgets showcased in infomercials.

I pondered many times what would happen if I called Chuck (from Chuck's restaurant) and asked him to bring me over a veggie burger from his place, and serve it to me in bed: I really think he would have done it. He used to hand me $1.00 bills at my restaurant, La Strada, and would ask me for a lap dance. (RIP Chuck!)

Sometimes I would just talk about whatever annoyed me. Finally, I would fall back to sleep. There were many times I would wake up the next morning, and hurriedly delete some of my insomnia reports. But my "insomnia followers" were very loyal to me, and looked for me every night.

One night I wrote, "I wish I had some potato chips." More than 100 people responded to that post. An old friend called me the next day. "How did you do that???" he said.

"Do what?" I asked.

"You wrote seven words! Seven words! And 100 people care about that!" He was flabbergasted.

"I don't know," I answered. Because I didn't know. I was just saying whatever I felt at the time.

MY FIRST STORY

Then, one day, I wrote a story. Not just seven words. Probably 500 words. It was about a man named Dave who had died; we called him Canadian Dave.

I went on a special concert trip in 2007 when I was turning 50 years old. I wasn't happy about being 50, so this concert opportunity came just at the right time. A large group of us from around the world began conversing online in an AOL chat room. We were excited about the upcoming concert, and were all making plans on what we would do when we met in person in London for the concert.

BTW, it was the fantastic Led Zeppelin reunion concert, that was only one night, and was held in honor of their late manager, whom they loved. The trip was beyond phenomenal, and lifelong friendships were created. One of our members was "Canadian Dave," who, obviously, was from Canada. Many of us in this "Led Zeppelin group" stayed in touch via Facebook.

One day, Dave told us he had cancer, and he was determined to fight it. But despite many treatments, he passed away.

I had been so moved about our friendship, that I decided to tell that story of how we all met in London, and how funny Dave had been, and what a good friend he was to all. Somehow, that one story, as long as it was, resonated with people. They didn't need to know Dave, to *want* to know *about* Dave. (I tell my whole story about him in the chapter called "Loved Ones I Miss.")

People liked reading about friendships and connections. Some could relate to his health struggle, and others related to the experience of losing a friend. Everyone could relate to the human condition. And they liked hearing about another ordinary person who had affected those around him in extraordinary ways.

That was the day I learned that people liked reading about human interactions, about how people misunderstand each other, and how we all learn from one another. So, I expanded beyond my Insomnia Report.

When I felt moved to do so, I would write another meaningful story. Sometimes the stories were about something funny that had happened in my business that night. Many of the stories were about some small kindness that someone had shown to me or to someone else—I was most moved to write about those experiences.

When I traveled, I would turn into a travel-blogger of sorts, and I wrote every night about the day's adventures. My audience grew, and people frequently asked when my next trip would be—they loved following along nightly on every adventure.

I told stories about my late mother and her dementia, and how my siblings and I had dealt with her illness. And stories about raising my children, from babies to teenagers.

Basically, I talked about real life, anything I saw, or felt, or experienced.

MY FIRST BOOK

In January of 2021, I had an important 30-year-date coming up. I could never call it an "anniversary" because that word sounds so celebratory. And it was not an event of celebration.

By now I had been writing stories for over ten years. But the stories that emanated from that monumental day had never been written. However, they had never left my head or my heart. I wanted to write these stories, even though it had now been 30 years. But I did not want anyone to feel sorry for me because I feel I am a very blessed person.

So, I was hesitant, and yet the stories seemed to be writing themselves in my brain and I could barely type fast enough to get them all down.

I decided to do it. I decided to write and publish these stories, one each day until each story was told. I let my audience know that I would be writing this series of 32 short stories about a long-time-ago event. I reassured them that I did not have any lingering sadness from this tragedy, and I was OK. I gave this warning because some of the emotional pain I experienced had been very deep, and I did not want anyone to worry about me.

On January 2, 2021, I began with what became the Introduction to my first book, "A Kindness I Will Never Forget." The story included a photograph that happened to be snapped on January 2, 1991, on my mother's front porch. It was the day before my whole life changed.

The story explained the happy smiles on mine and my children's faces, and noted how we had no idea of what was to come the following day.

On January 3, 2021, I told the story of 30 years ago, when on this day, I came home with my newborn and my 2-year-old, opened my front door, and saw my husband lying on my kitchen floor. He had died from a massive heart attack while I had been gone for a few hours.

Each day after that, I chronicled how the story unfolded, and about the new and unexpected challenges I was now facing. Many family relationships are complicated, and mine were no exception. But there were things I could never have predicted, scenarios I could never have dreamt of.

I continued the storytelling of what happened weeks and months after he died. Each story told of a kindness someone had done for me, a kindness I will never forget.

I could not believe the response to my stories of this event in my life. People were posting beautiful heartfelt comments, and they were also sharing their own experiences of loss. They resonated with what had happened to me.

One woman messaged me and told me her father had died when she was 10 years old. She said she had not been very kind or understanding to her mother; she had had no idea what the experience had been like for her. She told me she was going to call her mother that evening and apologize to her.

What I heard more than anything from so many people was, "I never knew this happened to you."

"What?" I would say. And then to some of them, "You knew my husband died a long time ago."

"Well, yes, but I didn't know you went through all of THAT!"

It was a common response. It actually made me feel proud to hear it, because I knew that I had built an authentic life beyond this terrible tragedy. The outgoing, fun, and full-of-ups-and-downs life I had created, was not a smoke screen to hide my pain. I had gotten past what happened, and had learned to accept life with all its moments. It had taken me a long time, but I learned to see the good in almost every situation.

The most special reaction I received was from my friend Brandon.

Brandon had owned the store right next to my restaurant—we had known each other for 10 years. He understood me well; I always referred to him as "my 2nd St. husband" because he could always predict my answer to everything, and always seemed to know what my next move would be.

Yes, in passing, at some point I had mentioned that my husband died, long ago when I was a young mother with two small children. But I didn't talk about it much because, as I always said, "I don't live in that place anymore." That was the best explanation I could give.

After he read my book, "A Kindness I Will Never Forget," he called me from Florida, where he now resided. "Jesus! You never told me this! I mean, I knew you were a widow, but you never told me all of that stuff! I had no idea what you went through. I just thought you were that crazy parade lady in high heels, who didn't have a care in the world!"

This was the best compliment I have ever received.

It meant I had truly found a way to live my life to the fullest, to enjoy and explore as many opportunities as I could. It meant I was joyful, and did not live my life in the past. The fact that Brandon had no idea what it had really been like for me, felt like a true testament to my full recovery from the loss of my husband.

This book is a collection of my stories: about cataract surgeries, my experiences with my handsome surgeon who fixed my rotator cuff, my challenges with motherhood, and how I traveled to Slovakia to meet distant relatives (and saw the Rolling Stones twice along the way!)

And what it was like to grow up as an introvert, with a job that required me to be an extrovert.

Every story is about a true event, and what the experience meant to me. It is real-life, through my eyes.

MY SECOND HOME, LA STRADA

FROM ENGINEER TO RESTAURANT OWNER

I was not your average restaurant owner.

Most restaurateurs have a passion for the business; it's in their blood, they love hospitality, or they were once a chef, or it is a dream they have always had. None of these descriptions fit me.

My prior restaurant experience had been pretty limited, and took place when I was a teenager. In fact, I seemed to be a serial "dessert thief."

The summer I was 15, my friend Marianne invited me to go with her to try to get a job at Woodies Goodies, located at the infamous Horny Corner at the bay in Belmont Shore in Long Beach. I thought, why not?

The owner immediately wanted to hire Marianne, but he was doubtful about me. I was small and a late bloomer and still 15, because I hadn't yet had my birthday that year. But I lied and said I was 16, and Marianne "vouched" for me—she was so convincing! We were both hired.

I had heard the original owner of Woodies Goodies was a wonderful person, but it had now been sold to an older, grumpy couple. They were not friendly or even very nice, and we were disgusted with how the man would reach in with his filthy bare hand to grab a fistful of pickles, to refill the container for the cook.

Minimum wage was $1.65/hour and he paid us $1.35, plus a free sandwich at the end of the day. Of course, at that time, I had never even heard of payroll taxes, or other expenses. We were annoyed that he was cheating us (he was actually cheating the government), so sometimes we took a Chico-o-stick when he wasn't looking.

We worked many days each week, and I loved working alongside Marianne—she was a great friend, always laughing and upbeat. After the afternoon wore down, we would sometimes lay on our towels at the Bay trying to get a tan—we oiled our bodies up with the cocoa butter we had "borrowed" from the stand. I could always justify these little indiscretions because in my mind he was cheating us. And he was mean too.

Later, when I had my restaurant, I reflected back on this many times, and how my young brain interpreted things at the time. I specifically discussed "unintended theft" with every new employee.

My next job was at Alphy's, a coffee shop on 7th Street, at Redondo Avenue. They only hired me because my older sister was such a good waitress there. I was a hostess, and I only lasted a month. They had these delicious Andes Crème de Menthe mints, and I'm pretty sure I ate an entire box. They found out, and fired me. I remember thinking, "What's the big deal about eating a few mints?"

After that I worked at Hof's Hut in the Marina for a couple months. They made us wear a ridiculous hair piece called a "cascade" that I was sure made me look 50 (or that's what I thought at the time. I probably just looked 16 with a ridiculous hair piece). They did have good pie and ice cream there, and we could eat whatever pies got messed up, which frequently seemed to "accidentally" happen.

I seemed to always have a justification for stealing desserts. After all, I was so humiliated to be wearing that cascade hairpiece, that I thought it was just fine for me to find a piece of "messed up pie" to eat at every shift.

I was not really cut out for the restaurant business. I had no interest in ever owning a restaurant, or even any kind of business at all.

Fast forward to an unusual situation in 1993. My father decided to financially back a new business endeavor for a man who already owned another restaurant on 2nd Street in Belmont Shore. My father really trusted this man, as he had befriended him by eating at his place for lunch almost every day.

My father, also an engineer, knew nothing about the restaurant business, but decided he would put up the initial investment, and the partner would manage the operation. The new space opened, and was called Caffe La Strada, meaning, the "Café on the Street."

It wasn't long before my father knew that something was going terribly wrong with his new investment. His partner had promised high profits that they would be splitting, but after many months, that was not happening. My father believed his partner was somehow stealing inventory and profits from the restaurant, but he couldn't figure out how he was doing it.

One day he called and asked me to come help him out. He wanted me to come to the restaurant one evening and just "be there," to walk around, observe and say hello to people. To "work" there, without really doing much. I told him I didn't know anything about the restaurant business, but he asked me to come anyway. My mother would watch the kids, so they would have a fun evening with Grandma. This would be a turning point in my life, even though I didn't know it at the time.

I had no idea how being there was going to help, but on the appointed evening, I decided I should look a little nicer than my usual stay-at-home-Mom style of jeans and a shirt covered in baby food stains. I put on a pretty dress, and it occurred to me that I had not worn a dress in quite a long time, not since Walt had died two years before. It felt nice.

I arrived in my pretty dress to my father's new business venture. I felt very uncomfortable and out of place because I wasn't sure exactly what my father wanted me to do. He introduced me around to everyone working there. Not being a hospitality-type person, it didn't feel natural for me to walk around and just talk to strangers. I stayed mostly with the wait-staff, asking them if they needed help with anything. They began to show me how they did this and that during the evening.

My father's partner was there, and I was a little afraid of him because he glared at me all night as if he didn't trust why I was there. As the evening wore on, I found the fast pace of everyone moving around me quite invigorating. I felt this palpable underlying excitement, I felt alive, and challenged.

Parts of me were waking up; it was like they were all screaming at me: Let us out! That night helped me to begin reclaiming all of those buried parts of myself. I hadn't even realized they were missing, until they all came flooding back.

I suddenly felt creative, and like I had done something constructive during the evening. And as much as I loved being a mother, I began to feel more like a complete person, like a woman again. I had buried so much of myself while I was in survival mode, because my focus had been on making sure my kids were OK.

It felt good to be a little more out into the world, to be of assistance to someone else, and to maybe make a difference. It really helped my father for me to be there as well. His suspicions of his partner grew and he doubted why he had ever agreed to go into business with him. My presence made him feel like he was not alone in trying to figure it all out.

It was a relief to be doing something other than taking care of my babies; I had been with them every evening for the last two years. Being at the restaurant, I could escape my grief and responsibilities for a few hours. And they were safely being watched by my mother who they adored.

I stayed a few hours, then went to pick up the kids and drove home. I wasn't sure exactly what to think after one night in the restaurant, but I knew something was different. When I got home, I carried my sleeping kids into the house, one by one, and put them to bed.

I barely slept that night. Something had come alive within me. I couldn't really explain it. I wasn't sure if it was the break from motherhood, or the break from grief, or that I somehow felt pretty again while wearing a dress.

After that first night, I began to return night after night, dropping my kids with my mother, and then going to work at the restaurant. My role expanded as I got to know the staff and started feeling more comfortable talking to the patrons. I slowly began to learn some of the inner-workings of a business, such as how and when products were ordered, and when they were delivered. How to schedule employees and manage their days off and any sudden illnesses. And I found being in the kitchen watching the chefs fascinating. They would make the same dishes over and over again, without measuring or calculating anything, and they turned out beautiful every time. I could never cook without measuring.

I never had to worry about my children because they were with my mother, and they absolutely loved being there. They were not yet school-age, so there was no homework to be done or lunches to be packed. My mother read to them and played with them, gave them baths, and afterwards always dressed them in my father's adult sized white t-shirts—they looked like little nightgowns.

Each night I returned to my parents' house, and my father would carry my sleeping children out one at a time, and put them in my car. And I would drive home and carry them to their beds, one at a time.

Eventually the partner's theft revealed itself. He was "stealing labor" by having employees use the Caffe La Strada time clock, and then go to work at his other restaurant down the street. He was stealing inventory by stopping all orders and deliveries to his other business. Instead, he would order everything through the Caffe La Strada accounts for both businesses. Then he personally transported all the inventory in his own car to his other restaurant. One afternoon I stumbled upon him filling up his car with huge bags of pasta, and 5-gallon containers of chicken base, among many other things. It suddenly became very clear just how much he was stealing, and how.

Eventually, the relationship between my father and his partner dwindled. They did not trust one another, and they ended up suing each other to gain ownership of the business. The restaurant court case took over a year to resolve. My older sister and I spent many long hours helping our father with research and documentation. We also went with him to court appearances.

At one point, the judge in the case ordered that neither partner was allowed on the restaurant premises at all until things were resolved. My father asked me to continue working at the business as his stand in, and I said yes. I worked almost every night for seven months. I probably spent too much time away from my children. But because of that, something magical happened. My kids were at my parent's house almost every evening, with both Grandma and Grandpa, and they became very close to their grandparents.

After some time, in a way, my parents had become the "other parent" in my children's lives that had been missing since their father had died. My parents stared at my children with so much love and reverence. Each evening when I returned they would tell me every single thing they had done.

My children felt so loved and so secure. This beautiful relationship between my kids and my parents was an invaluable gift that I could never have imagined would come out of this restaurant challenge.

And being at the restaurant night after night had offered me the chance to become a whole person again. I finally felt like I overcame my grief, and joined the living once more.

In the end, my father was awarded ownership of the restaurant by the court. He asked me if I still wanted to keep running it, otherwise he was going to close it. I thought about it. I was now fairly used to this routine of working in the evenings, and being home in the day-time hours. If I returned to an engineering job, I would have to find childcare for my kids every single day.

I told my father, yes, I would try running it for a while, and would see what would come of it.

I only had this very limited restaurant experience during the part-nership dispute. I knew if I wanted it to be successful, I would have to learn a lot more about business. It would be a huge commitment of time and effort, and research and learning. I felt I was up to the challenge.

Within a few years, I changed the name to simply "La Strada," and I had turned it into a healthy thriving business. Along the way, I paid my father back his original investment. La Strada was all mine.

My father always felt foolish for trusting his partner and open-ing a business he knew nothing about. He did not like to fail, and he considered it to be a huge failure on his part. Over the years he said to me many times, "Opening that restaurant was the biggest mistake of my life."

And I always answered him with, "*Your* biggest mistake was the best thing that ever happened to me."

It helped bring me back to life.

WHAT I REALLY LOVED ABOUT THE RESTAURANT BUSINESS

After the restaurant court case was settled, my father said to me, "Well I don't want to run a restaurant. Do you want to try doing it?" I had already been running it for a year and a half, and I had learned so much.

Some of my greatest teachers were the restaurant employees. They told me how things worked in other restaurants, how to make things flow better, what was important to customers. I had also gone to book-stores and bought books on business, on how to manage employees, and on how to market a business. There was no internet back then, but somehow I found out about business seminars and went to those too. I even talked to other restaurant owners; I asked a million questions. And I listened to the answers and implemented what I thought would work.

I told my father I would try it for a while. It wasn't long before I discovered my true passion within the restaurant business: my employees.

I had suddenly become a mother to 15 more kids, aged 18-25. Yes, that's what they felt like to me. They needed direction, they needed to be loved and appreciated, and they needed discipline. And I loved having all these extra "kids."

Originally there had been many seasoned employees, all hired by my father's ex-partner. But with attrition, I began to need new people, and I learned to always choose someone who had no previous experience in the restaurant industry. Why? I always said, "You can teach someone the job, but you can't teach someone 'to be nice.'"

I especially learned this one afternoon during the year my daughter, Hannah, was in kindergarten. A girl was coming in for an interview at 11:30AM. I picked up my daughter from school and brought her to the restaurant with me. I told her she was to sit at the table quietly, and work on her homework packet while I talked to this girl. Her homework packet was a week's worth of assignments, and she had the entire week to complete it. In our household, this was always an unpleasant experience for me and my daughter; she was always stressed about making it perfect. We were many times at odds with each other as I tried to convince her that what she had done was just fine.

Hannah and I sat at a front table when Marissa came in. She sat down, and said hello to me and my daughter, and was really friendly. Right about then my chef came out and said there was a plumbing problem in the kitchen that required my immediate attention. I asked Marissa to stay with Hannah for a few minutes as I ran back to solve the plumbing issue.

The plumbing issue took way longer than I expected, and I was in the kitchen for 20-30 minutes. When I returned to the table, my daughter gleefully held up her homework packet and, beaming, said, "Mom! I finished my homework!" I couldn't believe it. I turned to Marissa and said, "You're hired."

"But," she said, "You haven't asked me any questions yet."

"I don't have to," I told her. "You helped my daughter finish all her homework for the entire week, and you just met us. If you would be that kind to my five-year-old, then you will be that way with everyone." And she was. Marissa worked for me for six years.

I used this model of hiring from then on out. I hired the people that showed they cared. One time I had a long line of kids waiting to be interviewed. I spoke first to a boy named Zac and I knew he was perfect for the job. But out of respect for the others who had taken the time to show up, I continued with the interviews.

The very next young man, Andy, was very quiet and unassuming. He was nice, but I really only needed one person. At the end of Andy's interview, as the next guy approached the table, Andy stood up and looked at him and said, "Good luck." He had just wished his competitor good luck. How kind was that!

So, I hired him too. Zac and Andy worked for me for many years.

My employees were the heart and soul of my business. I loved watching them grow up and learn along the way. Mostly when they started working, they had never made a salad or even a cup of coffee, some of them didn't even know how to make change. But they would take direction from the older staff who were happy to teach them.

And along the way there was something else I treasured. My employees felt safe with me. As I explained earlier, my employees shared things with me that they could never tell their own parents. When they were afraid, I understood that fear. If they wondered if their thoughts or actions meant they were a bad person, I would always reassure them they were not, and that nothing they could tell me would shock or surprise me. They were part of my restaurant family, no matter what. I was there for them. And they knew that.

They were all safe in what I began to call, "My 2nd Home, my little La Strada." And my love for them, and how they took care of me and my business, was infinite.

THE RESTAURANT DOCTOR

I somehow did not realize I had just landed in a business that required a skill that went directly against my most primal nature. I had always been quiet and soft spoken, a true introvert. I did enjoy conversations with people I already knew, like my employees or friends, but I was never very comfortable meeting new people.

I felt this at an early age when I took walks with my mother along 2nd St. in Belmont Shore. I could never understand why she felt compelled to say something to everyone she passed, and why she started entire conversations with someone she had just met while waiting for the light to change so we could cross the street.

At the restaurant, I gravitated toward the business end of things, and enjoyed the scheduling, setting up a billing system, and doing the payroll. But I shied away from the "people-interaction" part of it. I honestly didn't think it mattered much.

Even though I had a fair number of customers, it seemed my business was patronized by those who already knew me: families from my kids' school, friends of extended family, etc. And, of course, there were always "walk-ins," people who just happened to walk by.

But I knew I needed more customers. I wanted to know, "how do I get people who don't know me, to come in and dine here?" Specifically, how does one get more customers, in an organic way? Not with advertisements, but with word-of-mouth? There was so much more I needed to learn about the restaurant business. Especially if I wanted to earn a living by doing it.

I had heard of a man in the community who called himself, "The Restaurant Doctor." He would go to businesses, survey them, look around, watch them in operation, and ask many questions. After doing his research and studying a business, he would give his opinions on how to improve that business. I knew he was helping a local coffee shop down the street, and it had become tremendously successful.

I asked him to come meet with me. We sat and chatted, and he observed my employees and my customers. He asked me a LOT of questions. I felt nervous during the entire meeting. I could not imagine what he thought I should be doing differently. But I wanted to learn, and felt I would be up to any challenge he presented to me. When our meeting ended, he said he would be in touch with me to give his recommendations.

A couple days later, the Restaurant Doctor returned. We sat down at one of my little tables with the red-and-white checkered tablecloths, and he handed me a paper with a list of seven things he thought I should do to improve my business. Seven things. "OK," I originally thought, "that's not very many."

Some were so easy. He didn't like that from the front door, you could see all the way down the back hallway, including the cart with the dirty dishes. We had some latticework that separated the service area from the customer area. I could have a handyman move it over to cover the hallway. Easy.

But then the suggestions became way more difficult. He suggested firing most of my employees! It seemed he had suggested this in the coffee shop down the street as well, and it had worked out because the current employees were "comping" so many items (e.g., giving out free pastries); the owner was losing money on the freebies. Every new employee there was taught they would be fired if they did that. So, it worked out for the coffee shop owner.

But I loved my employees! They were my favorite part of coming to work every day. They were my "teenage kids." I could never fire them, and I just refused to believe any of them could be stealing from me, intentionally or not.

The Restaurant Doctor could sense I was already alarmed even though I stayed quiet as he continued through the list. Then he got to the most daunting thing on the list. And not only was it something I knew I could never do, I vehemently disagreed with him. He had said, "You need to talk to every customer that comes into your business. Every. Single. One."

I sat back in my chair in disbelief, and in total defensiveness. What??? I thought he was crazy; I was completely skeptical. Why would I need to talk to any of the customers? And every customer? Why?

And it wasn't just that I disagreed with him—it was because the thought of it absolutely terrified me. There was no way I would be able to do this. And it was not logical to me. Why would anyone want me to bother them and interrupt their meal? I posed this question to the Restaurant Doctor.

He laughed. "Your guests WANT you to talk to them." Really? I was dumbfounded. How could this be true? I never cared about meeting any restaurant owner while I was out dining. And if they did come to my table, I perceived it as phony and fake, and not authentic.

He looked at me and explained how wrong I was: "You are in a VERY small minority. Almost everyone, 98% of the population, loves to know that the owner cares enough to stop by and say hello. You will not be interrupting them. They want to talk to you. You will have to do this."

I persisted. "I don't want to be a phony," I told the Restaurant Doctor. He just smiled.

I didn't know how to accept this. I couldn't believe that 98% of diners would enjoy this. I honestly had the thought, "I'm just going to close up this business. This will never work; I can never do this. I don't *want* to do this. Why would anyone want me to come over to talk to them?"

As we sat there, he challenged me. He wanted me to practice, right then and there. I was terrified. He told me to walk over to a table by the window where two people were dining, and carry something with me. I picked up a pen. "No, no, no!" he said. "Don't take a pen, hold a bread basket."

I felt so dumb and out of my element. Full of tension and anxiety, I grabbed an empty bread basket and nervously approached the table. I paused until they stopped talking, and asked how everything was. I was a wreck. But they were polite, smiled back and said "great." I turned back around feeling ridiculous, holding my empty bread-basket-prop and headed back to the Restaurant Doctor. I had to stop myself from running.

The Restaurant Doctor said I had done great, and as he stood up to leave, he encouraged me to keep trying and promised it would get easier.

But I hated it. I hated doing it. It felt so unnatural to me, and like I was interrupting people's meals and time together.

But I had been determined when I hired this man. He was called the Restaurant "Doctor" for a reason; he had helped many businesses. I had paid him for his advice, and had vowed I would do what he suggested.

But I couldn't do all of it. I would move the latticework, but I could not fire my employees. They were too special to me. And I was so unsure about this "talking to everybody thing," as I called it. I mentioned it to a few customers, and to my amazement, they completely agreed with him.

I decided I was going to have to figure out a way to do it. And I was scared to death. But I began to practice. Each night, I took a piece of paper and made tally marks of how many people with whom I had spoken. And each night thereafter, I tried to do better than the evening before.

To gain more confidence, I would first go to the tables where I knew the people who sat there. We had two long-time patrons, Connie and Laurie, who knew of my attempt to learn this new skill. They came in every Friday night and would check on my progress. They knew about my nightly tally and reassured me over and over again that I wasn't boring or interfering with them, or anyone else. Each time I visited a table and spent some time chit-chatting, I would then quickly return to Connie and Laurie, and add another mark to my paper.. And once again, they would encourage me and send me out to another table. They were my consummate cheerleaders.

Slowly, but surely, I became better and better at this new skill. I started to really see and understand how important it was to people for me to say "hello." It made them feel appreciated, and it made them feel respected. It made them want to return and patronize my business.

I made many mistakes along the way, the most notable I remember was asking a woman when her baby was due, and then she told me she wasn't pregnant. I felt terrible and like I had ruined her evening. I also learned that two women talking excitedly together, were much less likely to want a visit to their table—they were most likely girlfriends, catching up with each other. Long-married couples were the easiest to chat with—they had been together so long, they welcomed banter with a new person.

And towards the end of my business, I had a favorite customer who was 93. He would immediately call me over the minute he sat down. And he always said, "Kid, the food's pretty good, but I come here for the entertainment!" And then he would wait for me to tell him a funny story about this or that.

Over time and with great practice, I had learned to become an extrovert, in a way. It was not my true nature, so I always called it a "learned skill" that I had to practice over and over again in order to master it.

I learned that after I approached a table and said hello, it was OK to bring up whatever was going on in my life at the time. And my patrons would share their own experiences of something similar. For example, when I was teaching my kids to drive, everyone had a fun story to tell. When my kids became errant teenagers and I discussed it with my loyal patrons, they let me know it would get better one day, that my kids would grow up and become mature adults someday. Also, by speaking to so many guests in my restaurant, I got to know many wonderful people over the years.

I began to see my business grow and thrive. People would step in the front door and wave at me as soon as they saw me. They were excited to talk about the latest thing happening in my life or their lives, or in the world. They started to seem less scary to me, and I became more and more comfortable greeting everyone.

And another thing began to happen. When people came in, they would tell my staff, "I know Lisa!" and they would be proud and feel like they were part of my business. And in fact, they were. They were contributing to a family of employees and they became part of that family, sending us Christmas cards and celebrating our successes.

I had experienced many benefits of learning my new skill, but still, at heart, I remained a true introvert. And as exhilarating as an evening at work would be, with all the busy-ness, managing, and overseeing, and all the talking to "each and every person," I was exhausted at the end of the night. I always needed my very quiet home to rejuvenate my soul and spirit.

I learned such a valuable lesson, actually two really great lessons, by listening to the Restaurant Doctor.

First, I had been so wrong about his advice. 100% wrong. If I had not trusted him, and stepped out of my comfort zone, I would never have become the successful business owner I did. And I would never have met so many wonderful people.

And the second lesson, maybe even more important than the first: I discovered to take a step back, to listen, and to acknowledge I am not always right. I don't know everything. I can't know everything. And it's OK to trust other people's experiences and learn from them.

It was incredibly humbling.

"WE TAKE CARE OF PEOPLE"

"We aren't just serving food. We are taking care of people. That is our job."

I said this over and over again. To every employee I hired. I am fairly certain they were sick of hearing me say it. But that was my total philosophy and approach at my restaurant. It wasn't about taking orders and bringing out food; we were taking care of every single person who walked through the front door.

What did that mean exactly?

It meant paying attention, on every level. Watching what people did, listening to what they said or did. It meant noticing things they may not even notice themselves. And ideally, fulfilling their needs before they have a chance to ask, or maybe to even know they needed whatever it was they needed. For instance, when you heard someone banging the parmesan shaker on their table, trying to loosen up the cheese inside, they needed a new container of parmesan. And they needed it right away, so it was wise to immediately rush over with a fresh container.

Taking care of people also meant that when the same man comes in five times a week, and orders an iced tea and Penne Pomodoro, you have his iced tea already in your hand when you walk over and approach his table to greet him. This small gesture makes a world of difference to every patron—the feeling of being recognized and appreciated.

And sometimes taking care of people meant going to much greater lengths. For example, there was a time when an inebriated man needed to leave the restaurant and somehow get safely to his nearby home. I helped him up and accompanied him there, and made sure he got in the door safely. I also called Ubers for people who couldn't work their phones. When a lady left a Target Gift Card somewhere in the restaurant, we searched everywhere for it, even though she had accused the entire staff of stealing it (we later found it stuck in a menu between pages five and six).

Taking care of people also meant trying to get lost items back to their rightful owners; so many things were left behind—sunglasses, umbrellas, hats, credit cards, even action figures and a pair of black women's underwear under a corner table (I never saw that coming!)

On one particular evening, a woman called and said she was pretty sure she had left her lower denture at the first table on the right, wrapped in a napkin, and asked if we could look for it? Well, of course we could. And we did.

It was endearing to see the horrified faces of my young staff when I told them of the situation. They asked, "Do we really have to go through the trash??"

"Yes. Yes, we do. We take care of people. Follow me."

I carried our front trashcan to the back area and told the girls to go get gloves. They were still unsure; they weren't even sure what a denture was, or what it might look like. I asked them, "Have either of you ever lost a retainer? It's basically the same thing."

"Yes, yes," they answered, they both had. And one of them had wrapped hers up in a napkin in exactly the same way. "It's the same." I repeated. They now understood.

"OK, let's go through this together piece by piece and shake out every single napkin. Make sure we don't miss one." We all started looking, and going through every piece of trash. I helped too. I never asked my staff to do anything I wouldn't do myself.

We had almost gotten to the bottom of the trash can when one of them held it up, squealing with delight. "I think I found it! Is this it??" She held it as far away from her body as possible, not sure about how she felt holding it. Yes, there it was!

"What do I do with it??" she asked, now looking horrified. I smiled, trying not to laugh at her reaction. "I'll take care of it." I took the lady's denture and wrapped it in our green-and-white-checked bread-basket paper, and put it in a to-go box. I labeled it carefully so none of the employees would accidentally throw it away again. Then I called the lady back and told her we had it. She was absolutely ecstatic we had found it and so very grateful. In less than 20 minutes she arrived to pick it up.

And what about my two staff members? They felt proud and had even learned a few things.

1. they could conquer a fear
2. they could help someone
3. they now knew what a denture looked like.

And they learned first-hand, my motto:

"We aren't just serving food. We are taking care of people. That is our job."

TAKING CARE OF EACH OTHER—A RESTAURANT IS A FAMILY

In addition to taking care of the patrons while working at a restaurant, there is a much bigger caring experience that happens. Working together side by side, a group of restaurant workers become a family. And they take care of each other.

By working together night after night, sometimes in very stressful situations, familial bonds are created that are sacred. There is a level of trust one develops for their colleagues, and these shared experiences create lasting memories.

An understanding develops between employees, and between each employee and their boss. My employees "got" me. They knew what was important to me, and learned what to do first, and what to do next. I understood if they did not know what "on-the-side" meant, and I was willing to teach them. They knew I would never get mad when they broke a wine glass or a plate. They came to understand that I could forgive almost anything, as long as they told me the truth.

And I went to great lengths for them—I worked around their school and vacation schedules. I lent them money, I gave them rides, I made sure they were OK. Along the way, I always acknowledged their wonderment, and who they were as people. I felt this same way about my kitchen workers, who are known in the restaurant business as "back of house" staff.

One day I received a phone call from my server. She said my head chef was leaving to go to the hospital because of a burn. He told her that he didn't need me to come to the restaurant, he just wanted me to know. Uh oh. It took me all of 10 seconds to realize what this meant—I flew out the door, hopped into my car, and headed straight to the restaurant.

My head chef was a very private person. He and I were very much alike in many ways: quiet and analytical. And we were both "big-picture-people" who could see everything going on, and determine what needed to be done first. Yes, my chef worked for me, but we were definitely a team. He handled the "back-of-house" at La Strada, I ran the front. We had a deep respect and appreciation for one another.

He never complained. Ever. One time, during the Belmont Shore Chocolate Festival, he sliced two of his fingers pretty deeply and just wrapped them up and said "I'm OK." No. I took him to urgent care immediately. A week later I told him we needed to go back to have his stitches removed. He informed me that he had already taken them out himself. Yikes!

So, now, hearing that he felt he needed to go to the hospital, well, I knew it had to be bad. I was at La Strada within three minutes. I learned he had been lifting a large pot of marinara sauce and it somehow sloshed over the side onto his bare arm, from the elbow down. He was running it under cold water when I got there. He didn't look very good at all.

I called 911. The firemen came to the back door in the alley, and looked at his arm. They assessed that I could drive him to the ER myself. We hopped into my little red Fiat, and raced over to St. Mary's Hospital in Long Beach. He was admitted pretty quickly.

I reminded him that when they asked for his pain level, on a scale of one to ten, to say "ten!" I knew him well enough to know he would just say, "It's OK." And I knew it wasn't OK; burns are very painful.

He was called in, and they allowed me to come in with him. The nurses assessed his arm, and he gave the correct number of "10" when asked to indicate his pain level. Then they began to calmly apply topical medication, and wrap his arm. Everything seemed to be going so slowly. Why hadn't they given him his pain meds yet???

After about two minutes I nervously paced up and down the hallway. Then I'd come back and ask, "will he be getting the pain meds soon?"

"Yes, they have been ordered," I was told each of the six times I asked. I kept pacing and pacing.

I flashed back to a specific scene in the movie, "Terms of Endearment." In the film, the character of the mother is played by Shirley MacLaine, and her daughter is in the hospital. The nurses were a couple minutes late in giving the daughter her pain medication. The Mom character screams at all of them to give her daughter her pain medication. NOW.

I felt that exact same way inside, but I tried not to show it. I paced and paced. Finally, they gave him some medication along with a tetanus shot. After they were finished, he and I got back in my little red Fiat and headed back to the Shore where I dropped off his prescriptions at Rite Aid.

We then went to La Strada to get his keys. The minute we walked in, he immediately started working by moving things with one hand. No, no, no. I told him he had to go home, and he promised me he would after he picked up his medication.

I went home to change into nicer clothes for that evening. When I arrived back an hour later, I was happy to see my assistant chef busy in the kitchen making all the food. This meant my head chef had gone home and not stayed to work.

I then noticed the dishwasher guy was in the kitchen with him, acting as a sous chef. Weird. Why wasn't he washing the dishes? But then, as I passed the dishwashing station, guess who was in there loading and unloading the dishwashing machine with one hand? Yes, it was my head chef.

He was so devoted to me and to my restaurant, he refused to go home that evening and continued to work. I had taken care of him, and now he was taking care of me. We would both drop anything we were doing to help one another immediately, whenever and wherever we were needed.

And this respect and gracious spirit was evident among all the employees that evening. Without being asked, they jumped in to return the clean dishes back to their respective places, something the dishwasher would normally have done. Nothing needed to be said, it was understood that we took care of each other.

A group of restaurant workers is more than a team, it's a family. And this was the number one reason why I loved my job so very much.

A WORLD EVENT LIKE NO OTHER

Sometimes real-life events have a huge impact on business.

In 1994, I was at my restaurant on a Friday night. There wasn't a single customer in the place. We didn't know where everyone was. And there was no way to find out what was happening—there were no cell phones, no Twitter, and we did not have a TV.

Where was everyone?

Suddenly at 9PM, people started coming in in droves. They couldn't stop talking about what had happened—it was the night that OJ Simpson had been running away from the police in his white Bronco, and everyone had been glued to their TV sets watching the news.

As soon as he was apprehended, everyone left their homes and came out to eat. They were all hungry—there were no delivery services back then either.

After that experience, I knew to always pay attention to big events in the world and remember they might affect how busy my business might be on a particular night: State-of-the-Union addresses, big boxing matches on Showtime, Super Bowl, the World Series, and unplanned disasters and world events.

People stayed home when something monumental was happening in the country or around the world, because the only broadcasts, news, or updated reports came directly from their television sets.

Then . . . 9/11 happened. It was a Tuesday night and tragic for the whole country.

I wondered how business would be that evening at my restaurant— I assumed it would be very slow with everyone staying home to watch the news coverage.

I made my kids an early dinner, then headed to work anyway. Even though I expected very few patrons, I wanted to check in with my staff to see how they were doing; most of them were young and had never lived through a time of tragedy like this before.

When I arrived, every employee told me of what they were feeling and about how it was affecting their families, friends, and their schools. They were happy to be at work where they could share with each other, and be of service to others.

At first there were no patrons at all. But then I realized I could not have been more wrong with my expectations of the evening. It was nothing like what I thought it would be; I was absolutely shocked and surprised at how the evening went.

From 6PM on, people just kept coming in, table after table, and way more people than usual for a Tuesday night. And they weren't just coming in to eat, they were coming to my restaurant to be together.

As people entered, they did not go directly to their table. They stopped to hug me. They stopped and hugged each and every server, and the busboy too. If they recognized fellow customers at other tables, they went over and hugged them too.

A family of four might sit at their table on one side of the restaurant, but if they recognized a family or group arriving at the door, they didn't just nod or wave at them. They all stood up and walked toward each other and embraced each other. People were crying and speaking of the great loss of our citizens in the towers and in the planes that had crashed.

Suddenly the furniture started to be rearranged, and I didn't care at all. Rather than going to sit at a separate table, the adjoining table would be pulled over and the chairs placed around so they could all sit together.

Then another family would arrive and the same thing was repeated. My restaurant of 17 small tables was now a mishmash of neighbors, friends and fellow Americans, a room full of people talking, crying, and loving each other. It became one family, turning to one another for comfort and understanding of what had happened: it felt like 50 people sitting around one dining room table all together. More than anything, we all felt an intense pride about being Americans. There was no division amongst us.

For several more nights, this continued. People just kept coming in to reach out to one another, to be part of their community and they behaved differently too. No one got mad if we forgot to bring a salad. No one minded if the bread took too long to bring out.

Even in light of this tragic event, a greater purpose of kindness emerged. It became a memorable experience full of love and unity. I will never forget the tragedy that happened to our country that day. But also, I will never, ever, forget those nights of community spirit, and I was so happy to be able to provide a special place for people to come, and to be together.

100 RESTAURANT STORIES

This is one of hundreds of stories I could tell about my restaurant. It is one of my favorites.

There is a certain type of customer, usually a couple who have been together a long time, who don't just want to dine. They sincerely want to get to know each and every staff member.

Ray and Kay were the originals; they knew everyone by name. They came in every week, usually early on a Friday evening, and sat on the left-hand side of the restaurant that we called, "The Right." (because we were looking from the opposite direction).

They had been married a long time and they both ordered Lasagna Bolognese, and shared a half carafe of Chianti. Ray and Kay would chat with their server and get caught up on everything happening in their lives. They knew what they were studying in school, if they had a boyfriend or girlfriend, or what their future aspirations were. When they were all caught up, the server would go on to his or her next table, and Ray and Kay would motion for the next employee to come over and would chat with them too.

Every member of the staff loved taking care of Ray and Kay; they felt appreciated and loved by the two of them. In fact, every server felt it was an honor if they sat in their section.

One day, a staff member mentioned to me that Ray and Kay had not been in for a while, maybe for a few weeks. I didn't remember seeing them either, so I inquired of most of the staff and no one else had seen them either. I began to worry. It's hard not to be concerned about your regular customers.

Eventually there came a day when Ray walked in, right around 4:30 when the evening servers were arriving as well. I noticed he was carrying with him a pretty box, and I definitely noticed that Kay was not with him. He walked over and sat at table 5R, the fifth (and last) table on their side of the restaurant, the furthest table from the door.

I went over to talk to him. I leaned over and put my arm around his shoulder to greet him, and he asked me to sit down. Ray told me that Kay had died. He had been too sad to come back to La Strada without her. He couldn't face it. I reached over and held both of his hands in mine, and looked into his eyes to let him know the sorrow I felt for him.

Ray then reached for the box and opened it, then turned it so I could see inside. It was Kay's jewelry box. Kay loved "pins" and had many of them. Ray wanted to give a pin to each server to remember Kay. I thought that was so touching.

I told the two servers, Kendra and Sarah, to sit down with Ray. They had both waited on him and Kay many times, and I knew they had both been worried that we hadn't seen either of them for a few weeks. Ray told them that Kay had passed away, and they both started crying. Ray showed them all of Kay's pins, and told them to each pick one out.

I was in the back getting fresh lettuce for the evening rush. When I came back I saw there was a man sitting up front at a small table. He looked very impatient. The girls hadn't seen him because they were not facing the door. I took a menu out to him and greeted him warmly.

"Are you the manager?" he asked angrily.

"Yes," I said, "I'm the owner."

He looked disgusted and said, "Do you know I've been sitting here for 10 minutes, and your employees are just sitting down over there with that man?"

My blood began to boil. I thought about explaining that one of our customers had died, but I didn't think he deserved to know anything about Ray and Kay. I took his order.

When I walked back to hang up his order and get his drink and a basket of bread, the girls then saw there was a customer and offered to get up, but I told them to stay with Ray. He needed them, and I didn't care if this man thought I was the worst manager ever by letting my employees sit down while I ran around and did their job.

More tables came in and I took all the orders, brought drinks and fresh bread, and took care of everyone. I brought Mr. Grumpy out his food, and he glared at me. I was as smiley and sunshiny as ever. Kendra and Sarah continued to sit with Ray as I let them know I was doing fine, and keeping up with all of the patrons.

As I handled everything in the restaurant while the girls sat there with Ray, Mr. Grumpy grew madder and madder. I have to admit, this made me very happy.

He finished eating, I brought him his bill, and returned with his credit card. He glared at me each and every time I arrived at his table. As he got up and left, I said with complete sarcasm, "Thanks for coming!"

At some point I did need the girls to get up and begin to help. But I was glad they had had time with Ray to talk about Kay. And I was glad for Ray to be able to eat dinner with two young ladies who really cared about him and his loss.

No one tells me how to take care of my people and my patrons. I know them, I know what they need, what will make them feel better in this world: being heard and understood and cared for. That was what Ray (and my servers) needed that night. That was what my La Strada was all about.

I could tell many more stories about my 27 years at my restaurant—stories about staff, about customers, about weather, about plumbing (plumbing?), and about inebriated people and how to handle them.

But those stories will have to wait for my next book.

RYAN

MY KIDS

I can't write a book of stories without including some stories about my children. They were, and are, a pivotal part of my life.

For years after I started writing, I actually chose NOT to write about them. They were teenagers at the time, and did not want attention drawn to them. I embarrassed them enough already, and even the stories that had absolutely nothing at all to do with them, made them uncomfortable.

Also, the teenage years as a single parent were not easy. Maybe teenage years are never easy. Mine as a teenager certainly were not.

When we become parents and are now on the other side, I think we try to fix whatever it is that we missed out on. That's what I did anyway. I somehow thought if I did it better than my parents, then it would all go smoothly.

It didn't. I was wrong.

My main goal as a parent was to make sure my kids knew I loved them no matter what, and I would never turn on them for anything. That seemed like a good idea; I had the right intentions. But looking back, I was probably too lenient and didn't hold them accountable enough for whatever transpired. I can think of lots of things I should have/could have done differently, but I don't usually stay in a place of regret. It doesn't do anyone any good and it offers no peace.

And all that's changed now anyway, as they are all grown up. They are (mostly) OK with whatever I do now.

So, let's start with Ryan.

FINALLY A MOTHER

The day Ryan was born in 1988 seems like "forever-ago." My water broke early one morning and I called my doctor. He said I didn't need to come to the hospital until I was having regular contractions. Nothing was happening yet, so I told Walt to go ahead and go to work; I was fine.

By 5PM, my doctor called and said I should come to the hospital. I called Walt to let him know he should leave work soon. As I got ready, there was something I wanted to do before we left that would preserve the memory of what it had been like being that big and pregnant.

Back then there were no cell phones or home computers. And taking a picture of yourself pregnant was NOT something to do like it is now. So, I finished packing my hospital bag, put on my bikini, and waited for Walt to come home. He walked in, and just stopped. "Honey, what in the hell are you doing? Shouldn't we be going to the hospital?"

"Yes. We will. This will only take a second." I motioned for him to follow me into the backyard. "I want to remember it." I handed him the camera.

Even though he was concerned and wanted to leave, he obliged me. I struck a few poses in my bikini—those few extra minutes were worth it!

After a long night, Ryan finally arrived at 5:05AM before the sun came up. Those were the days when you didn't know if you were having a boy or a girl. I remember the doctor saying, "He's of the boy variety!"

They handed Ryan to me and I looked down at him. I was in heaven. There are not adequate words to describe the emotion a mother feels looking into her baby's eyes for the first time. And Ryan's eyes were blue like his father's (mine are brown). In fact, they were bluer than blue, almost turquoise. He looked so much like his dad that it felt like I was holding a clone of his father.

It looked like this baby didn't even have anything to do with me. And he was just perfect.

I have loved being his mother. And . . . he did turn out a bit like me, after all.

MY LITTLE BOY

After over eight years as a software engineer at Rockwell, I gave plenty of notice at my "rocket-scientist" job, and left to be a stay-at-home mother. I wanted to be with my new baby all the time, and I relished every single day.

Walt went to work every morning and always checked in during the day to see how we were doing, or if I needed him to pick up anything from the store on his way home. When he came home each evening, he immediately scooped up Ryan and included him in all his nightly chores and activities.

Walt had three daughters from a previous marriage, so having a son was a new experience for him. One evening he became rather reflective. He stared down at this little boy that looked so much like him, and said, "You know, honey, I never understood why it was so important to men that they have a son. But somehow, I sort of understand it now."

The two of them became inseparable.

Walt carried Ryan in one arm when he took out the trash cans. Walt loved to garden and he carried Ryan with him as he watered and checked in on all his plants. Once Ryan was walking, he followed his dad everywhere around the house. And Daddy coming home was the highlight of his day. Ryan would go running towards the door screaming, "Daddy's home!"

Walt also went on many business trips to Kennedy Space Center. Ryan always understood "Daddy's on a trip this week," and Walt called every night to check in and see how we were doing. If we weren't home, he left loving messages on the answering machine that I would play for Ryan.

By the time Ryan was two, he frequently joined his dad on errands. Walt loved to shop—I never had to go to a grocery store! The two of them did all the shopping together. Walt even took Ryan with him to get car repairs, or with him to the barber. They were inseparable every evening, and all weekend long.

But when my little boy was just two-and-a-half years old, he suffered a huge loss. Ryan does not remember, but I do.

We had been out to lunch, and when we returned, I had opened the front door, and Ryan ran in ahead of me, into the kitchen. I heard him say, "Silly Daddy! Don't sleep on the floor!"

I looked over and saw my husband lying on the kitchen floor—he had had a massive heart attack. Everything was a whirlwind after that. While the paramedics attempted to save him, I could only explain to Ryan that "Daddy was broken" and the men were trying to "fix him."

Later that evening I had to break the news to him that Daddy could not be fixed, and he could not come home anymore. Ryan nodded and said he understood, but he didn't really. For weeks after that, every day around 2PM, the mailman would come. Ryan would hear the screen door open, and run towards the front door with his usual, "Daddy's home!!" And then, I would have to again tell him that Daddy was not coming home anymore.

Every day he asked why he could not come home, and if we could go visit him. I would attempt to explain it again, and he always nodded, and then asked, "Mommy, why are you crying?" Because of course, I was crying again, trying to get my little boy to understand that his father had not wanted to leave him; he had not purposely abandoned his little boy.

Finally, the day came when Ryan stopped asking. The mailman

came and he didn't run to the door or say "Daddy's home!" I wasn't sure if he had actually forgotten his father, or if he realized that asking for Daddy always made me cry.

Either way, my heart broke, and yet I knew it was better for my son. I wanted him to have a happy childhood. And we had to somehow move forward so that every afternoon was not filled with tears.

These were difficult and solitary times for me. I had a sad toddler, and also a newborn baby girl, who had no idea that everything around her had changed. I lived about 30 minutes from my family, so it wasn't as if they could just drop by every afternoon to help out. Both of my sisters had their own babies and toddlers.

Plus, I didn't want to ask my parents for help. My father had said over and over, "What if you have kids with him and then he dies? Then what?" followed by his very stern, mean look. I was determined to prove I could do it, that I hadn't made a "mistake" by marrying Walt and having children with him.

Although relieved to see Ryan begin to be a happy little boy again, I was tormented knowing he would soon probably forget everything about his father. I didn't really want him to lose all of these memories completely. I wanted him to still "know" who he was, and who he had been. So as time passed and Ryan no longer really remembered his dad, I put a lot of pressure on him to at least know things about his father. I talked about him constantly, and reminded him of what his dad had been like, and what was important to him.

I explained how his father looked at almost everything in the "gray area" and never in black-and-white extremes, how he always gave everyone the benefit of the doubt no matter what their background, how he loved gardening and growing corn and green beans for us to eat as a family. I told him how brilliant his father had been, but how absolutely modest he was about that brilliance, how he was funny and fun to be with, and saw good things in people that they had not yet recognized in themselves.

I was relentless.

Ryan tried his hardest to retain all these facts about his father because he knew it was important to me. I was putting him in a difficult situation, but I couldn't see that at the time. Looking back, I know I did the best I could do under the circumstances.

I also leaned on Ryan too much for help with his sister. There were times when she was 3 or 4 years old, and would cry uncontrollably. Sometimes I would lock myself in the bathroom to have a couple minutes away. Then, through the door, I would hear Ryan coaxing his sister away to give me a break, "Come on Hannah. Mommy needs to be alone. Let's go watch TV and I'll put 'Barney' on for you." He had to accept a great deal of responsibility as a child.

And even though Ryan would not remember his father, it was a huge loss for him.

Ryan was always kind and thoughtful, dutiful and respectful. He looked out for me as his mother, and always felt very protective of me. He was always tuned into me and could read my emotions. Looking back, I realize what a burden this must have been for him to carry, to feel responsible for his mother's happiness.

HE WOULD TRY ANYTHING

Ryan followed rules, and did his homework. But he also had a whole other side to him that he expressed through his many hobbies. Ryan would try anything. He was fearless.

He once wrote in a school report that he wanted to be a clown when he grew up. Following that goal, he soon learned many "clown talents." He started doing magic tricks when he was 8 years old. He also taught himself how to juggle—balls, sticks, or oranges.

Next he learned how to make balloon animals. He had a little pump and hundreds of balloons and he delighted so many kids in the neighborhood by creating whatever animal they asked for.

He even learned to walk on stilts!

In 5th grade, he got a unicycle. Now, this made me so nervous—I thought for sure he would fall and crack his head open. He practiced for hours, leaning against the side of our house outside for support.

When I had all my nieces over to teach them how to crochet, he learned that too. His entrepreneurial spirit began to emerge and he went a step further. He set up a table in front of a bank, and sold all the potholders he had crocheted. He had hand-drawn signs that said things like: "Potholders for All Seasons" and "Make your Life Easier with a Potholder."

He tried his hand at many instruments, and I signed him up for every sport, so he could try different things. I was a little worried about making sure he had enough "masculinity" around, so I would put sports games on TV, and I pretended to be interested in them. But Ryan knew me so well—he knew I didn't care about any of that. He once said, "Mom, you don't need to pretend you're watching football. I know you don't really care about it."

I couldn't get anything past him. I tried to fill the role of his missing parent, but I was not good at being a "father." I was all "mother." And Ryan always knew that, and it was all he wanted anyway.

I WAS A GREAT SANTA

There was only one way I could get something past Ryan. And that was in my role as Santa Claus.

I loved being Santa Claus. It was one of my favorite things to do as a parent. It was so fun to buy presents that I knew my children really wanted. I strived to be the best Santa Claus ever, one who could make miracles happen.

I suppose this doesn't sound very nice, but leading up to Christmas morning I always expressed doubt that Santa could bring something they really wanted; it was "too big" or "too difficult." I would say things like, "Santa's really wonderful, but even he probably can't make that happen."

The fact that I "doubted Santa" made Christmas morning extra special when the present they were dreaming of was waiting for them. I loved watching how happy they would be.

But I had to be careful; Ryan was very smart and logical. Pulling off Santa surprises when he was little was easy. He didn't question Santa's existence until around age 6 or 7.

One year, I bought each of my kids a new bike that would be their big present from Santa. I knew I could just wheel the bikes into our family room on Christmas Eve after they were asleep, but I wanted to do something magical and extend the illusion of Santa a little longer.

Hmmmmm. I had a great idea! I would put the bikes on the roof, next to the chimney. But could I actually do that?

Late on Christmas Eve, I went out to my garage and got out my ladder. I went to a low spot on the roof where I knew I could easily get from the ladder to the roof. I picked up one of the bikes and started up the ladder, one step at a time. It was easier than I thought it would be. When I got just one step from the top, it wasn't difficult to lift the bike and put it on the roof. I then went down the ladder, brought up the other one, and then carried each bike over to the chimney. I was so excited!

I left a note from Santa for the kids that said he couldn't get their presents down the chimney and would leave them nearby.

On Christmas morning they bounded out of bed and ran to our family room. They checked their stockings and the gifts on the floor, and then read the note. They looked confused, and I said,

"Let's go look outside!"

We all ran out into the yard. They both searched and searched, but neither of them thought to look up. They seemed discouraged, and Ryan said, "Mom, I guess he didn't leave anything after all. We need a bigger chimney for next year."

I said, "Well, he did say he couldn't 'fit' them in the chimney. But they were nearby."

Ryan immediately looked up at our roof and then went running to the front yard to get a better view of the chimney. When he saw the bikes up on the roof, he started jumping up and down and screaming with delight. Hannah soon joined him. "But Mom, how will we get them down?"

"I don't know. Let me get the ladder and see if I can find a way." Of course, I got the bikes down, and they went on a test ride in their pajamas. I felt so excited and pleased with myself that I had pulled that off! It was a great Christmas.

The next year I wasn't sure how I could top that. And many of Ryan's friends were speculating that Santa Claus was not real. But Ryan was steadfast. "Are you kidding? There has to be a Santa Claus. My mother could never have gotten those bikes up there on the roof all by herself. Santa had to have left them."

I knew Ryan wanted a computer desk for his room so his computer would have a proper place instead of being on a wobbly table. I bought one and put the box in the garage. It would have to be assembled, but I wasn't worried about following the directions to put it together because I was blessed with an engineering brain. But if I built it in the garage, I would not be able to carry it into the house all by myself. It would be way too heavy. So, I made a plan. I would build it in his room.

Ryan asked lots of questions about the existence of Santa; wondering if maybe his friends could be right. He felt bad about doubting me, but I told him it was OK. I suggested that at bedtime on Christmas Eve I would go into my room and close the door, and Ryan could sprinkle powder on the hardwood floor outside of my room. This way he would know if I had come out in the middle of the night and put out presents, because my footprints would show in the powder on the floor.

He loved this idea. Christmas Eve came and when it was time for bed I went into my room and shut the door. Ryan sprinkled the powder on the floor outside my door and said, "Goodnight Mom!" through the door and headed to bed.

But he forgot that I had a back door from my room into the yard, and I could enter the family room from a different outside door (that I had conveniently left unlocked).

After the kids were asleep, I headed out to the garage and began to bring in the boards and shelves of the desk, piece by piece, through the family room and into Ryan's room. He was a sound sleeper, but I kept an eye on him. After I had all the parts in his room, and with the light very low, I slowly and quietly put it together using mostly just an Allen wrench. Then I set his computer in place. I slipped back out of the family room door, and went through the yard and back through the outside door to my bedroom.

On Christmas morning when he woke up, he jumped up and down with excitement at his brand-new computer desk. He quickly checked the hallway and looked at the entrance to my room and saw that the powder was undisturbed. He was so happy, not only because of what Santa had brought him, but also about being able to still believe in Santa Claus.

I can't remember when he finally realized who Santa Claus really was, but he never held it against me for tricking him all those times. Instead, he always appreciated that I would go to so much trouble to make sure he and his sister always had a memorable Christmas,

These moments remain some of my fondest and funniest memories of motherhood, and Ryan tells me he always brags about what a phenomenal Santa his mother was. He tells the story of how I carried bikes up onto the roof myself, and about the desk I quietly built, one piece at a time, while he slept.

PRIDE AND WORRY

Each year I went to a school Open House, to see what Ryan had learned throughout the year—I would hear the same thing each year. Once I extended my hand and said, "I'm Ryan's mother," they would gush, "Oh! Ryan is so wonderful to have in class. He does all his homework and helps everyone." I was always so happy to hear that. And he was a happy kid.

But when he was 9 years old, something new started to happen; I wasn't sure how to deal with it—he started to panic whenever I left for work in the evening. He would start crying uncontrollably and would beg me not to go. I couldn't figure out what was wrong.

Finally, I took him to a highly recommended therapist, Dr. Matt. After 30 minutes, Dr. Matt had Ryan step out into the waiting area. He looked at me and said, "This is a simple problem, with a simple solution. But it won't be easy for you."

I was floored. I had tried for months to calm down these sudden outbursts. What was this doctor seeing that I was not? He continued, "You are treating him too much like an adult, like your partner. He wants to be a child. He needs to be a child. He feels responsible for you and your happiness. He is worried every time you go out the door, that something might happen to you, and he won't have any parents at all."

It hit me like a ton of bricks. "So, what do I do?" I asked.

He continued, "Take away all of his choices. You are now in charge. He doesn't decide where he goes while you are at work or what time he goes to bed. The only decision he gets to make is whether he wants an apple or an orange in his lunch. Do not discuss anything at all about what did or did not happen at work. He thinks it's his job to listen to you and help you solve problems—it is not his job. His job is to be a kid. Tell him nothing about it, and find someone else to discuss that with."

Oh my gosh, what had I done? I suddenly felt so lost and overwhelmed; these were the times when I so missed having his father around. And now, I had to "undo" the damage.

Dr. Matt added, "Oh and it won't be easy. He will put up a fight. But don't give in. Remember, you are the parent; he is the child."

And Dr. Matt was 100% correct. I stopped talking to Ryan about my work and any of my problems. I stated I was dropping them off at

Grandma's or a friend's when I was going to work, and walked him to the door even if he was crying.

He did put up a fight, but with steady diligence on my part, it worked and Ryan became a happy little boy once again.

Trouble started up again the summer before Ryan started middle school. He had heard stories about eighth graders picking on the sixth graders by lifting them up and putting them in trash cans. He spent his whole summer worrying about it.

I think it was mostly because he was one of the shortest kids in his class, which wasn't surprising because I am not tall, and neither was his father. On the first day of 6th grade, an older kid DID put him in a trash can. But Ryan just stood up and started dancing. And then it was over. I think that gave him confidence that he would be OK.

After that, he really developed his comedic and leadership skills. What he thought would be a defeating experience, instead brought out that hidden comedic side of him. It gave him the freedom to be himself; he was finally comfortable being in his element.

Even though most of his friends were a foot or more taller than him, he was the ringleader. Throughout middle school, the same group of boys spent every Friday night sleeping over at our house. On Saturday mornings, I made Mickey Mouse waffles for the whole gang.

Ryan graduated from middle school with all of these boys, and he was still the only one who had not reached puberty. Almost all of them were now a head taller than him, but it no longer bothered him.

In high school he dedicated himself to being the highest achiever ever; he took more AP classes than any kid had ever taken at his school. He was relentless in his goal to get straight A's.

But along the way, besides being the highest achiever ever, he also managed to get into the most trouble, more than any of his friends. And he was rather proud of this distinction. He reminded me so much of his father at that point. He managed to hit the "trouble" jackpot, over and over again.

There were so many things that happened, and I always say "these are Ryan's stories to tell," but here are a few highlights:

- "How my son helped all his friends with their homework and didn't realize he was an entrepreneur (by accepting all those free lunches)"
- "The famous '420' (4/20, meaning marijuana) party filmed in the Ramelow backyard."
- "The famous 'blown-up' party in the Ramelow front yard."
- "How my son got thrown out of England on the third day of a month-long program."
- "Why I made my son chop tomatoes every day at my restaurant (see above sentence)."
- "That time my son mounted a protest at the school against how many AP classes the students had to take."

I can say as a mother, these times were not easy for me. I worried a lot. Some of the things he did were ordinary goofy teenage pranks and antics. But some of his behavior truly frightened me. I was actually more than worried; I was really scared. Some of his actions resulted in serious consequences, and could have been much worse. Navigating all of these experiences proved a big challenge for both of us.

After high school, Ryan went off to college at the University of California, Berkeley. He was thrilled to go there. He loved the rebellious spirit he perceived the school to have. During that first year, he ran into difficulties once more, and came back to Long Beach to get back on a better path for a while.

Ryan was a rebel of sorts, so very much like his father. He took lots of chances, and some of them were very risky. He seemed to carry with him the same indomitable spirit as his father.

And while I loved his perseverance, he seemed to believe he was immortal, just like his dad had believed about himself.

The difficult challenges for me as a mother continued. I was worried beyond belief, and many times, I thought he would die. And there were times he almost did die.*

I had no idea how to help him. I felt like such a failure. I was his mother, why couldn't I fix this?

So, I had to do what was hardest of all for me. I had to learn to step back and do nothing. I had to stop worrying because it did absolutely no good. With lots of support, I learned the importance of staying in your own lane, and to stop trying to run other peoples' lives.

I had to let Ryan figure it out on his own. He was his own person and I needed to trust he would find his own way. After working very hard, he eventually returned to Berkeley, and he finished his degree on time.

I was so proud as his mom, to be at his graduation and watch him walk across that stage.

We all want our kids to turn out "OK." I'm very grateful that Ryan turned out much more than OK.

TAKING CHANCES

One day Ryan came to see me. He said, "Mom, don't freak out." So of course, I freaked out!

"Mom, I'm moving to New York."

What???

He had recently come home from having a blast spending New Year's Eve in New York City with his cousin Jeff and their friend, "Romanian John." They stayed in my niece Claire's tiny studio in the Upper East Side. But, moving there? What?

The first thing I said was "Honey, going there on New Year's Eve, and living there, are two very different things."

---

* I cannot tell those stories here because they are personal to my son, and I respect his privacy.

"I know Mom, I know what I'm doing."

I had a zillion questions, of course, but before I could even start asking them he said, "Don't worry Mom. I'll work it out."

And he did. Just a few months after his 23rd birthday, he had it all set up. He brokered a transfer with his company to their New York office, and they even paid his moving expenses. He let go of his apartment in Venice Beach, and moved his things back home the last few weeks before he would go. The day came when the moving van arrived to get his stuff. I tried not to cry.

I was proud of myself for staying calm while he prepared for his big move. I hadn't cried or interfered in any of his plans (although at times I wanted to). This was what he wanted to do and I planned to support his decision. The day came when I drove him to the airport. As I hugged him goodbye, I couldn't hold the tears back any longer. "Don't fall in love with a girl back there! Make sure you come back one day!"

Then he was gone, moving 3,000 miles away from home to New York City, at just 23 years old. It wasn't an easy thing to accomplish, but he made it happen.

On Christmas eve of that year, he sent me a photo of the Empire State building lit up in red and green lights. "Mom, don't worry. I'm the happiest I've ever been in my life." I looked at that photo often. It reassured me he was happy, but I wondered if he might come back home to California one day.

STAYING CLOSE

I began to visit Ryan at least once a year, actually more than that. He always worked many hours, but would have dinner with me every night that he could.

I started noticing small changes in him on my visits. When he talked about the city, he would say "our mayor." At first I thought he was talking about the Long Beach mayor. And then I realized he was talking about the mayor of New York city. That was his mayor now. I could see in small collective ways, how New York city was becoming "his city." His home.

I couldn't believe my son wanted to live in such a fast-paced and high energy place. I liked visiting, but I don't think I could ever keep up. And every time I left New York to return home, I felt like I was leaving him behind, even though he was completely happy.

After eight successful years in commercial real estate, he did not feel the same way about his job. It didn't make him feel like he was making a difference. Nearing 30 years old, he wanted to do something different and he did not want to wait until he was 35 when it would be even more risky.

He thought back to his creative days of magic and juggling, and missed that *figuring-out-how-to-do-something* part of himself. One day he googled how to make a hand-made felt hat. He reached out to hand-crafted hat makers and became intrigued; it became a challenge for him, and Ryan always liked a challenge. Working out of his apartment, and using a steam iron, a wooden spatula, and a piece of rope, he started learning to shape hats around a hat base he had found on eBay.

He loved it from the start. A friend of his who he looked up to, listened to him talk about his dissatisfaction with his current job. The friend then asked, "What do you think will make you happy?"

Ryan told him how much he enjoyed his new interest in making hats. His friend looked directly at him and said, "Dude, then go make fucking hats." That was it. He left his job on good terms, and started his own hat business.

He researched all about hat-making, and even traveled to Oaxaca, Mexico because he heard it was a creative place to visit. He came upon a hat stand run by an older man, Armando. He had made all the hats himself with special equipment. He spoke no English and Ryan's knowledge of Spanish was not very extensive, so the two of them communicated via Google Translate.

Ryan visited his workshop and loved seeing all the hat-making tools and machinery, and watching the man explain his process. He was amazed, and Armando loved having Ryan there as an apprentice, a young person so interested in this old-time craft of hat-making.

He returned to New York city and continued to make hats in his apartment. The experience was very fulfilling to him. He frequently told me: "Every time someone puts on a hat I've made, they smile." He liked helping people feel better about themselves. This was everything to him. He never had that experience at his previous job of negotiating commercial real estate leases. But now, every day, he felt like he was making a difference, and making people feel happier and more confident.

After some time, he leased a small office space in the Noho area of Manhattan, on the 9th floor of a building on Broadway at Bleecker. He slowly added equipment to his shop: sewing machines, special presses to shape the body of the hats and smooth out the brims, a machine to sew the lining inside, and one to add a decorative band around the outside.

He built his website and developed "hatty hours," where people could come enjoy drinks and try on his hats. As he came up with idea after idea to get publicity and word-of-mouth going about his hats, his business grew. He provided outstanding customer service, and would readjust a hat as many times as necessary to make sure it fit perfectly, and the wearer was 100% happy.

Ryan put away the suits and ties required for his real estate job, and went back to his more bohemian California-way of dressing. He even returned to his childhood mode of transportation, his skateboard, which made him quite the fixture in New York City.

Eventually one of his networking efforts led to him being asked to be a part of a fashion show happening during New York's prestigious fashion week. It was a great next step, but as in any business, it takes step after step after step.

As Ryan's hat business grew, it brought us closer together. He began to call me more often with business-type dilemmas. Every single time, I could remember a similar experience when running my restaurant, whether it was about a city permit, an employee, or how to decide which task to tackle first. He had watched me sort out many business challenges.

Ryan would always say that everything he learned about business, he learned from me. But he is really the one who has made himself who he is—with his tenacity, his dedication, and his desire to make a difference in the world.

On one of my visits to New York City, Ryan planned a party for me and invited all his friends I had met there over the years. I was honestly excited and touched that he wanted his friends to come see me, and some of them I would be meeting for the first time.

We walked over to one of his favorite restaurants and his friends began to arrive. So many people showed up; it became clear he had put down solid roots in the city.

One of my favorite encounters was when I met one of his newer friends. He walked over to me and introduced himself and said, "I just had to come. I had to meet you! Because the way your son talks about you, you sound like a unicorn. I had to see if you actually existed!"

I felt so proud, especially after everything we went through together when he was a teenager. I always loved when he said, "I want to be as cool as my mom" and "I am who I am because of my mom."

At the end of the party, Ryan called a car for me and walked me out, opened the car door, and made sure I was safely inside. And he told the driver, "Thank you. And take good care of her. This is my mother."

He was always looking out for me.

A STOREFRONT IN A LITTLE NEIGHBORHOOD, IN THE MIDDLE OF NYC

Ryan's hat business had been slowly growing for three years, and he decided to move his business to a storefront location. He looked at many potential spaces and neighborhoods in the "villages" and the Soho area, and finally settled on one he thought would be perfect—a small storefront, 107 Sullivan St., in Soho, New York city.

It had previously been a dry-cleaning store. There was a lot that needed to be done, but he wasn't worried. When he learned the price of the needed demolition work, he decided to do it all himself. He had spent many hours with his grandpa, my father, fixing things on his apartment buildings.

Eventually he finished the demo, reconstructed the brass work on the ceiling, and installed shelves and many other needed things on the walls. Then he moved all of his equipment to his new location.

And in July of 2022, he opened his new store, on Sullivan St., between Prince St. and Spring St. He was so happy to be in a first-floor storefront space, and he would soon discover the magic of his new neighborhood.

On my next visit, I experienced something entirely new: I got to see, up close, a small community that is part of one of the biggest cities in the world. I met all of his neighbors.

First up was Angelo from the hair salon next door, "Anonymous." He gave me a huge hug and said he told my son he needed a haircut before his mother arrived, so he had cut his hair for him the day before.

We were standing on the sidewalk chatting when an elderly couple walked by. My son told them I was his mother, and they immediately hugged me and said, "We love your boy!" They both had that quintessential NYC accent, and explained to me how they had lived in the neighborhood for over 50 years. They told me all about the "mob days" from long ago.

Then we went to the sandwich shop, "Alidoro," a couple doors down. Their sign read, "Open 11:30AM to 4PM. Or until the bread runs out." I met Walter, the shopkeeper—he had a thick Italian accent, and told me all about the beginnings of his shop, and how he had leased it just six months before 9/11 happened, in 2001.

Walter explained how on that morning, all the neighbors had come outside when they heard the first plane flying over the city. That in itself was so strange because there are never planes flying over New York City. And then that first plane hit. Walter called his mother in Italy to tell her what happened. He was still on the phone with her when the second tower was hit.

Walter turned and pointed south down the street and explained how there had been a clear view of the twin towers, right down Sullivan Street. Now looking down the street, was a clear view of One World Trade, looming in the distance and yet appearing so close.

Inside his shop, Walter showed me a photo from when he had opened, and in the photo you could indeed see the twin towers right down the street, standing tall over all the brick buildings in this part of Manhattan.

I had been home in California when I watched 9/11 unfold on TV. I remembered scenes of the towers crumbling to the ground, and the debris and smoke billowing up through the small streets of the city. I realized I was now standing on one of those small streets. Walter said it had been exactly like that. It felt surreal to stand in that spot looking down the street to where the towers had been, and where the new building now loomed majestically in their place.

Later that evening, Ryan and I went to dinner and sat on an outside patio. Many people passed by, saying hi and waving. He was now a fixture in his community. And every time, he would point to me and say, "This is my mom!" with a big smile.

I loved meeting my son's neighbors, and hearing the love for their neighborhood. My son was now an integral part of this small community, within this giant city. He had created a place where people can come to be cared about, listened to, protected, appreciated, and made to feel beautiful.

MY SON WAS NOW A NEW YORKER

I had traveled to the Hamptons in 2019 with my friend Michele, and we then went to the city for a couple days. We had dinner with Ryan, and she asked him many things, like how he knew he wanted to move there after he had visited on New Year's Eve in 2011.

He explained how fascinated he was watching the high energy level of the people living there, and he kept thinking, "Wow, I didn't know people lived like this." Everyone worked so hard; he had great respect for that and knew he would fit in.

I always knew he was happy in New York, but now after eight years, I could see how he not only loved this city; he had become a part of it.

I finally understood.

On that visit, when I got to the airport to leave New York, I no longer felt like I was leaving my son behind. It wasn't because he had lived there for eight years; it was because I now understood it was now his home and represented all he had accomplished. He had taken a big chance at age 23, moving to the city without knowing a soul, and adjusting to how different it was from where he grew up.

He had made a difference in so many peoples' lives; he had become an important part of his small community, in this very big city. And now I'm OK with him staying there forever, and "falling in love with a girl back there."

I now finally understood. My son had become a New Yorker.

Ryan still has the remarkable spirit I saw in him from the day he was born. Sometimes we will chat about the long-ago past, when many times things went awry, and could have turned out so differently. He knows I worried about him a lot back then.

He had been such an easy little boy to raise, so those teenage years really threw me for a loop. It was especially hard being a single mom—I never thought I was being strong enough for him, or tough enough. I could barely sleep. I remember waking up many days and thinking, "how will I make it through another day raising a teenage son?" And not just any teenage son, but the son of Walt Ramelow.

But that was years ago and now it's different. He is now taking chances on following his dreams. With emotion in his voice, he told me how important it has been to him to live his life in a way where he is always giving back. He shared about the many people in his building who stop in and let him know they feel safe with his shop below them. He has really become a protector and a leader there.

Ryan also shared with me some of the reviews people leave for him after an experience in his store:

"Ryan Ramelow is hands down one of the nicest, most knowledgeable, stylish and helpful hat makers. Ryan's shop is a true old school hat shop and Ryan is a true old school hat maker and fixer who wants his customers to be happy. This is all capped by the privilege of being able to leave and wear such art. Grateful for having met Ryan Ramelow."

Sometimes in life we start something, and we don't know where it will lead. This was my own experience: I started off as an engineer, became a mom, and then somehow became a restaurant owner. I then turned it into a place where people felt connection, love, and acceptance.

I often referred to my business, "La Strada," as my "2nd home." In a way, the same thing happened to my son.

I think Ryan would be OK with me calling his hat shop his "2nd home."

HANNAH

MY QUIRKY GIRL

Hannah was born in the days when you didn't know if you were having a boy or a girl. I so badly wanted a girl; I wanted to be a mom to a daughter, as well as to my son. Whenever anyone asked what I wished I was having, I lied and said I didn't care, "as long as it's healthy!"

It felt wrong to say it out loud that I wanted a girl. Because what If it was a boy? I didn't want to have openly declared that I had wished he was somebody else.

But on that day in the delivery room when she was born, I felt overjoyed when I saw that she was indeed a girl. They put her into my arms and I stared into her gorgeous blue eyes. I was now the brown-eyed mother of two blue-eyed babies.

She was feisty from the start. I remember looking at her in the hospital bassinet and asking the doctor why she looked so "jittery." He assured me she was just fine. At a few months old, it became clear she did not want to sit still. Once she became mobile, she never stopped: running, dancing, wiggling, jumping, and talking.

She always registered at the bottom of any growth chart, so as a baby she felt like my own little "dolly." She was little and cuddly, and every day I swung her from side to side to special lullaby music. She was definitely the daughter I had been waiting for, this sweet little baby girl.

Even though having a newborn was exhausting, the first three months of her life were joyous for me and her father.

But soon after she turned three-months-old, my husband, Walt, died suddenly of a heart attack. After that, much of Hannah's "baby stage" became difficult for me. With the father of my children now gone, I went into complete survival mode trying to raise two children alone without him. The rest of her first year, I really did not fully enjoy motherhood or appreciate (or notice) the growth she made from being a newborn to being a toddler. I just tried to get through each day and be the best mother I could.

As I recovered from this major loss in my life, I began to better know and appreciate my little girl. Busy as ever, she barely sat still, but she also had this huge personality. She never ceased to make me laugh.

Diagnosed with asthma early on, at times she had to undergo breathing treatments in the middle of the night, with the side effect being a caffeine-type surge from the medication. I have fond (sort of) memories of lying there at 3AM exhausted, while she would sing and dance a jig all over the bed as I tried to sleep. She was just so cute; how could I be mad?

When Hannah was crying or frustrated, her tears came from frustration of not understanding something, or of not being able to adjust to something. I always understood this about her, and once she calmed down, she would hug me and cling to me in a very "grateful" way, as if she knew I understood her so well.

Her delightful personality was a constant source of entertainment as I watched how she perceived the world. When her babysitter told her that her dog had to go to the dog hospital, Hannah asked if all the doctors and nurses in the hospital were also dogs.

She said funny things every single day. But I started to feel worried. One day when she was 5 years old, I handed her shoes to her, and told her to go put them on the shoe bench by the front door. She ran down the hall towards the living room. But when she got to the end, she turned and ran back.

"Which one is the front door and which one is the back door?"

I mostly found her confusion about everyday things very endearing, but it began to worry me. I knew she was bright, but how could she not know the difference between the front door and back door?

When she was in first-grade, she was tested for the gifted program and she scored at 99%. This surprised me. I asked her teacher if they had scored it correctly. The teacher scolded me, " Mrs. Ramelow!!"

Her intelligence would show up out of nowhere. One day I sat with a group of first graders as they passed a book around, reading one paragraph each. I watched as each girl read every sentence very carefully, trying to sound out any words they did not know. But when it was Hannah's turn, she just read through the paragraph immediately without pausing or hesitating at any words at all. I honestly did not know how she could do that—I hadn't done anything extra to teach her to read better. She just seemed to know how.

By third grade it became obvious she had a math brain like both of her parents. She had a homework assignment to help learn calculator skills. Each student was to go to the store with their mom or dad, and write down how much various produce items cost per pound. Then when they returned home, they were to use their calculator to determine the total cost of three pounds of each item.

We went to the market and she carried with her the assignment paper and her pencil. We headed over to the apples. She wrote down 89 cents per pound. But then on the line for the total for 3 pounds, she immediately wrote $2.67. She did that for every single item, all the calculations done in her head.

When I asked her how she knew $1.29 x 3 was $3.87, she looked up at me, confused and somewhat annoyed, and said "Mom! It's obvious!!" Maybe to her, but she didn't understand it was not obvious to others. It was something she could just do, the same way I was born with a sharp sense of direction.

And yet so many other things were not obvious to her at all. I always looked for things to point out to her that I thought maybe she didn't know, like the difference between the microwave and the toaster oven. But I had to be careful because sometimes it would hurt her feelings if she thought, I thought, she was dumb.

I never thought she was dumb, just quirky. Her uniqueness awed me, and I was proud to be her mother.

ANNIE

A good description of Hannah would be "small but mighty." She was so little. But, her big bold personality was way bigger than her tiny little body.

In eighth grade Hannah tried out for the lead role of "Annie." She got it! It did make sense as she totally fit the role of a child, but her teacher told me later it wasn't just her size—she knew Hannah well enough to know she would put in the many hours of practice to learn all the lines and songs.

I wanted to take my parents to see the Annie performance; they both adored Hannah and I knew they would be so proud. At this time though, my mother was a few years into having dementia; she didn't know who everyone was exactly, but she did know when a person "belonged" to her. She had also lost her ability to act appropriately in many situations. But still, I knew she would love to see the play, so I decided to bring her to the day-time performance that was put on for the other students at the school. I knew if she did anything inappropriate, I could quickly take her out of the auditorium.

We got there early, and I explained to my mother many times that we were going to be seeing a play, and Hannah would be singing. She seemed to understand. I knew she would not recognize Hannah in the red wig she would be wearing, so I told Hannah to come out into the audience before the performance to say hi to her grandma.

Hannah came down the steps from the stage wearing the traditional little red "Annie dress" that is so well-known from this play. She walked over to her grandma and gave her a big hug. It was clear my mother did not know who she was, so Hannah pulled part of the wig up to show her her hair underneath and said, "Grandma, it's me, Hannah!"

My mother hugged her tight. She knew she was someone important to her. Then she held onto her shoulders and stared lovingly at her. Hannah kissed her on the cheek, and then ran back up the steps to the stage and behind the curtain.

The play started and there were kids filling the aisles singing "It's a Hard-Knock Life." My mother was really enjoying it. Hannah appeared on stage singing and my mother looked as happy as ever.

Then came a scene with Hannah and another girl, who was playing the evil Miss Hannigan. As part of the scene, Miss Hannigan yells at Annie, shoves her, and she then goes stumbling backwards. The girl playing Miss Hannigan did exactly what she was supposed to do—she yelled at Hannah and then shoved her, and Hannah stumbled a few steps back and fell to the ground.

My mother was livid. She stood up and pointed at the girl on stage and shouted, "Don't you do that to her again!" She was ready to go up on stage and rescue Hannah. I was horrified, but I got her to sit back down, and reassured her as best I could that Hannah was OK. I just kept saying, "Mom, it's a show. Hannah is OK. I promise Mom. It's a show."

Somehow calling it a "show" seemed to make sense to her, and she calmed down after that. I was glad I had brought her to the day-performance where the audience was almost all students, with very few parents there to see their own kids.

Later that week, I took my father to the evening performance where the audience was filled with parents and grandparents. He had long ago nicknamed her "Squeak" when she was just a baby. I knew he would not interrupt the show the way my mother had done, but I had a whole different issue with him.

Shortly after the play began, he leaned over and whispered to me, "How old are all these other kids?"

"Dad, they are all the same age, 13. 'Squeak' is just really small for her age, like she always has been."

He looked at me as if he just couldn't believe it. When the boy who was playing Daddy Warbucks scooped Hannah up in his arms, and carried her across the stage, my father pointed at him, and said, "But how old is that kid?"

"Dad, he's 13. Shhh."

Then he pointed at a shapely girl who was playing a governess. "But how about that lady in the skirt?"

"Dad, that 'lady' is 13 too. They are all 13."

He finally stopped asking. But I don't think he ever believed me. He was really proud of her that night though, and had tears in his eyes when he hugged her after the show.

In retrospect, the antics of both of my parents created wonderful memories for me. They were who they really were, always, until the very end.

At her 8th grade graduation Hannah received a special award. Before they called her up, they described her as a powerhouse, both academically and in life, and they also noted she was a good friend to all her classmates.

Then she was asked to come forward. Hannah exited the row she was sitting in, and made her way up the center aisle. I could see people looking surprised as the "powerhouse" walked past them, and up the steps to the stage, wearing her (children's) size 7 dress, with her black and white converse shoes.

She was quite the powerhouse. She was my tiny little powerhouse.

"DADDY, DADDY"

Once Hannah entered high school she was still very small in stature. She was definitely a late bloomer, and looked years younger than her actual age. I had been exactly the same way. She took a drama class, and they would be putting on a short one-act play for the parents.

The story was about a single father with an elementary school-age daughter. I don't remember the plot exactly, but there was a scene where the father went into an office and had a conversation with a secretary.

Hannah was 14 at the time, and she really wanted to be cast as the office secretary. But instead, of course, she was cast as the 7-year-old little girl. She came home from school that day and was absolutely livid that she had not been cast as the office secretary. The thought of wearing a costume that would make her look like a little girl, upset her. I headed out to the garage and looked through a box. I knew exactly what I was looking for—her treasured purple coat from second grade.

Her Grandma had given it to her for her birthday that year, and she just loved it so much. It was soft, and the buttons were big giant pink roses. It was well-worn, and the fabric had little fuzzballs all over it; she had continued to wear it even when it was far too small on her.

I brought it in the house. "Honey, I bet you can still put this on." She took it from me, and slipped it on. We both smiled. The sleeves were too short, but yes she could still wear it. It would be perfect for the part. She finally accepted her role, and learned all her lines.

The evening came for the performance. I had a tiny gold locket that had Walt's picture on one side, and tiny pictures of my children on the other side—the ages they were on the day he died. I always wore the locket whenever my children were doing something in school, something special that their father would have attended. It felt like I was bringing him along so he would not miss out. As my children got older, I didn't wear the locket regularly anymore. But on that night, I remembered to put it on.

The play began. When I saw the young lady playing the part of the secretary, I smiled to myself. Hannah would never have looked right in this role, as this girl was wearing a tight turtleneck with a pencil skirt. Hannah would have been a stick figure in that outfit.

And then she appeared in her purple coat playing the little girl—she was perfect for the part. Towards the end of the play, the single father entered the room. And then Hannah said her lines:

"Daddy! Daddy, please can I go? Please Daddy!"

I felt my heart stop. I reached up and held onto the small gold locket around my neck as tears welled up in my eyes. I was not expecting that. It had now been fourteen years since Walt had died. I was "well recovered" by then, but at that moment, I realized I had never before heard my little girl say the words, "Daddy, Daddy!" Because she had been an infant when he passed.

I sat there in the audience in the dark and thought about all that Walt had lost. And I thought about how my daughter had grown up without a father who adored her.

After the play I went down to congratulate her. I kept my other thoughts to myself though; this was her celebration.

But I was so very grateful that her teacher had cast her as the little girl. I got to experience something I never even realized I had missed.

MY 13TH GRADER

Every year, when Hannah started a new grade, I would hoist her up on my left hip and say:

"Yep, I can still carry my 1st grader."

"Yep, I can still carry my 2nd grader."

"Yep, I can still carry my 3rd grader."

I think 4th grade was when we stopped that tradition. She didn't like it anymore, and felt I was babying her.

In high school, Hannah tried out for cheerleading and earned a coveted spot on the team. Her team put on the type of cheerleading stunts seen at sporting events. They would form a "base" and would then throw one girl up high in the air—that girl was referred to as the "flyer." Guess who wanted to be the flyer?

She definitely was the smallest one on the team, but she also possessed all the necessary qualities of working hard, practicing every day, and trusting her teammates.

There came a time there was a demonstration at the school to show their progress to the parents. The music began and the cheerleaders ran out in formation, danced, and shook their pompoms. But then they started getting into formation, and suddenly Hannah was in the middle being boosted up by several of the girls, who were holding her feet and part of her leg. She kicked one leg up and out, and did some hand motions and dance moves.

And then, suddenly, they just tossed her in the air—her body was completely straight and her arms were crossed in front of her, and she just went spiraling through the air before dropping down into her teammates' waiting arms. I could barely watch. They threw her up over and over again. I was so scared every time I saw her tossed up in the air. But she loved it and was dedicated to it. She was her own person, and I respected that so much about her.

When it came time to take her to college, at the University of California, at Berkeley, we packed up everything she needed into the car for our 8-hour drive up to Northern California. We walked out the front door of our house and I locked it, as Hannah headed towards the car. But I stayed on the front porch.

"Honey, wait, come back here for a minute."

"What is it Mom?" she asked as she walked back towards me.

"Come stand here" I motioned to my left side, next to my left hip.

She did, but said "What Mom?" I leaned over and put my arms around her, sort of scooping her up (in a sense), and she immediately realized what I was trying to do and started laughing.

"Mom!" she said. But she was smiling. And then she did a little jump up, to make it easier for me to hoist her up onto my left hip. She was all grown up now at 17, and maybe a bit silly for me to be doing this, but still, I held her and said, "Yep, I can still carry my 13th grader."

She smiled and had a very sweet look on her face. I think we both thought it was the perfect way to say goodbye to her childhood home, and head off to college.

WHO IS THE PETULANT TEENAGER NOW?

I wondered when the mother-teenage girl conflict would ever be over. It had now progressed far into her 20's.

"Mom, you're chewing too loud." "Mom, you're breathing too loud."

I could barely take it. And she was always frustrated at things she had inherited from me: thin hair, wide feet, overly-analytical and being an over-thinker. She mentioned these things frequently. I would remind her that I also gave her intelligence and good eyesight, big boobs, and her big beautiful blue eyes (I have the recessive blue-eye gene!)

Still, she would roll her eyes at me.

One day a package for me arrived—I had ordered some pants that had some type of cutouts down the sides of the legs. I took them out and put them on. Hannah was horrified that I would order something like that.

Hannah: "Mom, you didn't really order those did you?"

Mom: "Why yes, honey. I ordered a few things from the Venus catalog."

"How many? What else did you get?"

"I don't remember how many—I just got some Vegas-type things."

"Vegas!! Mom, when will you be going to Vegas?" Poor thing. I had become her difficult, petulant teenager. Now she had to deal with me!

Also, because we used to watch "The Dallas Cowboys Cheerleaders" show together, I ordered a Dallas Cowboy Cheerleader costume. "Mom!!! You can't wear that!!"

I laughed. "Well, maybe I can if I lose five pounds."

"Mom, MOM!!! Promise me you will send back that costume."

"OK, honey, I will."

OK, but I didn't. I still have it. It's in my hallway bottom drawer. I've never been to Dallas, and when I go there one day, I plan to see a Dallas

Cowboys game. I don't care about the football players; I just want to see the cheerleaders from the show. And I will be taking my costume with me, and will probably wear it under a trench coat.

Don't tell Hannah I still have it!

A MOMENT I HAD MY BABY BACK

There was one time, though, when Hannah forgot to be annoyed by me. It was the night of the Belmont Shore Christmas parade.

Belmont Shore is an area in the city of Long Beach, California. My restaurant was located there on 2nd Street, which is the heart of this community and has many shops and stores. I had moved to the Shore area when my kids were teenagers, after raising them in a neighborhood about three miles away. It was so helpful to be living so close to my business, and to my parents, who were requiring a lot of help at that time.

Hannah was now about 25, and she and her friends had come to my restaurant to watch the parade, and had then gone out on 2nd St. very late before returning to my home to spend the night. I was already upstairs in bed, but I could hear them talking and laughing as they devoured the last of the Mississippi Mud brownies I had made for the parade. It was well past 2AM.

About 15 minutes later I noticed that all was quiet. I went downstairs, and saw all of them were asleep—on the floor, on the couch, sitting upright in chairs. They were out. I went back to bed.

Around 5AM I heard someone coming up the stairs. Hannah quietly came into my room, "Mom, everyone's asleep downstairs." And then she added, "I'm so cold Mama."

I told her, "Honey, I have my electric blanket on. Why don't you get in on the other side and warm up?"

She walked around, and got under the blanket. But then she moved over to my side and rested her head on my chest like she used to when she was a little girl. And promptly fell asleep.

I couldn't believe it; she hadn't done something like that in many years. I think she was too tired to remember to be annoyed at me.

For the next few hours, I just lay awake with my arm around her watching her sleep, looking at her, remembering all those times she slept like that on my chest, from being an infant, to a baby, to a toddler, to a little girl.

I felt so blessed. She was now a grown woman, and it had been forever since she had been cozy like this with me. I remained still and quiet and barely slept at all, but I didn't care. I had my little girl with me, my baby taking comfort in my arms.

WE ARE MATHEMATICIANS, NOT FLOWER ARRANGERS

I think my daughter tried very hard her whole life to **not be** like me. But the writing was on the wall. We both analyzed everything to death. We both asked way too many questions. We both needed the other person to understand how we felt even if they did not agree with us.

I remembered a small turning point when she was frustrated at her wide feet. She went on and on, and then suddenly she just stopped and turned to look at me. She said in complete exasperation, "It's true, isn't it? I am just like you!!" It was one of my happiest moments as a mother—she was somehow (just slightly!) accepting that we were quite similar.

She once came home for a few days to celebrate her cousin's 27th birthday. She stopped at Trader Joe's for groceries and bought a few of their bouquets of flowers so she could put something together for her cousin. It was Friday evening, and I headed off to work at my restaurant around 5PM, like I always did.

I got home from work around 11PM, and found Hannah in the kitchen cutting up the bouquets of flowers. She had every vase I owned sitting out on the countertops. She had put the cut flowers in some of them, but other vases remained empty. There were cut-up stems everywhere. It was a hodge-podge, a big giant mess. I walked in and set down my work bag. "Hi honey!"

"Mom! What am I doing wrong?? All of these flower arrangements look terrible! No matter what I do, or what I cut, or what I add, it just looks worse! What am I doing wrong?"

Answer: "Honey, I don't know! You know I'm terrible at flower arranging. I've never been able to do it."

Then I went over to try and help: "Maybe you should put this weird green thing in this one."

"No, Mom, that will look even worse."

Then she just stopped and looked at me. "This is another thing I've inherited from you, isn't it?"

We both smiled. Yes. It was. But this time, she wasn't mad. Her face was full of acceptance.

On that flower-arranging night, it was really nice having her over to visit. She had asked for my help, and accepted me for who I was. And she had accepted herself, even though she was so much like me.

Because, we are mathematicians, and not flower arrangers.

MY JURIS DOCTOR

There was another thing that bothered Hannah, her birthdate: 09-23-90. "Mom!" she would say when she was a little girl, "Why didn't you have me the day before?"

"What? What do you mean?"

"Mom, if you had had me the day before, I would have been born on 09-22-90. Then my birth date would be a palindrome, just like my name is." She was quite serious.

"Well, honey, believe me, I would have liked to have had you earlier. My water broke on a Saturday morning at 5AM, and you were not born until the next day on Sunday at 5PM. That was a really long labor! You just took forever." I heard about the "palindrome" thing many times as she was growing up.

She was never sure what she wanted to do or be when she grew up. With so many choices, her analysis and indecisiveness would kick in. That frequently kept her from making any decision, or choosing any direction. She would become stuck in some sort of abyss. She even had trouble deciding what to order in a restaurant.

Her friends called her extensive thinking, "Hann-alyzing."

After she graduated from college, she returned home without any sort of plan. She wasn't sure how to even look for a job. I had been the exact same way. I had come home from college with no plan, and after about a month of hanging around, my father got mad at me and made me put together a resume.

When Hannah returned home, I had become quite used to living alone. It had definitely taken a long time for me to get used to both my kids being gone, but then I had become rather accustomed to it. Still, I told Hannah it was fine if she moved back home for a while.

It didn't work out very well. Hannah would turn on the TV every day, and then basically get stuck there almost the whole day. I left for work around 5PM and returned around 11PM. Every night when I came home, there she was, still watching TV. And she wasn't doing anything to help me around the house, or to help with my business, like she used to do when she was younger.

After about three weeks of this routine, I came home one night and just lost it. I was so angry.

We got into a huge fight. I knew she was not being lazy, she was just stuck and did not know how to move forward, just as I had been.

Also, this was a time when jobs were scarce; I had young people coming into my restaurant every day asking for jobs. She knew I was mad and she agreed to take some bussing shifts at my restaurant.

Not long after, she became a server. She was actually an excellent employee. She was on time, neat, polite to every customer, and she "noticed things"—this is an important quality to have in the restaurant business. You must be able to notice when a customer needs something. Hannah was perfect at all of it.

She ended up working for me for two years. She did grow tired of people asking her when she would finish school and get her degree, because after all, she already had her degree.

I told her she needed to move on, and she started some sort of clerking-type job, and then tried being a financial planner. But that job was really mostly a sales job; it required a great deal of cold-calling and trying to convince every person you know to invest their money in this finance company. Hannah is not a salesperson, and neither am I, so I totally understood and was supportive of her leaving that job. It was definitely the wrong thing for her. She moved out and was living with a friend, but she just did not seem happy or fulfilled.

My brother, Fred, was in Long Beach one afternoon and we went to our usual spot of Ruby's Diner in the Marketplace Shopping Center, and placed our usual order.

I told him how worried I was about Hannah. He looked at me and said, "Everyone always said she should be a lawyer one day. Maybe she should go to law school." One of his sons had already gone through an MBA-Law School combo program, and his next son was now in that program too.

"Well, I really don't love the idea of paying for that," I said. "And wouldn't she have to take a test or something?" He explained she would have to take the LSAT, a requirement before applying to any law school. The next test was only six weeks away, and there wouldn't be another test for six months.

I started to think about it. For Hannah's entire life, everyone always said she should be a lawyer. She asked a million questions, she noticed things, and she remembered details. She could also talk non-stop to the point that a family friend had nicknamed her, "Filibuster." Also, being logical and compassionate, she could look at both sides of any issue, and try to see it from someone else's perspective.

I called Hannah and asked her to come see me. I explained this idea. She was unsure, and questioned whether she could study enough in six weeks to get a good score on the LSAT. I think we got into several more arguments.

I insisted that if anyone could do it in six weeks, it was her. I reminded her that she had learned all the lines as the lead in a play. She had practiced countless hours to be a cheerleading "flyer." She was a straight-A student who could learn facts very quickly and retain them. I knew she could do this too.

She signed up for the LSAT, studied the next six weeks, and got a great score. We visited several law schools; she applied and was accepted at Pepperdine Law School. I was so proud of her—she had done it.

Once Hannah started law school, I had never seen my daughter so happy. Law School was logical for her—it fit her brain perfectly.

During that first year, they had a "Parents Day." Not only were we invited to the campus, but we would be allowed to attend one of our student's classes. I was so excited! I told Hannah I was going to attend dressed all in pink like the character, Elle Woods, from the movie "Legally Blonde."

"MOM! Don't you dare!"

Well, of course I wasn't really going to do that. I also told her I needed to be prepared in case the professor called on me in class. I had heard of "torts" since she had entered law school, but I had no idea what they were. "Honey," I asked her. "What exactly is a 'tort'?"

"Mom. You don't need to know what a 'tort' is! No one is going to ask you anything," she reiterated.

The next day in class I was a perfect student. And I was a perfect mom. I sat quietly and listened. I said nothing and asked no questions. Many other parents were videoing their students or trying to impress the teacher. Their kids were clearly embarrassed. I thought I was so well behaved that I deserved an A+ as a mom that day!

I did point out to Hannah just how good of a "student" I had been compared to the other parents. She did have to agree with me, "I guess you were, Mom."

Just a month later after Parent's Day, was Halloween. So that year, I DID dress up as Elle Woods from "Legally Blonde," and handed out candy in front of my restaurant as I did every year. It was one of my very best costumes. One man asked if I was Barbie, but every single child knew exactly who I was.

Around the time she started school, Mattel had put out its new edition of Barbie—"Judge Barbie." I ordered one with blonde hair and blue eyes, like Hannah. I put it on the mantle over my fireplace in my living room. I considered it a good luck charm, and I liked the constant reminder that my daughter was now on a good path.

And when the day came for her graduation, I brought the Barbie doll to the ceremony with me, and of course I made her hold it while I took a picture.

It had taken some time, but my daughter had found her calling. And when the day came and she earned her degree, called a "Juris Doctor," or J.D., she was now a lawyer.

As a mother, there is nothing better than seeing your child thrive and be happy.

"NO ONE THINKS YOU DON'T LIKE PEOPLE IN WHEELCHAIRS"

When I owned my restaurant, I was sued by someone who was part of the American Disability Association. It was a blanket-lawsuit that covered many businesses in our district. The person suing had never actually been to any of the businesses; his lawyer knew that almost every business owner would settle for $5,000 or more.

One day at work I told my employee that if anyone came and asked for me, to say I wasn't there. I explained to her I did not want this paperwork. A guy walked in an hour later and I could hear him ask if I was there, and my employee said "no." Then, being the cheerful girl that she was, she said, "if you need to leave something I can take it!" The man scribbled something and said, "you've been served" and walked out. I felt so upset. I wanted to run after him and throw the papers at him.

I was a nervous wreck having to face a lawsuit. I had always welcomed anyone in a wheelchair or with any other special need. I always told everyone who worked for me that we weren't there to just serve food, we took care of people. And we did.

Hannah was in her 3rd year of law school at this time. I texted her to ask if she had an email address for the judge she had interned for the summer before. I knew he was aware of some cases about a "repeat plaintiff" or something. She called me. "Mom, I only have a few minutes because I'm studying for a major midterm, but I didn't want this to come off wrong in a text."

"OK." I was just happy to hear her voice, but then I got even more emotional.

"Mom, it would not be appropriate for me to email the judge. He is a federal judge and this would be out of his jurisdiction."

"I know honey, I just feel so emotional all of a sudden. I told my server not to accept paperwork from a process server."

"Mom. You should not have done that. Don't have your employee lie for you. He would have left the papers anyway."

"I know. I also want to call this creepy lawyer and say, 'You are a total M*ther F*cker A$$hole!!'"

"Mom. Mom. Mom. Do Not Do That. Promise me you won't do that."

"OK. I'm just mad. Why would anyone think I would be mean to anyone in a wheelchair?"

"Mom. You're taking this personally, and it isn't personal. Everyone knows you would help anyone in a wheelchair. But you may or may not be following the legal rules for wheelchair guests. These are people who make it their job to sue businesses, but there are rules that have to be followed, and you could have more than one violation."

I understood. Hannah was clearly Hann-alyzing this for me since I couldn't think straight. She made so much sense. And I realized I really didn't have things set up in the correct way to accommodate all people with disabilities. She calmed me down and I promised to be patient. I don't know what I would have done that day without her understanding of who I was.

And I just wondered . . . When did we switch roles?

When did my little girl become the mother, and I became the quirky little kid?

How did this happen???

BABY BOOMERS VS. MILLENNIALS

It is so wonderful when your kids grow up and are finally less annoyed by you (or at least they have learned the grace of keeping it to themselves).

One year at Christmastime, Hannah and her dog Finley came to stay with me for six nights. One night she came into my room and sat on my bed. I had the news on. "Mom, does this TV have any Apps on it?"

"I don't know, probably. It's only about a year old. Let me find the controller." I found it and handed it to her, and went back to work on my laptop. "Mom, you have everything, all the Apps. You even have HBO Max that I got so you could watch 'Friends,' remember?"

"No, I forgot about that."

"Mom, you can use all these Apps."

"I just want to turn on the TV and have it work."

"Mom, it WILL work. I can show you again."

The "old Hannah" would have been too frustrated with me to say that. Instead, she was patient and showed me such compassion by explaining it all to me yet again. I stared at her in awe; I was pretending to listen to the instructions she was giving about the TV, but all I was thinking about was how proud I was of her.

The next morning, I got up cheerfully and said, "Honey, let's take Finley on a long walk!" She didn't look enthusiastic; she didn't want to get up and get out of the house. She sighed, "Mom, how long do you want to go for? How far?" she asked.

"Come on, it'll be fun!" I was extra cheerful.

"OK, but I need some coffee first."

"I have coffee here."

"Mom, all your coffee is from Target. Let's go to Starbucks. I'll order on the way."

We headed up the street; I had the dog leash, and she was looking at her phone. "Oh Mom!" She sounded so dismayed.

"What's wrong?"

"Your Starbucks doesn't have the Chestnut Praline syrup."

I just started laughing. "Who cares about Chestnut Praline syrup?"

"Mom, it's really good. I'll have to get something boring now." I just smiled inside thinking of how unimportant all this was. The "old Lisa" would have said that out loud. But now I was also learning the grace of keeping some thoughts to myself.

Hannah sighed. She sounded defeated. "I ordered the Brown Sugar Vanilla. I hope I like it."

"I'm sure you will," I said, cheerfully once more.

"But what if I don't?" she asked, sounding worried. "Then you can order something new tomorrow. And you will see that you can live with disappointment."

Then I started laughing, and so did Hannah. It was so wonderful to laugh together instead of having a silly argument over something so unimportant.

We got to Starbucks and they had a chalkboard out front with all the specials on it.

Guess what was the first thing listed??? Chestnut Praline!

"Ugh!" Hannah said. "Why wasn't that on the App???"

She didn't want to cancel the order; she didn't want to make the employee take the time to make her a new drink. She just accepted the Brown Sugar Vanilla. There was no need for an argument like there would have been in the past; we could now laugh together.

We went on our long walk. She ended up enjoying her drink. But mostly, we enjoyed each other. The "old Lisa" and the "old Hannah" were now replaced by a mother and daughter who love, respect, and accept each other.

MY MOST LOVED STORIES

HOW I CAME TO LOVE HIGH HEELS

No, I did not love high heels all my life. They were just OK to me. My love for my high heels happened when I was almost 50 years old.

My friend Diane and I sat at the Catalina terminal one day, waiting for our middle-school-aged daughters to return from a camping excursion. She giggled, lowered her voice and said, "I took a pole dancing class! I saw it on Oprah—I have the shoes and everything!"

"What? Really?" I'd never heard of such a thing. She made me promise not to tell her daughter. When I got home I looked it up. I was intrigued; they had a $40 one-hour introductory course. I enrolled.

The studio was in Los Angeles, at La Cienega and Wilshire Blvd., pretty far from Long Beach. It took me an hour to drive there. During the two hour class, we spent the first hour doing yoga moves and listening to the teacher. After that, she did a routine to loud, pulsating music.

I loved it! I was sold! I signed up for the eight-week, Level 1 course.

It would be quite the investment of time, because of the drive and the long class. But I chose Monday evenings—there would be less traffic and I would be home by 10PM. My children were now teen-agers so I could leave them for a few hours doing homework, while I secretly drove off to pole dancing class.

The class was rigorous! The first hour always started with very slow yoga, followed by at least 30 minutes of abdominal work. Strong abdominal muscles were essential to be able to flip upside down on the pole and do many of the other pole tricks.

But the real emphasis throughout the class was on getting in touch with your "erotic creature;" in essence, feeling beautiful within your own skin. Every movement was done with grace. The teacher encour-aged us to move in sensual and fluid ways, to be in touch with our nat-ural femininity.

For the third class in the series, we were told to arrive with our own pair of 6-inch platform heels. Luckily Hollywood was not located far from this part of Los Angeles, and they gave us the names of two great stores that carried them.

Right after class I went to one of those shops while still wearing my yoga pants and sports bra. I felt a little embarrassed going in at first, because there were hundreds of platform shoes displayed everywhere, along with a very large selection of erotic clothing and stripper-type accessories.

I somehow felt the need to explain to the clerks that I was not actually a stripper. But they didn't care why anyone wanted to buy their products. They were helpful and encouraging, and probably would have thought it was great if I actually had been a 50-year-old stripper.

I bought two pairs of beautiful 6-inch platform shoes, one was patent-leather shiny red, and the other was a clear plastic that I thought would match any outfit (I don't know why that was in my brain because I had no plans to wear them anywhere but in class).

The day came for class number three, and I headed off with my plat-form shoes in my bag. Tension filled the unusually quiet room, because we all knew it was "shoe night." Our teacher began with our usual one-hour warm-up of slow yoga and abdominal work.

Then it was time. She told us to put on our shoes and hold onto the wall for support. I felt ridiculous, but kept telling myself that this thought in and of itself was ridiculous, because we were all doing it! It was brand new to everyone in class.

With nerves on edge, everyone wobbled as they tried to stand and walk slowly towards a wall without falling over. I could tell others felt a little embarrassed as well; I was not alone. It was more difficult than I thought it would be, and took enormous concentration. I had to purposely lift each foot slowly, and walk heel-to-toe. I could not shuffle my feet or walk improperly in any way.

Then we had to take it to the next level.

Our instructor had us take turns walking around the room, before making our way to one of the poles. We then had to hold onto the pole while we walked slowly around it three times before heading back to the wall. We were reminded to slow down and walk with grace, with our heads held high.

Everyone in the class was different: young, mature, thin, overweight. It didn't matter, we all began to feel pretty and light, and free to be ourselves as we strutted around in those 6-inch platform stripper shoes. Slowly but surely, by the end of class, we were all able to walk gracefully with way less fear.

At each new class, we were taught basic moves, ways to walk, how to bend over towards a wall, how to put our backs to a wall and slide down. All of these were eventually combined into an entire routine. This was so helpful, because it gave us structure and direction when we weren't sure what to do next. Everything was done with a great deal of intention.

During each class, we also learned a new pole trick. We would take turns walking, approach the pole, and then practice the new trick. The tricks had fun names like the Firefly, the Half-pint, and the Corkscrew.

Some of the dynamics of the pole tricks were hard for me to grasp. The direction needed to spin for each trick seemed backwards to me some of the time. I just couldn't get them down.

One Saturday morning, wearing my sneakers (not my heels) I walked over to my kids' old elementary school—I knew they had tetherball poles on the playground. They seemed to be the same circumference as the dance poles at the studio. I looked around to make sure no one was watching, and I slowly walked through one trick to understand it better by getting down to the mechanics of it. I kept checking to make sure no one was around. I didn't want anyone to figure out what I was actually doing!

Eventually I purchased my own pole. The great thing about the pole setup was that I could remove it after any dance/exercise session. There was an attachment for the ceiling, and by lifting the pole it could slide out of the attachment, and then I would hide it safely under my bed. This was a must for me because my kids were teenagers, and I didn't think a 17-year-old boy would want to know that his mother was taking pole dancing classes, even if it was for exercise.

So, it remained hidden.

As the classes progressed, we all became more confident. We had learned the routine and were now taught how to peel off different layers of clothes in a sensual way. This was not a requirement of any participant and there was absolutely no nudity. It was just another element in learning to be OK with our sensuous selves.

After I finished the eight-week Level one course, I took every level course they had, and then I repeated the highest level for over two years.

In these more advanced classes, we already knew all the basics, so there was more time to actually dance and perform. Each week we were given an assignment for the next week's class. It might be based on a musical selection (your favorite song from the 70's or from your favorite movie), or on a piece of clothing (e.g., wear your favorite cocktail dress).

For the last 20 minutes of each class, one at a time we put on our three minutes of music and took a turn dancing to what we loved. It didn't matter how technically accurate our pole moves were, it didn't even matter if we even touched the pole at all and just danced and crawled (yes, there were two types of crawls!)

The point was to get lost in the music and feel beautiful. Believe me, my fellow dancers were fantastic at cheering each other on! You never heard a group of ladies whoop and holler so loud when one of us really "got into it." These classes were fun, and my teacher was so nurturing. I also got into great shape. It was truly the only exercise class I've ever loved; it was so much better than any gym I had ever been to.

In that little studio, I learned how to slow it down, hold my head up high, and to be comfortable with my "erotic creature." Walking in high heels makes me feel pretty, and allows me to be my true gracious self. And, after two years of walking in those 6-inch heels, they felt like slippers to me.

So, whenever someone asks me, "How are you wearing those high heels all the time?" or when someone points to my high heels while I walk in a parade, I just smile a secret smile, knowing it was my two years of pole dancing classes that showed me the way.

MY FAVORITE SOUVENIR—A BEAUTIFUL DRESS IN NEW YORK CITY

I'm not someone who collects many souvenirs on my travels. I only buy things that will provide a long-lasting memory for me, not something that is part of a collection like spoons and keychains. For instance, I purchased a small hand-drawn painting of the Eiffel Tower that I had bought along the River Seine in Paris—it has been on display in a corner of my living room from that time on.

My friend Michele had gone home after our trip in the Hamptons and New York City. I was staying one extra day in the city. The day before, Michele and I had been looking in shops trying to find "coasters"—it was her way of remembering the places she had visited. She liked displaying them on her coffee table and around her home. We had not been able to find anything she liked.

It was now only an hour before I needed to head out to the airport, but I ran out to check some of the shops around my hotel in the Lower East Side.

I couldn't find anything like what she wanted, so I was rushing back to my hotel on a small quaint street, when I passed a very small dress shop. There was a dress in the window that made me stop in my tracks. I practically gasped; it was so "me." The dress was made of a beautiful pure silk cream, with a pink and red flower print, cinched at the waist but flowing out femininely below.

I knew I really had no time to try on a dress; my flight was in just two hours and it is always difficult to get to JFK airport. But I went in anyway, and right in the front of the shop, another woman was trying on the exact dress, AND she had on the "only one" in my size. Ugh! She couldn't decide whether or not she wanted it, and was taking her time turning this way and that.

I only had five minutes before I would have to literally run to the hotel. I couldn't miss my plane because of a dress!

I met the owner of the shop, Anya Patastrovka; she was from Russia. We chatted as I anxiously waited for the other lady to decide. Anya explained that she makes all the dresses herself, and she only makes one in each size.

The sales lady gave me a similar dress in a different fabric to try on. There was only one dressing room, and the other woman had all her stuff spread out in there. They asked me if I would mind going into this storage closet to try it on. No, I didn't mind at all!

I put on the other dress and came out of the storage closet to look in the mirror. No, it just wasn't right, and I didn't like the colors as much either. I then quickly tried on a red satin dress also, but it didn't look right either. Oh well. Time was ticking down. I needed to get going to make my flight.

Suddenly the other woman came out of the dressing room and handed the dress to the sales lady and said, "No, I don't think so." The sales lady turned to me and said, "Here it is."

I ran back into the storage closet, put it on, and came out to look in the mirror. Something was a little off with the hem of the cream silk lining underneath. They said they could hem that little part up. But I didn't have time for that—I had to make a quick decision. "I'll take it!" I said. I knew I could always fix it myself if need be; it was just too feminine and beautiful to leave behind.

They began to run my credit card, but something was wrong with their machine. They couldn't get it to process. They tried over and over again.

I had no more time left. I had already been there way longer than I should have been. I told them I had to go, and asked if they would trust me and let me take the dress. They could run my credit card later. They looked at me dubiously and I pulled out my driver's license as well and suggested they take a photo of both. I reassured them that I would pay them no matter what. "I promise," I said.

Anya, the owner, looked me in the eyes and decided to trust me. She handed me the bag and said, "Go! It's yours."

I ran back to my hotel, gathered my things, and jumped in a taxi. The dress was right next to me in a bag on the seat—I didn't dare smash it into my luggage. I carried the dress with me right onto the plane.

Later they were able to process the payment.

I wore that beautiful dress on Valentine's Day of 2020, the very last Valentine's Day of my restaurant, La Strada.

This dress is my most treasured "souvenir" from any trip I have ever taken. And it wasn't just the beauty of the dress, and the fact that it came from a quintessential little shop in New York City. It was also the actual experience of seeing it at the last minute, waiting and waiting, trying it on in a storage closet, earning the shop owner's trust, running back to the hotel, and carrying it wrapped in delicate tissue paper in a little shopping bag onto the plane.

Every time I see it in my closet, those rush of memories wash over me. And I smile, every single time.

THE RED SILK DRESS

In December of 2019, I had a secret.

I had made an important decision. I sometimes wavered on whether or not I was doing the right thing and I wasn't absolutely sure about it. So, I stayed quiet and told no one, until I could be sure, and also so I had time to get used to it myself.

My decision was that I was going to finish out the last year of my restaurant lease, and close up my business by the end of August 2020. That meant that every event or holiday coming up, would be the "last one" of whatever it was.

So, after 22 years participating in the Belmont Shore Christmas Parade, the year 2019, would be the last time there would be a "La Strada" entry in the Christmas Parade.

In August of that year, I visited my son in New York city. While shopping the streets on the lower east side, I happened upon a small dress shop, and I had purchased a gorgeous handmade, cream floral silk dress. I absolutely loved that dress, and planned to wear it on the final Valentine's Day at La Strada in February 2020.

But now it was December, and it was just one week before the Christmas parade. I looked in my closet, hoping to find a perfect dress for this final parade. I had some red dresses, but none of them seemed right. I kept being drawn to the beautiful floral one I had purchased in New York. But it was red and pink, and didn't look at all like a Christmas dress.

Hmmmmm. I decided to check out the website for that small shop in NYC. And there it was . . . the most gorgeous red dress ever! It was the identical style as the floral one, but it was in glorious, red silk.

I remembered the shop owner very well. She was Russian and her name was Anya. We had chatted a lot that day back in August, when I had bought the floral and cream dress. But, now it was December 1st, and the parade was December 7th. Anya custom makes every dress. Knowing it was a long shot, I nervously picked up the phone and called the shop.

"Hello, this is Anya."

"Hi Anya," I said. "You may not remember me, but I bought a dress from you last summer. Another lady was trying it on, but I waited even though I was late for a plane. In fact, I tried it on in your storage closet."

"Yes, yes!" she said. "I do remember you! We talked about you after you left. About how you looked like you were from the 1950's with your shape, and how beautiful you looked in my dress. And how nice you were."

I smiled thinking back to that day; it had been a very special experience. "Anya, I have a very big favor. Can you make me that same style, but in a beautiful red silk?"

"And," I paused. "I know this is an even bigger favor to ask, but I want to wear it next Saturday in a parade. No one knows this, but it will be my very last parade, and I would love to wear the most beautiful red dress ever. I know it's a lot to ask of you."

Anya was quiet. "Hmmm . . ." she said, "I do special orders, but there is almost no way I could make a dress and send it out to you by December 7th. I'll think about it."

"I understand," I said. "I just thought I would ask." I thanked her and said goodbye.

Ten minutes later, Anya called back. "I know it's crazy. But I'm going to do it for you. I'm going to make you the dress and will do my best to get it there on time."

I thanked Anya profusely before hanging up. I was so grateful and emotional; it wasn't just that she was making the dress. It was because she understood how important it was to me, and how wearing something so beautiful would mark such a turning point in my life.

I had owned my business for 27 years, and it was such a big decision for me, to close out my 2nd home of La Strada. I think I was also emotional because I had now said it out loud—I had actually told someone of my plan to close my business and take my life in another direction.

A few days later, I started checking my porch multiple times each day to see if a package had been delivered. By Friday, I was beginning to lose hope. The parade was the next day and still no package had arrived. Late on Friday night, I began to pull other red dresses from my closet, realizing it probably wasn't going to happen—the custom red dress would not make it on time. I wondered why I thought it was so important anyway. It was just a dress.

I had so many things I needed to do before parade night anyway. I let it go, and thought, "If it comes, then it will be my miracle." Saturday morning, I got up and made the Mississippi Mud brownies I made every year for those coming in on parade night. I made a run to La Strada to drop off the Mississippi Mud and other supplies.

I returned home and parked in my driveway. The dress was now the furthest thing from my mind. I walked up to my front porch, and there was a very small envelope, only about 5 x 7—it looked like some type of office correspondence. But . . . could that be it? Could a dress fit in there?

I picked it up and saw Anya's name. I was trembling. I ran inside and opened it, and gently pulled out the most beautiful, flowing, red silk dress.

I ran upstairs and put it on . . . it was perfect. I immediately called Anya. Through tears I could not thank her enough.

That evening at the parade felt magical.

While in the parade lineup, my staff and I waited next to my little red Fiat with the perfect sound system to play our Christmas music. As it became our turn to walk onto the route and enter the parade, I walked carefully and with intention, like I had learned in my pole-dancing class. My dress shimmered and flowed with every step I took. I felt like I was floating on air in that beautiful red silk dress. I walked ever so proudly.

I know, it was just a dress. But, was it just a dress?

To me it was a sign. Something clicked for me that night, as I walked the parade route. It had now become so clear; I knew I was making the right decision. This would be the last time I would be walking for La Strada, but I was OK with that. And as I continued in the parade, I held my head high, and a new sense of purpose and excitement came over me. I waved at all the parade spectators, and smiled the biggest smile ever.

The dress became more than just something beautiful I wore that night; it symbolized the new direction of my life.

PAUL MCCARTNEY IN THE HAMPTONS

Remember my childhood friend Michele (with one "l")? We remained friends throughout adulthood. In 2019, she and I decided to take a trip to a place neither of us had ever visited.

The Hamptons. In New York.

Michele flew out from Seattle, and I left from Los Angeles. Our flights arrived within one hour of each other at JFK in New York City. From there we took a car to the Hamptons.

When we had made the initial decision, Michele had offered to look into restaurants for our trip—she is great at that! She loved the menu for "Nick and Toni's" and noted that in the description it said, "don't be surprised if you see Paul McCartney leaning against the pizza oven." Well, I didn't believe that would ever happen, but the restaurant did sound good.

I had always heard of the very famous "White Parties" in the Hamptons where the elite attended dressed all in white. I didn't know how we could possibly be invited to any of these parties, but Michele and I packed white dresses anyway, just for fun.

The night had come for us to go to Nick and Toni's, and we decided to wear our white dresses that evening. We were seated at a small corner table, and we loved everything about our meal and our experience. We paid our bill and were winding up our conversation, and were about to get up to leave. Then Michele suddenly grabbed my arm and whispered, "Lisa! Don't get up. There's Paul McCartney!! He just sat down at the next table!"

I looked to where she had indicated. She was right. The large table in front of us had been vacant all evening, and now his party of five were milling around and taking their seats. We were so busy wrapping up and paying the bill that we didn't even notice them walk in. We froze and tried to act nonchalant. But we were frantic!!!

A couple patrons approached Sir McCartney, but the restaurant staff shooed them away. A man at the table next to him turned and kept talking to him—Paul actually seemed to enjoy it. The woman beside him looked patient, and smiled as if she had seen this many times. I wondered who she was, and thought maybe it was one of his daughters.

I secretly snapped a clandestine photo of the woman and sent it to my sister. I knew she would know who it was; she was the most avid Beatle fan I know, and she reads every edition of People magazine and follows pop culture. She and I have seen Paul in concert over a dozen times as well.

I asked if she knew who the other people at the table were. She had texted back, "the woman next to him is his oldest daughter, Mary." Ohhhh, so Mary had seen this many times in her entire life, her dad chatting with his fans.

Michele and I sat there mesmerized. We decided to order another glass of wine and a dessert; we were now in no hurry to leave! Our entire conversation for the next hour centered around what we should, or should not, do. What we should (or would) say. We analyzed the situation from every angle.

I had no intention of approaching him because I don't think it's right to bother the famous people that bring joy to my life; And I have no interest in autographs, they mean nothing to me. But a photo? I would have loved that, but still, I wasn't going to ask.

I wished I had been that person sitting at that table next to him to whom he was talking to—I would have told him I had just seen him at his concert in Orange County, CA where a young lady had come up on stage dressed as a walrus (from the song "I am the Walrus"). But all I could do was stare from our corner table.

We did note that Sir Paul looked directly at us for more than several seconds, no less than five times!!! We discussed what we would do when he got up to leave (we were NOT leaving first!!!). Would we get up and follow him out? Would we say anything?

Finally, their group got up. He walked right past us and we said, "Good night, good to see you."

He looked right at us, stopped for a second and said, "Good night."

Sigh. We sat there star-struck.

On our way out, I chatted with the manager and asked if he came in a lot. She said he was not staying at his house in the Hamptons as much as he used to do, so they didn't see him very often. "Only every now and then anymore," she said.

Oh my gosh, how lucky were we?!?!?!

When we got back to the hotel, we mapped out where he lived and how to get there—it was only 4.9 miles from our hotel. I told Michele we should show up at his house in our same white dresses from that night and say, "Remember us????"

Then we could get arrested!

I LOVED the Hamptons!!!!

THEY WILL ALWAYS BE 7

A family of five came into my restaurant, La Strada, for dinner one evening. They arrived with their 7-year-old boy twins, who were celebrating their birthday, along with their little sister. The mother gave me some cupcakes, along with two "7"-shaped candles, and asked me to bring them out after they finished dinner.

They sat down on the right side of the restaurant at a table, directly below a black-and-white photo of my son eating a bowl of spaghetti. He had been 5 or 6 when the picture was taken.

After dinner, we brought out the cupcakes topped with the "7" candles. Everyone in the entire restaurant joined in singing "Happy Birthday"—it warmed my heart.

Soon after, the mother, Nina, motioned me over.

"Lisa," she said. "You might not remember this, but this was the first place we dared go to after our twins were born. We came in early for dinner at 4:45PM. We sat over there—she pointed to a table up near the front door. You made room for our stroller with our sleeping babies right next to the table. We were so nervous they would wake up and get cranky, causing us to get up and leave so as not to disturb anyone. But you came over and talked to us, and laughed and reminisced about being a new mother with a newborn."

She continued, "I hope this doesn't embarrass you, but you told us a story that I couldn't relate to at all. I don't know if you remember, but it was about how you accidentally bumped your baby's head into a wall."

Ah, yes. I totally remembered the story. My son had been a week old and I was exhausted. As I changed his diaper, he peed, and it went into his eyes. I frantically scooped him up and rushed him to the bathroom to rinse out his eyes. But on the way, I banged his head into the doorjamb. He screamed and I cried. After we had both calmed down, I called my husband at work and told him that I was a terrible mother. He assured me I was not.

I laughed and told Nina that I remembered the story very well.

She said, "I thought it was so strange when you told us about it—you smiled and laughed like it was no big deal—you were trying to make us feel confident that we would be able to handle anything that might go wrong with the twins. I didn't get it at the time, but now after seven years, and three kids, we have been through everything! I get it now."

I pointed at the picture on the wall above their table of my son eating spaghetti. "That's my son, the one whose head I ran into the door jamb. He's 30 now. He's just fine."

Then I added, "He has his own hat business now, and sometimes he lights his hats on fire while creating them. One time he did it while wearing one of them. You have a lot to look forward to."

She looked confused. I realized I had just filled her head with too much information. "Oh, it's a long story," I said. "Don't worry about it. But see these adorable little faces?" I gestured at her children who looked up with wide eyes and chocolate on their faces.

"They are always going to be this age in your eyes. They will always be 7. Always. You'll see."

I smiled, then left them to enjoy their family celebration. I expect to see Nina again in about 20 years, when she comes back to tell me she gets it.

THE PARADE: IN HONOR OF MY MOTHER

My mother, Rita, had always loved the Christmas parade and had supported it from day one. She loved Belmont Shore so much—this was her community for over 40 years. She had attended the very first parade ever, with my niece Claire, and my nephew Josh, when they were just toddlers.

Together our family celebrated many Belmont Shore Christmas parades. When they were older, my mother and father never missed a parade. They came every year to sit in front of my restaurant.

I had been sponsoring groups in the Belmont Shore Christmas parade for years. But in 2010, my friend Robert suggested that I do my own float.

Robert was very creative. He came up with the idea of re-creating the atmosphere of La Strada on the back of a truck. We were able to borrow a gardening truck, and Robert went to work putting up lattice, stringing up lights, and adding a table and chairs from the restaurant.

I had a full staff that year who wanted to walk in the parade, so I ordered our very first set of matching costumes, and made alterations on many of them.

My mother had been diagnosed with Frontotemporal Lobe Dementia eight years earlier—it's a long, drawn-out illness that takes away your memories, then eventually your physical functions as well. She lived at home with my father, and caregivers, and by 2010, she no longer spoke and knew little of what was going on.

A few days before the parade, a hospice nurse came to check on her. They let us know that her final time had now arrived. We asked if it was days or weeks. The nurse said, "not weeks."

I started to wonder what I should do about the parade. I wondered if I I should just cancel everything? I wanted to be by my mother's side as much as I could; to help care for her and hold her hand.

Being part of the parade was a big investment of my time and effort. There were so many things I still needed to finish and organize: getting the sound system together, having everything decorated, making sure all my staff were outfitted and ready. I would have to be at the restaurant a lot. The kids who worked for me were so excited about being a part of our first parade entry.

I didn't know what to do.

I went round and round in my mind. What if I didn't cancel? But what if on the parade day itself, she became suddenly worse? I would never forgive myself if I was off waving in a parade while my mother slipped away from this world.

Anxiety filled me. I went to a very quiet place, closed my eyes, and settled myself. I asked the universe for an answer and waited. I could somehow hear my mother speaking to me in my mind.

"No! Do not cancel the parade. Live your life. Keep going."

It became so clear. Even though my mother could not speak to me in her current state, I knew her well enough to hear her words if she had been able. She wouldn't want me to cancel. She loved that parade too much. She would have wanted me to follow through on my plan. So, I decided to go ahead. We would walk all of Belmont Shore in her honor.

The night of the parade arrived. With everything in place, I was so excited; I knew I had made the right decision to move forward. There were 60,000 people on 2nd St. waiting for the parade to begin. My restaurant was full of people happy to be celebrating together. My staff were all there, and those who planned to walk in the parade wore their parade costumes.

My sister agreed to stay with my mother that evening so that my father could attend the parade for an hour. It was the first time he had come without my mother. He arrived and sat down in the chair we had reserved for him right in front. When I saw him there I ran over to hug him and tell him I was so glad he came. I think he felt conflicted about leaving my mother. But he lit up seeing four of his grandchildren: my two children, Ryan and Hannah, and two of my nieces, Rachel and Marissa, were part of our parade entry that year.

Our group headed to the parade staging area to wait our turn. The time came and we began walking. My restaurant was just one block from the start of the parade route, so it wasn't long before we passed in front of it. I waved at my dad and could see tears in his eyes; he waved back and beamed with pride.

That night, as I walked the parade route, I thought of my mother with every single step; I felt her right next to me, in spirit. I knew I had done the right thing.

My mother died five days later, with all of us by her side.

"YOU DON'T NEED YOUR MOTHER!"
My mother was a wonderful grandmother, especially for kids over three years old. She was not a new-baby type of grandma.

She started a tradition—she loved Hawaii, and took any grandkids who were old enough to go with her over Easter and Spring Break. She found a kid-friendly hotel on Oahu, and a Catholic church down the road. She brought fantastic Easter baskets for each kid, and they all rode the bus to go to church on Easter Sunday. Every grandchild could not wait for the day they were old enough to "go to Hawaii with Grandma."

So, when my son Ryan was six years old, it was his turn, and my mother included him along with his cousins, Claire and Celeste. He was so excited to go he could barely wait for Spring break. My mother always began packing weeks ahead of time, picking out bathing suits, shorts, and beach outfits. He was excited every time he went to her house and saw what she was packing for him.

I was so excited for him.

The day of the trip finally came. My mother believed in taking the very first flight available so that "we can be on the beach by 11AM!!" I had Ryan promptly at my mother's house at 6AM, where the Super Shuttle waited to take them all to Los Angeles International Airport.

My mother had made a large handmade poster that said, "Hawaii 1995!" She gathered up the three kids and they sat around her on her front porch and she held up the sign while I took their picture. It didn't matter how early it was, they were all so excited to go on this adventure.

After the suitcases had been loaded up into the back of the van, I leaned down and hugged and kissed my son goodbye; I had a lump in my throat but there was no time to be emotional and I would not have wanted him to be worried about me if I looked upset in any way. He reciprocated with a quick hug, but couldn't wait to clamber up into the van with his cousins and Grandma. They rolled down their windows and waved goodbye, each of them wearing bright new sunglasses Grandma had brought them for the trip.

The van pulled away and it was suddenly quiet. I was happy though knowing they were all together laughing and full of anticipation.

As the week went on, I was finding it very difficult to be away from my son for such a long time. I had only been away from him for one day at the most. And this was going to be for seven days!

I just worked and stayed busy, telling myself that he was having so much fun, that he was OK with my mother and his cousins. I did have the hotel phone number, but I didn't want to call and interrupt their vacation. I was a little surprised though, that my mother never called even once to check in.

The week crept by, but finally, the night came when they were all flying home. I went to LAX to pick them up. In those days, you could even walk to the gate and wait for them to come off of the plane. I waited and waited. I paced and paced. I worried about the plane landing safely. But mostly, I felt overcome with emotion and was trying to hold it all in at the thought of seeing my son after a week of being apart. I had missed him so much; it was almost unbearable.

Finally, I could see them!

They walked off the plane and into the terminal. I knelt down and could not hug my son fast enough. I was beyond relieved that they had made it safely back. My mother had a huge smile and was carrying lots of souvenirs. Both my nieces were chatty and smiley; they were talking over each other about the beautiful beaches, and how much fun they had, and all about the red-headed birds they had seen everywhere.

My son only smiled slightly, and was super quiet; he said nothing. My mother could not stop talking about how great their trip had been.

We piled into the car and I drove everyone to my mother's house. My nieces were telling story after story about the International market where they went every day to get this special soup. And how Grandma got them ice cream every day. Ryan remained quiet.

When we arrived at my mom's house, she and my nieces headed inside while I unloaded the luggage. My son stayed outside with me. We stood by my car. He looked up at me. "Mom."

"What is it honey?" I asked.

I looked at him and big giant tears ran down his face. "Mom," he could barely say. "Mom. I missed you so much . . . that I thought I was going to die." I threw my arms around him. I understood because I felt the same way. "Oh honey, I thought you were having a great time with Grandma!"

"I was Mom. But I needed to talk to you. I missed you so much. And I kept telling Grandma that I wanted to call you, and she just said, 'you're with your Grandma now, you don't need your mother.'"

Oh dear. She probably wanted him to see that he would be OK without me.

After that, I was (quietly) mad at my mother for a while. I was grateful she had taken him on this wonderful trip. But it broke my heart she had not let my little boy call me when he so desperately needed me.

As the days went on though, he began to talk about all the fun things he had done on the trip. And how he felt even closer to his cousins, because they had consoled him every night when he missed me. Soon after, only the good memories remained.

With a little time and perspective, I got over being mad at my mother. Her wonderful "grandma-qualities" far outweighed this one indiscretion. And, after that, my son went to Hawaii many times with his grandma and his cousins. And he did just fine.

But I never forgot that night.

Because . . . I don't think anyone else has ever missed me so much, that they thought they were going to die.

THE BEST PRESENT I EVER RECEIVED

I do love Christmas decorations.

Once my home is decorated for Christmas, it always feels so peaceful. I loved returning home every night from work, and seeing the Christmas tree glittering in my front window. And I loved waking up in the morning, and walking down the stairs, alongside a lighted Christmas garland on the banister.

But I absolutely can't stand the actual decorating part. I hate getting all those boxes down in the garage, and figuring out what goes where. I detest it, even though I love the end result.

In November of 2009, my daughter Hannah was away at college at Berkeley in Northern California. She called me on my birthday to chat and to wish me a happy birthday.

"Mom, I have a present for you, but I can't give it to you for about two weeks. I promise you will like it." I had no idea what it would be.

By the time two weeks had passed, I had already forgotten about the upcoming present. The Belmont Shore Christmas parade was just days away, and I had so much to do to get the restaurant ready. And as usual, I had done nothing to get ready for Christmas in my own home.

One morning, my doorbell rang around 9AM. I ran down and opened the little window in the door and peered out to see who it was— there was Hannah, standing right on the porch! I was so confused.

Hannah looked at me through the little window and said, "Hi Mom! I didn't want to use my key because you didn't know I was coming, and I didn't want to startle you."

As I opened the door, Hannah smiled. "Mom, I'm here to give you the birthday present I told you about, the one you had to wait two weeks for. I am just here for today, and going back to school tonight. But today, I'm going to decorate your whole house and we are even going to get you a tree and decorate that too."

I stood there dumbfounded. I wasn't even all the way awake yet, and Hannah was supposed to be away at college. I finally said, "Well, how did you get here, honey?"

"I took the first flight out at 7AM and Rachel picked me up at the airport. I have to be back at the airport by 6PM to get the last flight back." I just stared at her, my heart feeling so full.

We headed to the garage and Hannah pulled out every Christmas box, bucket, and bin. "Mom, go do whatever you need to do right now, I've got this." And she did.

A few hours later we headed out to pick up a Christmas tree. We got it home and she started on the lights, and then completely finished it. I could have cried tears of joy.

Of course, this present was wonderful because I didn't have to put up any Christmas decorations. But what it really meant, of course, was my daughter understood me SO well, that she knew just how much this would mean to me.

I drove her to the airport that night for her flight back to school. It had been a wonderful day. I returned home and sat down on the sofa in my beautifully decorated living room, and stared at the twinkling Christmas tree. My gaze then went to the fireplace, where the stockings were hung and the mantle was all lit up, just like I liked it.

It was all so perfect. Not just because of all the beautiful Christmas decorations and the sweet and sentimental day I had spent with my daughter.

It meant so much to me because my daughter and I did not always get along. It was a time when she still found me annoying, and she would lose patience with me many times. I had even recently written her an email telling her not to call me unless she could be kinder on the phone.

And yet, she let all that go. She let all that go just to come home and give me the best present I had ever received: a gift of love, of understanding of who I was as a person, and what was important to me. A gift of time and creativity, from someone who loved me enough to make it all happen for me.

I sat in awe thinking about what a perfect daughter God had given to me.

THAT TIME I WAS A DALLAS COWBOYS CHEERLEADER

Remember that Dallas Cowboys Cheerleader costume I ordered? The one I was thinking of "maybe" wearing for Halloween? My daughter, Hannah, and I had become big fans of "The Dallas Cowboys

Cheerleaders" show. And because I gave out candy every year in front of my business, La Strada, I had purchased the costume along with a few others to wear on Halloween.

You may recall that Hannah was absolutely horrified at even the thought that I would wear it anywhere at all; she did not even want to see me try it on and model it for her. She had said, "Mom, promise me you will send it back!" I told her I would.

But I never did send it back; I just stashed it in a bottom drawer in my hallway and forgot all about it. I never could figure out a way to "appropriately" wear the costume while giving out candy on 2nd St., so it remained in my hallway drawer for years.

But now, years later, my nephew Nick, who helped me take apart La Strada after I closed it, had gotten a job that required him to move to Dallas. I thought about maybe visiting him one day. And then, last year I was getting my hallway painted, and I had to empty all of the drawers and cupboards in my hallway, and guess what I found? The costume!

My thoughts started churning: I wondered if Nick would mind if I visited him in Dallas. I wondered if I could bring the costume and wear it to the game. I wondered if there was a way to meet some Dallas Cowboy Cheerleaders at the game.

I called Nick and asked him about visiting. He excitedly said yes! "Well," I then asked, "Would you go to a football game with me? To a Dallas Cowboys game?"

"Are you kidding?? Of course, I will!!"

"OK, but what if I'm wearing a Dallas Cowboy Cheerleaders costume under my coat?" I waited for his answer. Nick busted up laughing, and said it was no problem for him, he loved it. And he would be happy to be my photographer! Another bonus about going to Dallas was my other nephew, Josh, now also lived there. They were both excited to go to a game with me.

I looked up the Dallas Cowboys home games, and Nick and I decided on the Monday, Nov. 18 game against the Texans. I had never been to a "real" football game (only a high school game when Hannah was a cheerleader), and it sounded especially fun to be at a Monday Night Football Game!! And I had never even heard of the Texans, but I didn't care.

I checked in with my other nephew, Josh, and asked if he wanted to go too, and would he mind if I was wearing a cheerleading uniform? He started laughing and said, "Aunt Lisa, if you are buying the tickets, you can wear whatever you want!!" That was a definite yes! Now it was time to plan, and I LOVE planning, especially for adventures.

I found these adorable team shirts and ordered one for me and each of my nephews. Then I ordered Cowboys earrings and Cowboys sneakers, and cowboy boots to go with the uniform.

I bought the tickets in section 208, and signed up for the "Meet and Greet" that is held the day before.

Now . . . about my sweet Hannah. I had gone to visit her on my birthday about a week before I was leaving for Dallas. I told her about the trip and showed her the pictures of the jerseys I had ordered for me and her cousins. She thought they were great.

As I was leaving her apartment, I mentioned I had been eating a lot and how I hated to go on a trip feeling fat. "Well, Mom," she said, "don't worry about it. At least you're only wearing a football jersey to the game. It's not like you're wearing a Dallas Cowboy Cheerleaders uniform."

Uh oh. I turned to her and told her the truth. "Honey, actually I am wearing the uniform. I'll have it on under my coat." I searched her face for what she might say next.

"That's OK, Mom. I understand." And she gave me the biggest hug ever.

This was the daughter who knew me so well, that she wasn't even surprised by my new upcoming crazy adventure. For my birthday, she had bought me a full set of skincare products, but had taken the time to label each and every one with a post-it note, because she knew I would not be able to remember what to do with each product. She had bought me a couple slices of coconut cake (I love coconut!), but was worried I wouldn't like the pineapple layers (I'm not a big fan of pineapple).

The mother-teenage daughter phase was now over. She was now the daughter who took care of me, the daughter who told me to text her when I made it home.

I hugged my beautiful adult daughter goodbye.

A few days later, I flew off to Dallas with my costume safely packed, along with the white "cowboy-ish" boots to complete my outfit.

I loved Dallas, it is a beautiful city. Nick was a great host and was excited to have me there. The day after I arrived was the Cowboys Meet and Greet. Nick agreed to go along with me. There would be many players from the Dallas Cowboys football team, but I had no interest in them—I didn't know the name of even one player. But there were also supposed to be two Dallas Cowboys Cheerleaders there as well.

On the appointed morning, Nick left early to go to work for a few hours, and said he would be back in plenty of time for us to get to the Meet and Greet. I started to get ready, but I was a nervous wreck. I was quickly losing my nerve. Why was I doing this again???

I put on the outfit anyway, and waited for Nick. When he got there I gave him photo tips, and apologized to him in advance for having to see his aunt dressed like this, but he didn't care. He took some pictures of me and we headed out.

The event took place at a Renaissance Hotel in a 2nd floor ballroom. I felt so conspicuous in my pale blue trench coat and white cowboy boots as we walked up the stairs. But Nick became my most avid cheer-leader—cheerleading the "cheerleader!"

We could see ahead to the check-in area, and Nick noted that many people were dressed in Cowboy gear, mostly Cowboys shirts. And there were some little girls with white boots and Pom-poms (my Pom-poms were carefully hidden in a plastic bag!)

We checked in and took our seats. The emcee first announced the two Dallas Cowboy Cheerleaders who were featured that day: Megan and Marissa. I didn't recognize either of them from the show, but that was OK. Probably most of the ones I would have known had moved on to other things in their lives. It had been many years since I had watched the show with Hannah.

After being introduced, Megan and Marissa went to the back of the room to stand by a backdrop so people could take pictures with them. There was no line yet, so Nick and I headed over. These two young ladies could not have been nicer or more accommodating to me. They were so sweet when I took off my trench coat, and they directed me to stand between them. They told me to "pop" my leg up, and where to hold the Pom-poms.

Nick then asked them if they would sign my boots, and they were delighted to do so!

We left before any of the actual players showed up, not only because I wouldn't know who they were, but also, they wouldn't be in uniform so I had no interest in taking pictures with any of them.

As we got up to leave, this older man at the next table begged me for a picture and I obliged. His daughter said it would mean the world to him. Another man walked by and asked "what year were you?" I suddenly realized that both these men thought I was a "retired" cheerleader—they had no idea I was just wearing a costume. Nick and I ran out of there laughing!

The next night was the big game. Nick, Josh, and I went to AT&T Stadium for the big Monday Night Football Game—the Cowboys vs. Texans!

We got there early and I was so nervous to ditch my coat and pose in my "uniform" with the huge football field as my backdrop. But Nick, still my most avid cheerleader, was so supportive and he took lots of pictures for me. Then I put my coat back on and we sat down and relaxed and watched the game. It was a wonderful experience!

This was one of my most favorite adventures ever. It happened so organically. My love for a TV show led me to ordering a costume. My nephews moved to Dallas. I had my hallway painted and found the costume in a bottom drawer. I came up with the idea. I made the calls and asked the questions. I did the planning and made it all happen.

And it could not have worked out more perfectly.

And this is what I meant in my introduction to this book: any person can move on from disappointment and tragedy. We can all look for ways to find other directions in life in which to go, and to be part of adding to other people's lives. There is no roadmap or steps, just know that "if that person could do it, then so can I."

MORE THAN ONE MOTHER

My very first nephew, Josh, my brother's oldest son, got married in Mexico City in November of 2022. The wedding was held on the grounds of a very old convent; it was so very beautiful even though it rained during much of the ceremony, but thankfully it was only a very light rain.

There were many special moments, but this one stood out as the most special of all.

Josh's parents were fairly young when they had him, and it didn't work out; they divorced when he was about six years old. They both remarried, and each of them had more children.

Over the years, as in many divorce situations, sometimes they did not agree on decisions for their son. And Josh also now had a stepmom and a stepdad who were a big part of his life; there were disagreements over the years, as those situations are not always easy.

We were all assembled for the wedding at the convent. My brother and his wife, Sherri, sat in the front row. Josh's mother, Judy, stood at the back of the venue with Josh, waiting for the ceremony to begin; she was going to walk him down the aisle. But then, she left Josh's side, and walked to the front row. She leaned over to my sister-in-law, Sherri, and spoke quietly to her.

The two of them whispered back and forth, and then Sherri stood up, a little hesitantly.

Judy assured her that it was OK, and the two of them walked back and stood at his side. His two mothers, together. Then the music started, and the ceremony began. It was so moving to watch my nephew walk down the aisle, with both of his mothers, next to his side, beaming with pride. My heart swelled.

It was such a sign of unity.

Not even the rain could dampen such a beautiful moment.

I AM NOT A RUNNER

I had some regulars who came to my restaurant all the time: Ed and his lovely wife, Pauline. Their daughter Kristen worked for me long ago. I just loved her!

They came to La Strada often, and Ed invited me to join his running club. He said it was a great social group and he had met many long-time friends there.

They sounded really fun!

There was just one problem: I hate running.

I always feel nauseous and I have never gotten that magical "endorphin" feeling.

But Ed said to come anyway, so I showed up at the Sunday morning 10AM run.

I tried to keep up for a bit, but eventually I was in the back of the group with a few mothers pushing strollers.

After the run, they assembled at some location. This is where I learned why they called themselves "a drinking club with a running problem." Tons of beer appeared out of nowhere.

I continued showing up a few more weeks to the running events, even though I didn't think it would work out for me. On one Sunday, there was going to be an induction ceremony, but I wasn't given any details. That day had arrived.

The run was over and everyone was gathered under some trees in a park. Another lady was being inducted first, and she was led up in front of the 100 or so people (mostly guys). She was introduced, and then handed a beer. But it wasn't just a mug—it looked like a quart of beer! And she was told to chug it.

And she did. All the way down, and then held up the glass triumphantly. Everyone was cheering.

Oh no. I was next. And guess what?? I hate beer. I can't even take a sip without gagging. What was I going to do???

I stood there, a nervous wreck, while the man introduced me. All I could think of was how I was going to be a total disappointment to this crowd. The guy handed me the huge container of beer, and the crowd started chanting.

I looked down at the beer, and I suddenly had a thought! I had on shorts and sneakers. But I was also wearing a white shirt. A thin, white t-shirt.

As the chants grew louder and louder, I raised up that giant glass of beer . . . and then instead of drinking it, I poured it all over the front of my white t-shirt. The crowd roared, and I heard someone say, "she's one of us!"

I was glad I was "quick on my feet," in coming up with something to do at that induction ceremony. But, while they were all very nice, I never went back again.

After all, I couldn't stand running OR beer.

HE WAS IN HIS ROBE, I'M SURE!

Recently there was a fraud alert on my JetBlue credit card; I called, and learned I would have to get a new card. The next morning, there were pending charges from places I had never heard of.

I called JetBlue again—a man named Charles answered. He had a low, deep voice, and sounded like he had just woken up—he gave the usual "thank you for being a longtime customer" speech in a slow drawl. Then he did a long, low-pitched, clearing of his throat.

By now I figured he was sitting up in bed with his feet on his (hardwood) floor. "No problem," I said, "take all the time you need!"

Charles chuckled in his low, deep voice. "Hmmm," he said as he logged into my account and saw the charges. "Do you recognize any of these?"

"I've only used one recently, the Farmersdog.com."

"You didn't order from 'Stripe'?"

"No! I don't even know what that is."

"Hmmmmmm," said Charles, "how about Apple Pay?"

"I don't even know how to use Apple Pay. If my credit cards are in my 'wallet'—does that mean I've used Apple Pay?"

I added, "Can you tell I'm 65?" Charles started laughing. "You're good."

"Thank you Charles." We were now on a first name basis. In my mind, Charles was now in his robe walking around and making his coffee.

He continued, "Let's go through some of these. Have you ordered from Etsy?"

"Yes! I ordered some dog stuff from Etsy."

"Air BnB?"

"No, I only stay in hotels!"

"Uber?"

"Yes, yes Charles! I know how to work Uber!" More deep, low chuckling.

"Macy's?"

"Yes, I ordered this blue coat but the sleeves are too long. I have to take it back, it's still in my trunk."

"Yandy?"

"Well, Yandy is a lingerie company, but I did order a Halloween costume from them, a space-age-type outfit!" I almost offered to send him a photo.

Charles now knew that I was 65, had a dog, stayed in hotels, took Ubers, liked the color blue, and ordered from lingerie companies. I was really nervous about what else was in my account.

"How about 'Felix Huttenbach'?"

"I don't know who that is, I swear!" I declared as if Charles wouldn't believe me. He laughed, long and slow. "I believe you," he said, as I imagined him sipping his coffee.

Charles finished going through each and every charge with me before saying goodbye. I hung up and felt a rather wistful longing. I imagined Charles was still in his robe, relaxing with his coffee.

The next morning, I thought, "I hope there are more fraudulent charges on my card today." Or, I could just call the credit card company myself:

"Hello, JetBlue? It's Lisa Ramelow again. Please let Charles know that I am single. Thank you."

LOVED ONES I MISS (WHO HELPED ME ON MY JOURNEY)

LOSING LOVED ONES

"Time heals all wounds." Is that true?

It might not "heal" exactly, but it certainly does help. When people you love leave this earth, it makes an impact on you, whether it's sudden like my husband's heart attack, or a long-drawn out illness like my mother's dementia.

From my experience, the unexpected situations are the most difficult. It's like you've been punched; you can't breathe. Your mind keeps playing tricks on you, convincing you that your loved one is still present. You dream that they are alive and it was somehow all a mistake, and then you wake up and within a few seconds, the truth hits you in the face one more time; "Oh, they really are gone. It's true."

I wrote about the sudden loss of my husband in my book, "*A Kindness I Will Never Forget.*" It details what it was like for me, having a two-year-old and a newborn, and the difficulties and growth that I experienced.

The loved ones that are ill and are aware they are going to die, are also painful situations to experience. You must watch them suffer. You must watch their angst and grief and guilt knowing they are leaving you behind. You wonder if it would be better if they could have died instantly so they would not be going through what you are watching them experience.

Then you feel guilty for having these thoughts.

Sometimes they hang on for a very long time, more than anyone expected. And you are glad they are still with you . . . and yet, they aren't who they used to be—they are only part of who they once were, because whatever illness they have has taken away part of their body or mind. Then you wish that they would just go already, so that they (and you) could be spared. And then even more guilt follows after those thoughts.

And it is still painful when they leave.

There does come a time though, when you must find a way to live without those lost loved ones—it is imperative for your survival. Your thoughts must go to finding a way to honor them the most. You must find a way to not be so sad anymore. You must find a way to accept they are no longer here . . . but you still are. What can you do? What would they want you to do?

LIVE.

They would want you to live. And to live your very best life.

So . . . wake up every morning and find something, even the smallest thing, to feel peaceful about—that peacefulness will grow from this small start. Do the things you love, and sometimes do the things that *they* loved. Think about them. Celebrate them. Do things that would make them proud.

Then, one day, something very strange will happen. You will wake up, and they will not be your very first thought. They will be your second thought. It feels scary when you notice it.

Some guilt may follow . . . but trust me, when this happens, it is the very first sign that you are now getting better. That you will indeed be OK without them being here anymore. And it doesn't mean that you will ever forget them. It just means that "time" is working, helping to heal your wounds.

And it's OK. Your loved ones understand. They want you to LIVE.

"BLOND HAIR AND A PINK COAT"

In 2009 I was relatively new to Facebook and only posted short things about my restaurant. But in that year, my friend Dave died. I didn't know him very well, but we crossed paths in an unusual way, and I was moved by his death at a relatively young age in his 50's.

I decided to write a "long" story about Dave, how we met, how we continued our friendship over a long distance, and how we were united by our love of music.

I posted the story on Facebook, and I was completely flabbergasted at the response. People loved reading about Dave—they felt they got to know him through my words, and they understood and empathized with what it was like to lose a friend. The comment section was filled with people sharing their own stories of loss and friendship.

The outpouring of love and support really surprised me; I had no idea Facebook could be used for storytelling, and I especially did not realize people really wanted to read these real-life stories.

But because of that first "long" story, I began to write other stories, about life, death, love, accomplishment, and growth. So, in a way, I have Canadian Dave to thank for turning me into a writer.

I didn't know Dave for very long or even that well, but he was part of one of the most memorable experiences of my life.

In December 2007 I got on a plane for London. I had a concert ticket in my hand, as well as the phone numbers of about a half dozen people I had "met online." I was on my way to the event of a lifetime, the Reunion Concert of Led Zeppelin at the O2 arena, playing for one night only, to honor record producer Ahmet Ertegun.

It was sort of a last-minute decision for me. I had a milestone birth-day coming up (I was turning 50), and I was not happy about it. I decided to borrow from my home equity line of credit to buy myself a ticket. I navigated onto a Zeppelin web site and quickly became friends with a community of people who had been discussing the upcoming concert for some time. They welcomed me into the fold. I made my travel arrangements.

Once I arrived in London, I was excited to meet all the people I had been conversing with via AOL messenger. I had purchased an international phone to take with me so that I could contact everyone.

Dave was from Vancouver, Canada, and we had chatted many times online. His online name was Canadian Dave and I could tell from all our chatting that he was a very funny guy. Dave was married, but was coming to the concert solo as were many of those in the group.

Once I settled into my hotel, Dave was the first person I called. There was already a plan in place for everyone to attend a party at a place near Hyde Park, which was close to my hotel. Dave's hotel was near the O2 arena, so he suggested he would grab a taxi, and come over to pick me up, and we would head over together.

Never having met him before in person, I added, "OK. And I have blond hair and a pink coat."

"OK," he laughed. "I'll be in a cab. Oh, and I have brown hair and a brown coat."

I think he didn't really need my description of myself if I was going to be standing in front of my hotel.

When the cab pulled up and the door opened there he was, this bright smiling man. He did indeed have brown hair and a brown coat.

"Hi, I'm Dave!" he said.

"Hi, I'm Lisa!" I said.

Normally I would not jump into any car with a man I did not know, but it was a taxi, and it was so obvious it was Canadian Dave. I hopped right in and we took off to the meeting place.

Once there, we met a dozen or so other fans from across the world: Les and Jon from Australia, Chris from Texas, Marc and Steve from

LA, Sharon from Washington DC, and many others. We were united by this wild and ridiculously crazy thing we were doing, flying off to another country to see a band play a one-off concert.

Our group became fast friends. We spent the next three days together pretending we were 17 again. We had dinners together, shopped at Christmas markets (it was in December), and we all went to the O2 Arena the night before the concert to pick up our wristbands. While we were there, we could hear the band inside practicing for the big event the next evening. Our excitement grew.

At our party the evening before the concert, I remember Dave telling me, "Lisa please pray for me that they will play 'The Ocean,' it's my very favorite song." I didn't particularly like that song, but of course I would hope so for Dave's sake; after all it was a foregone conclusion that my favorite song, "Kashmir," would be played because no Led Zeppelin show would be complete without it. In fact, there were giant billboards outside the arena with printed lyrics from "Kashmir."

"I hope they play it for you Dave!" I said reassuringly.

The next evening was the concert and it was more than fantastic, it was just indescribable. The whole experience was definitely a once-in-a-lifetime event. Led Zeppelin did indeed play "Kashmir," but they did not play "The Ocean" that evening.

And, side note: Led Zeppelin has never again done another concert. So, this memory will always be extra special.

After returning home from London, one of the ladies in our group, Sharon, shared how her college-aged daughter had told her all about this new thing called Facebook. This was 2007, and Facebook was mostly used by young people. But Sharon sent out friend requests to each and every one of us, and most of us accepted.

Through Facebook we could all keep in touch with each other and see what everyone was up to. And every December, for many years, we all reminisced about our special time in London in 2007.

Dave and his wife loved to travel and because of social media I was able to see all the photos from his various trips to Hawaii and other places.

At some point, Dave's son enrolled in a prestigious music school in Los Angeles. The entire family came down to set him up in school that September, and they all came to Long Beach one evening to eat at my restaurant.

Dave and Barbara often visited their son in Los Angeles, and would stop in for dinner to see me as well. On the last visit I saw him, they talked a lot about how the healthcare system in Canada was quite different from ours in the US. They hadn't said anything publicly, but Dave had completed chemo for cancer and had recovered. He was in remission.

But it wasn't very long after he was in remission, that a sudden complication from that illness took his life. He was only in his 50's. His wife Barbara let everyone know about his funeral arrangements.

I was not able to attend Dave's funeral in Canada. But, while Led Zeppelin never did play "The Ocean" that night in London at the O2, on the day of Dave's memorial, I listened to it in his honor . . . rest in peace my Zep friend. It was such an honor to know you.

MY CRAZY UNCLE BOB

My Uncle Bob was unusual because he had two such distinct parts of his personality; and both completely defined him. On the one hand, he was a brilliant physician. He loved being a doctor and worked many hours.

The other side of Uncle Bob was the irreverent and inappropriate side. He loved to curse and tell jokes—they were actually "stories," most were at least five minutes long. He told them over and over ever since I could remember. Every single one ended with a filthy punch line. I laughed every time.

I'll start with his brilliant physician skills.

My mother had two brothers: her older brother Bob who became a physician, and her younger brother, Joe, who she raised herself from when he was 8 years old, after their mother had died.

Every year, she took all of us kids back East to see her family in the Philadelphia/New Jersey area. Uncle Bob and my Aunt Doris lived in Cherry Hill with my five cousins.

The summer when I was 12, my mother sent me and my older sister to stay with them for a whole month. We loved it. There were trips "down the Shore" to Atlantic City and Ocean City. And every day, when we were in Cherry Hill, we would walk to Uncle Bob's medical building about two blocks away, on Covered Bridge Road. Out in front would be his big shiny Cadillac—he loved those cars and got a new one every single year.

Right across the street from his office was a "7-11" store, and we would walk there every day to get TastyKakes—they were prevalent on the east coast, but unheard of in California. I loved the chocolate cupcakes with chocolate frosting.

That particular summer, my mother had asked Uncle Bob if during my visit, he would test me for allergies. My asthma had gotten worse and my many allergies were not helping. On that day, my cousins walked me over to my uncle's office, and then went on to get their TastyKakes before heading back home.

Uncle Bob performed a standard allergy test on me—on the underside of your forearm they make many tiny scratches, then apply a small amount of each potential allergen onto each scratch. After 30 minutes, if there is any reaction, then you are allergic to that particular allergen.

All I remember was that my forearm turned into one giant swollen mess. I was allergic to everything. I then threw up and passed out in the office bathroom. I woke up hearing Uncle Bob talking to my mother on the phone telling her that it wasn't a good idea for him to test further while I was there on vacation.

Uncle Bob then walked me out and put me into the back seat of his big Cadillac so I could lie down. He drove across the street to the 7-11. He told me to wait there in the car while he went inside. He seemed very uncomfortable. He and my Aunt Doris had a traditional "50's" type of relationship; his job was to be a successful physician to support his family. Aunt Doris was to take care of the kids, and by extension, any visiting kids, like me.

As my uncle, he was usually more serious and formal around me, and wasn't one to tune into the emotions of the kids.

He soon returned from the 7-11, and handed me a big brown paper bag. "Here, this is for you," was all he said.

I looked into the big bag—I think he had bought me every flavor of TastyKakes in the store. He didn't know the chocolate ones were my favorite, and he wanted to be sure he had covered all his bases.

Uncle Bob got back into the car and quietly drove me the two blocks to their house on Pine Valley Rd.; he walked me inside, and went back to work.

He did not need to say anything more to me about the events of that day: buying me all those TastyKakes was his way of letting me know he felt bad about my reaction to the testing.

He was always protective of me after that.

Forty years later . . . he took care of me again. By taking care of my daughter.

I was at an event on a Friday evening. My daughter, Hannah, was now grown up and had come home from college for the summer. She texted me that she had a bad headache, and wanted to know where my migraine medicine was.

I returned home an hour later and was surprised to find she was still in intense pain. I didn't want to overreact, but we had a family friend whose granddaughter died from bleeding in the brain. I was so worried that something similar might happen to my daughter. It was strange that her pain had not eased at all after being on the medication for over an hour. I was scared to let her go to sleep because I thought maybe she wouldn't wake up.

I wasn't sure what to do. I kept telling myself, "It's only a headache." But then another hour would pass and I wondered why it still persisted. By midnight I was no longer confident in waiting; we went to the emergency room at Long Beach Memorial Hospital.

They controlled her pain with medication, and she was suddenly seeming like her old self.

But the doctors wanted to do all these other tests on her to check for other things. The tests sounded invasive and made me nervous—a CT scan and a spinal tap. I felt so unsure.

I tried to reach out to some local medical professionals to ask for their advice, but it was 1AM on the west coast. I couldn't reach anyone. My anxiety grew with each moment.

All I wanted to do was to call Uncle Bob. But he was now 85 years old, and even though he was completely "with it," he lived in an assisted-living facility with my Aunt Doris. And it was 4AM on the east coast in New Jersey.

But I felt so desperate. I picked up my phone and called.

"Hello?" he answered groggily. He sounded nervous and apprehensive.

"Uncle Bob, it's Lisa in California. I'm so sorry to wake you up. No one has died. Everything is OK, but I need your medical expertise."

His voice changed and he suddenly sounded wide awake; he turned into the calming professional doctor that I had always known. He didn't sound at all like he was 85 years old.

"Tell me everything," he said.

And then he listened.

"Uncle Bob, I brought Hannah to the ER." I explained about how she was feeling better, but how they still wanted to perform these medical tests.

He told me exactly what to do. He explained that the tests were necessary, and that the doctors would not be doing their jobs if they did NOT do them. Yes, it was probably just a migraine, but better to be safe than sorry.

And he told me not to worry.

I again apologized for waking him up, and he reassured me that it was 100% OK that I had called. It didn't matter how many years it had been since he had retired; he was still a brilliant physician, and I know he didn't mind helping me at all.

I was so relieved. And Hannah was just fine; all the tests came back negative—it had just been a persistent migraine.

At 85, Uncle Bob was still professional, and he still took care of me. And now, for the other side of Uncle Bob. . . .

If there is anything weird or nutty or "out there" about me, believe me, it came from my mother's side of the family. I don't know who was crazier—my mother, or her brothers, Bob and Joe.

A few years ago, when both my Uncle Bob and cousin Bunkey were diagnosed with difficult cancers, my sisters and I flew out to visit them. I asked Uncle Bob to take us on a Philadelphia history tour.

But not the actual history of the city of Philadelphia, or of our country—we wanted a personal tour of our family history in that city. We had seen many of these places before, on our many visits to Cherry Hill, New Jersey. But now we would see everything with Uncle Bob's narrative.

Uncle Bob wore one of his crazy pairs of colorful baggy pants, and we headed out in his giant Cadillac, from New Jersey over the Walt Whitman bridge to Philadelphia.

He drove us to their very first house in Philly on what looked like a tiny alley. They had only lived at this place for a very short time when he was a baby, and they had then moved to a row house in the Fairmount Park area, where they all grew up.

As we reached their old neighborhood on our way to the house at 2123 Green St., Uncle Bob began to point out different landmarks.

"That's the bar I snuck into when I was 13."

"That's the parish where a visiting priest from Spain tried to molest me. When my mother found out, she wrote letters to all the parishioners and had him sent back to Spain."

"That's the Church of the Pink Ladies. My mother, your grandmother, went to mass every morning there. Every single morning."

He then pulled up to St. Francis Xavier's church where my mother and father had gotten married in 1952, and he and my Aunt Doris had gotten married in 1953. It was their neighborhood parish.

We all got out of the car and were able to go inside and walk through the church; it was relatively unchanged from 50 years before. I had brought photos with me of my parents' wedding, and it was so magical to walk toward the altar, picturing my mother making this trip down the aisle to her waiting groom, my father.

After that, we piled back into the Cadillac for the 2-block drive to the home on Green St. where they had grown up.

Over the years I heard my mother mention "2123 Green St." or "St. Frannie's Church" so many times. She had wonderful memories of growing up there, even though she had lost her mother from cancer when she was 16 years old. She adored her father and her two brothers, and in a way, had become the de facto mother for her 8-year-old brother, Joe.

We got out of the car and stood in front of 2123 Green St. Uncle Bob pointed at a house across the street, "That's where Aunt Suzy lived. That's where I went when my father threw me out of the house."

Uncle Bob regaled us with his stories. I can't tell most of them here, but it was easy to picture all of these scenarios.

He had adored his mother, and was devastated when she died. He had been 17. But her death was what had inspired him to go into the medical field and become a prominent doctor. It was such a special experience to take this personal family history tour with Uncle Bob.

Besides his well-known story-telling, Uncle Bob was known in his community for the many eccentric and over-the-top escapades he created over the years. His home on Pine Valley Rd. was known for having more Christmas decorations than any other home in their township or beyond. And every New Year's Eve, Uncle Bob would put on his best tuxedo and meet up with his three best friends. They would drink all night, and when the sunrise came, they headed to their favorite golf course and played 18 holes, still wearing their tuxedos.

Uncle Bob developed cancer of the jaw. He participated in as many cancer drug trials as possible, always trying to help the medical community in any way he could.

As his illness progressed, he understood that his final day was coming, so he had plenty of time to plan and prepare for it. He picked out just the right tuxedo. And he chose a gravesite right next to the curb at the cemetery.

He told us, "I picked that spot so that when you come to visit me, you don't even need to get out of the car—just roll down the window, and throw the flowers right out and onto my grave."

We now do that every time I go visit. My cousin Patty and I pick up some flowers before heading out to the cemetery. She slowly drives down the right road in the cemetery, and then we roll down the window and yell out, "We're here! Here come the flowers!" as we toss the flowers out the window and onto his grave. We know he sees us.

I really do miss Uncle Bob, and all his crazy energy, and even his jokes.

There was no one else like him.

Goodbye Uncle Bob, thank you for always taking care of me.

An Ode to Uncle Bob:

In 2011, I attended an exhibit about Princess Diana on the Queen Mary in Long Beach. I wore a long black evening gown, something I almost never do—I don't have evening gowns and I rarely wear black. But this was a black-tie affair, and my friends were wearing their very sharp tuxedos.

At that time, I was dating a man who owned a jewelry store. I stopped to see him and asked if I could borrow something special for that evening. He brought out a beautiful diamond necklace; I knew it would be just right. As I was leaving the store, he gave me a gentle reminder, "Just be careful. The necklace is valued at $32,000."

What?!?! I couldn't believe it.

My friends and I attended the event and then wandered the ship, looking at the long hallways of staterooms and the gorgeous observation bar, still decorated in 1920's Art Deco style.

We made it up to the top deck and walked by the three very large, orange-painted stacks that are a hallmark of the Queen Mary ship. Each orange stack had a ladder that went up the side, all the way to the top.

We were at the middle stack, and the ladder reached all the way down to the deck. In front of it was a small sign that said, "No Entrance." It was held in place by a simple chain. The ladder was right beyond the sign and chain.

I thought it would be a great idea to climb up the ladder in my evening gown and high heels!

My friends were not keen on the idea, but I handed them my camera, and then headed past the chain and up the ladder in my high heels. When I got up high enough, I posed brazenly with one foot in the air, hanging off the ladder. My friends got a great picture for me.

It wasn't exactly what Uncle Bob had done in his tuxedo at the golf course, but for me, it was in the same spirit.

I think Uncle Bob would have been proud of me.

MY COUSIN BUNKEY

It was so very hard to say goodbye to a presence like Bunkey's. There is no way to replace her with anyone else, the best we can do is live up to those things that were important to her: enjoying every day, every moment, and finding ways to laugh.

Bunkey, my cousin on my mom's side, loved to talk—in fact, she almost never stopped. And she always added in the person's name to whomever she was speaking with—I think it was her way of accentuating whatever topic she was speaking about.

"You know what, Lisa?" or "I think you're right, Lisa!"

We were the same age, and even though we lived on different coasts, our parents kept us close. When we were teenagers we spent alternating summers at each other's houses.

The summer when I was 12, we went to the Atlantic City Boardwalk. Bunkey and I headed to Steel Pier, where they had musical shows, rides, and other amusements. We wandered around, buying cotton candy and playing carnival-type games.

Suddenly Bunkey pointed and screamed, "There's Danny Partridge!! Let's go meet him!"

I looked past a Merry-go-round, past a man holding about 100 balloons, and saw the bright-red-haired boy.

It was indeed Danny Bonaduce, the child actor who played Danny Partridge in the TV show, "The Partridge Family." That show came on every Friday night right after "The Brady Bunch," and we never missed it. All the stars on that show had become instant celebrities, and had graced many teen magazine covers.

Danny Bonaduce, easy to spot with his bright red hair, seemed to be a year or two younger than we were. Normally, I would never have chased him (or any celebrity) because I would feel I was disturbing someone else's privacy. Bunkey, however, immediately ran straight towards him, and of course I followed . . . because why not? If Bunkey thought it was OK, then I followed along.

When he saw us, he took off in another direction. But still we persisted until we caught up with him.

I had no idea what we were going to do once we reached him—I thought maybe Bunkey would ask for his autograph.

But instead, she exuberantly asked, "Can we cut off some of your hair as a souvenir?!"

I was completely horrified. By the look on Danny Bonduce's face, he was as well. After all, he was just an 11-year-old kid out having a good time on the pier, and some star-struck 12-year-old girl (followed by her much smaller cousin) chased after him and now wanted to cut off some of his hair!

He looked stunned, then turned and ran away from us as fast as he could. He seemed to have an older brother or someone else with him looking out for him, so at that point we did not chase after him again.

"Darn, Lisa," Bunkey said, "I don't know why he didn't like us."

I didn't want to tell her that it probably had nothing to do with whether he liked us or not. But more with the fact that we had just chased him across the pier and her request had been quite unusual. I'm relatively certain he had never heard that before (or since).

"Bunkey, we don't have any scissors with us anyway," was all I managed to say.

"You know what, Lisa? He may have had some, you never know."

That thought felt almost as ridiculous as what we had just done. But Bunkey always had a different take on things.

And that was how Bunkey and I did things from then on out. We winged it. And if it didn't work out, we laughed.

The year that Bunkey and I were 13, she and her sister Patty came to our house on Covina Ave. in Long Beach, California. Every day we walked down Division Street to the Bay; Bunkey loved to lather up with baby oil and "lay out" trying to get a deep summer tan.

And every night after dinner, we played pinochle.

My mother had taught us all how to play. My sister, Julie, and Patty were always on the same team, and Bunkey and I always played together as a team. The cards were dealt and then we'd make a bid depending on the cards in our hands. It was a really good hand if you and your partner had many cards of one particular suit. But of course, you were not allowed to communicate that to your partner. They would have to guess what you may have, depending on your bid.

But Bunkey had a plan (she always did). She developed a "system" for us so we would have a better idea of what cards we each had been dealt.

One day, while we were at the Bay, Bunkey said, "You know what Lisa? When we play pinochle tonight, I have a way to let you know what my cards look like. If I have a lot of hearts, I'll tap over my heart. If I have diamonds, I'll point to my finger (as she pointed to her ring finger on her left hand indicating a diamond ring). If I have clubs, "I'll do this," and then she pulled on her ear lobe a few times. I had no idea why that meant "Clubs" and I can't remember the signal for Spades.

"But, Bunkey," I asked. "Isn't that cheating?"

"You know what, Lisa? I really don't think it is, I think we're just helping each other! And as long as Julie and Patty don't know, who cares?"

So, we continued to play cards every night, over and over, and used our little cheating skills. I can still so clearly envision her tugging on her ear lobe, and widening her eyes to make sure I got the signal. I don't think Julie and Patty ever figured out how much we had been cheating.

We had so much fun that summer.

Bunkey was especially close to my mother, Rita. They were so much alike it was uncanny. In fact, Bunkey was born on my mother's birthday, April 3rd, and her given name was Kathleen Rita. Her father had given her the nickname of Bunkey at some point when she was a child and it stuck. Every single person in her life called her Bunkey, except for my mother, who called her Kathleen. I never knew why my mother refused to call her Bunkey.

Bunkey visited California frequently with her two children. She always stayed with my parents and made the most out of every visit. In 1990 she came after Christmas and stayed one week before returning home in the new year, 1991.

On January 3, 1991 my husband suddenly died. Bunkey had flown home with her children a day or two before. She called me as soon as she found out.

"Lisa, do you want me to come back?"

I usually had a difficult time accepting help, and never wanted to have anyone go to a lot of trouble on my behalf. But I immediately answered, "Yes, Bunkey. Please come back."

She had just flown the 3,000 miles back to New Jersey with her kids, but she got on a plane the next morning to come back to help me. There were so many things she did during that difficult time to make things easier for me—too many to count, and they are detailed in my book, "A Kindness I Will Never Forget."

Bunkey and I both loved watching the TV show the Bachelor. We would talk about all the dates the Bachelor had gone on, and who he eliminated. They would always have a two-on-one date when the bachelor would have to choose one girl, and then he and the chosen girl would often fly away in a waiting helicopter, leaving the other girl behind standing on a beach.

During one summer I visited, we stayed in Ocean City, NJ. One night, Bunkey experienced severe abdominal pain, so she woke me up to take her to the emergency room. I drove her car and she directed me to the small hospital a couple miles away.

After learning of her medical history and her cancer complications, the staff decided that she should be airlifted to a larger hospital with more resources. They called for a helicopter and prepared her for the transport—they strapped her on to a special hospital gurney. There was somewhat of a delay before the transport got going, and her anxiety was rising. She was not at all thrilled about being in a helicopter, but she was trying to remain calm.

Two men arrived who would be tending to her during the 30-minute ride. They checked her vitals and the straps on the transport bed. Bunkey remained cheerful and upbeat and never stopped talking to the two men (she still loved to talk). She told them she was also a nurse, and expressed her gratitude over and over for their help in getting her to the larger hospital. The men were smiling—she just had that effect on people.

She told them more than once though, that she was not at all excited about this upcoming helicopter flight. But then something occurred to her, something from the Bachelor TV show.

She told them, "I am not excited about going in this helicopter, but I'm going to pretend that the three of us are on the Bachelorette, and this is a two-on-one date. One of you will be eliminated at the end, and be left behind when it's over. So, both of you better work really hard at keeping me happy on this helicopter date!"

As they wheeled her out, I told her to enjoy her date, "Bye Bunkey!! Have fun on your two-on-one!!"

"I will Lisa! Don't worry! These guys are going to be fighting over me!" she yelled back as they loaded her into the helicopter. The two men smiled.

In 2013 I went to New York to visit my son at the same time that Bunkey was visiting her daughter who lived in Brooklyn. We had lunch and then she asked me to go with her to a museum where she needed to evaluate some paintings for an art class she was taking for fun.

"Bunkey, I don't do well in museums. I am horrible at understanding art; I never get any of it."

"You know what Lisa? You are going to surprise yourself. These paintings are really beautiful and I know you will love it. You will!"

"OK, Bunkey, but you are the only person in the world who could get me to go to a museum."

We walked into the museum, and Bunkey learned that the paintings she was to evaluate were on another floor. Along the way were lots of statues. I love statues, because I like to take pictures posing next to them. Bunkey obliged me at every one, filling my phone with many photos of me posing, this way and that.

Finally, we made it to the paintings she needed to analyze as part of her homework. I had no idea about any of them—the artists, where they were from, or the year they were painted, or what any of them were trying to portray.

Bunkey pointed at one. "OK Lisa, what does this one look like to you?"

"I'm not sure. It looks like a husband and wife and a chicken, maybe they're going to a market."

"Ok, you know what Lisa? That is a good guess and maybe just another interpretation. How about this one over here?"

"Well, that lady is sitting backwards on a horse. Maybe she wants to go back in time?"

"Lisa, maybe that could be it."

By the 3rd painting, after I gave my guess as to what it meant, Bunkey finally turned to me and said, "You know what Lisa? You really ARE horrible at this; I don't know why I made you come here. You should stay out of museums forever!"

"See? I told you!" I said.

We couldn't stop laughing.

Bunkey had been trying so hard to make me feel positive about my art ability, but after a few attempts she had realized it was hopeless.

We finished evaluating her paintings, then breezed right by some Indian artifacts and went to lunch.

Later that night we watched the finale of the Bachelor together with her daughter Kelly.

Thank you Bunkey, if it wasn't for you I would never have gone to the Museum of Metropolitan Art in New York City.

Bunkey died in June of 2017. She had just turned 60.

I had seen her just a few weeks before; we held hands and watched a movie. She told me that she was not afraid to die, she was just so happy because I was there. She had such a gift for making people feel special. I cried when I left because I knew it would be the last time I would see her. I told her I would miss her so much.

She lived way longer than anyone predicted with her type of cancer. But being an RN with a PhD, she had researched every option for treatment. If appointments with specialists weren't available, she brought cupcakes and donuts to the office until something opened up. She made a quilt for every doctor who helped her along the way, to show her love and appreciation. For all of them, every single one.

We were there for each other during the significant moments in our lives: deaths and loss and heartbreak. But what was more important, was what we did with the moments in-between. We took the smallest things and made them enchanting. We celebrated everything around us, and most of all, we celebrated one another.

I will love you forever Bunkey, "a bushel and a peck, and a hug around the neck."

SHE KISSED ARNOLD SCHWARZENEGGER!

I met Sandy, a real estate agent, in 2006 when I decided to move back to the Belmont Shore area of Long Beach. I had lived for 15 years in a different part of the city, where the lots were bigger and we had room for a lawn and a basketball hoop. Sandy and I hit it off immediately and became fast friends.

Besides being a lot of fun, Sandy also did something very helpful for me. When I met Sandy, my kids were teenagers. On the day we were shopping for a new house, the kids came along, and over the course of that day, she asked my kids all about themselves: what was important to them, what were their dreams and aspirations.

Sandy found me the perfect home and after I moved in, we did all kinds of fun things together. We went to SO many Long Beach fundraising events over the years. And we were always game for each other's antics.

If I told Sandy, "Let's go sit on that motorcycle over there! It will make a great picture!"

Well, Sandy would do it with me.

And when we went to the desert for a couple days, Sandy took us to this restaurant that had dancing. We were on the dance floor all night.

At some point I said to her, "it's getting late, isn't it?"

And she said, "The music is still playing!" and off she danced. Sandy loved to dance.

She was so genuine. I knew it, and my kids felt it too.

Being teenagers, sometimes my kids would drive me crazy. One day I might be annoyed at my daughter's disrespect towards me. Another day, I might have been devastated at a choice that my son had made.

But no matter what happened with my kids, if I needed to talk to someone, I always called Sandy first.

She would listen intently, never interrupting me.

And then, always, always, she would say something wonderful about them. She took their side in a way, not against me, but with her voice full of kindness and compassion.

She would say things like, "Maybe she had a bad day at school, she didn't mean it. She loves you."

Or, "I know you're sad, but I bet your son is feeling even worse than you. He loves you so much."

I think this is why I always called Sandy first. Subconsciously, I knew she would say just the right thing to remind me that things would be OK. That my kids were still good people even when raising them alone was tough for me.

I honestly don't think I ever thanked her properly or told her how much her support helped my heart.

Sandy went to The Belmont Athletic Club every morning at 5:30AM. She never missed a day, and even returned some afternoons.

Fitness was a way of life for her; her father had been a fitness guru and had owned gyms back in the day when there were very few of them—and mostly only famous people worked out there. Sandy had a picture of herself with Jack Lalanne and other notables, including

Arnold Schwarzenegger. She told me she worked out with Arnold often. Once she went on a date with him, and even kissed him!

Over the years, we attended many Long Beach charity events together. We enjoyed supporting the community, and with Sandy, something fun or memorable always seemed to happen.

In 2008 we went to the Women's Conference hosted by Maria Shriver. Arnold, then the governor of California, was there as well. The conference was held in the Long Beach Arena, which hosted many concerts and speakers. There were several seating levels, and Sandy and I were seated way up at the top in the highest tier.

From our spot way up high, we could see the stage, as well as all the floor seats surrounding it. To the left of the stage, Sandy spotted Arnold sitting there listening to the speakers. It was easy to tell it was him because members of his security team were all wearing black and seated around him.

Sandy was delighted to locate him way down on the floor from where we were sitting. She turned to me and kept mentioning it.

"There's Arnold!"

"I'm so happy he's here!"

"Oh my God, there's Arnold!"

Soon after, the conference was having a 20-minute recess.

I stood up, planning to go to the restroom. Sandy practically jumped out of her seat, and excitedly announced, "Let's go down there. I want to say hi to Arnold."

"Sandy!" I said as we headed out of our aisle. "You haven't seen him in 30 years. Do you think he'll remember you?"

She just smiled and I followed her down all the escalators until we got to the floor level. Sandy headed toward the seats at the base of the stage. We had to cross the entire arena from the back, to the front, where he sat with all his security guards.

Sandy walked quickly and headed straight towards him. "Arnold! Arnold!" she yelled, holding up her hand and waving it wildly.

I couldn't believe she was doing that! But I continued to follow her anyway as she kept walking quickly towards him.

But then . . . Arnold turned and saw her. He immediately stood up and grinned, and yelled back, "Sandy! Sandy Nista!" He walked right past all his guards and gave her a big hug. I stood dumbfounded.

Sandy had not seen him for 30 years. Yes, she was still beautiful and in fantastic shape, wearing her signature pencil-style straight skirt from Banana Republic. I swear she always looked like a fashion model. But still, it had been 30 years.

They spoke for just a few seconds before the security surrounded them, and he let them know it was OK.

Later, Sandy and I went to lunch. As we ate, she acted like it wasn't a big deal at all that she had just run up to the Governor of the state of California, who also happened to be one of the most recognized movie stars in the world. And she wasn't the least bit shocked or surprised he had remembered her.

I just looked at Sandy and said, "OK, Sandy, I think you did more than just kiss him!!" She laughed with that special twinkle in her eye.

A few years later, it became apparent that her mind was slipping. Her husband Ross lovingly cared for her in their home until he needed more assistance, and he found a safe place for her.

I went to visit her, and she had her big bright smile. "Hi Sandy!," I said.

She extended her hand and said, "Hi, I'm Sandy."

My heart sank. I had watched my mother deteriorate over 10 years from dementia. After that experience, I thought I was prepared on this visit to see Sandy. But I could barely contain my tears as she introduced herself to me over and over again.

I walked out of the double doors of the care facility and as soon as they closed behind me I was already crying. I stopped right out front and fumbled through my purse to find my phone. I knew I wanted to call my daughter, Hannah—she understood that Sandy meant the world to me.

As soon as she answered I felt this wave of emotion come over me, and I struggled to sound as "normal" as I could to immediately let Hannah know that I was OK even though I was crying uncontrollably.

"Honey, I'm just fine even though I'm crying. I just visited Sandy at her care facility."

"It's OK, Mom. How was she?"

I told her how I thought I would be OK, that it would be like seeing Grandma all those years. How I thought I wouldn't react so much because I had known she was sick for so long. And I repeated how I thought it would "be like Grandma." We had years to adjust to my mother's slow long progression into dementia.

Hannah listened intently and kept saying, "I'm sorry Mama." She really helped me that day.

Sandy had this very special quality—she could find delight in anyone. She saw something wonderful in every person, way before she saw anything bad at all—and usually she couldn't see anything bad in anyone at all.

She truly loved people.

On my last visit to her, we were sitting in a visiting area. She didn't talk very much. And she looked down most of the time.

But then, this little old man walked through the room. He looked angry and mad, and seemed to almost be snarling. He walked bent over. I remember thinking, "what's wrong with him?"

As he passed, Sandy got a glimpse of him and suddenly came to life. She sat up with the biggest Sandy-grin I had ever seen. Pointing at this angry-looking man, she said, "Isn't he adorable?? I just love him." She laughed and kept smiling at him until he left the room.

This moment reminded me that even though Sandy's disease robbed her of a lot, it never took her essence. That part where she only saw the good in people, never left her.

Rest in peace Sandy, I loved you so much.

"DO YOU KNOW WHAT IT MEANS TO BE 'OCCUPIED'?"

I don't always remember why I have done some of the things I have done in my life, and I may not remember the details correctly of a situation or experience.

But I always remember when someone did a small kindness to help me, whether it be an action or explaining something to me. I tend to best remember those things that seem to be obvious to others, but completely confound me when I learn them. I always wonder how I did not know something that everyone else seems to know.

Some of these kindnesses are stored way down deep in my memory, and then something will happen that makes them rush to the surface. When this happens, I love reliving the grace or gift I received from someone, no matter how small.

I had this experience in 2022 because of the war situation in Ukraine. There was a lot in the news about the Baltic States, and these states are located in proximity to Ukraine. Many times, I heard about "Lithuania" in the news.

"Lithuania" reminded me of Mr. Domas. If it wasn't for him, I would not know anything about this part of the world where the war was now taking place.

I was 22 when I started working at Rockwell International as a software engineer. Mr. Domas was a fellow engineer, an elderly gentleman; I had heard he was from Lithuania. I wasn't even sure where that was.

His first name was actually "Domas" and his last name was Vailokaitis, but he was respectfully always called "Mr. Domas" by everyone who worked with him.

Mr. Domas was probably around 65 or 70 if my memory serves me correctly, and this was 1981, so he had been in his 20s during World War II. He had a thick accent, and was the most gracious and respectful man I think I had ever met. He seemed like he was from another era.

When I was introduced to him, he asked if my name was "Lisa" as in "Elizabeth."

("Lisa" can actually be a rare nickname for Elizabeth).

I answered, "yes" to clarify the pronunciation of my name, but Mr. Domas thought my actual name was Elizabeth, and forever after that, he called me "Miss Elizabeth."

Mr. Domas did not talk a lot about where he had come from or what had happened to him, but one day I asked him about it. He said, "Miss Elizabeth, do you know what it means to be 'occupied'?"

"No," I answered. I didn't know.

"To be occupied means to lose all freedom. Our country became occupied during the war. We lost all freedoms and had to live in fear. We were not allowed to continue at the university. We must be home by dark. People were suddenly deported and taken away. We never knew what would happen to us, or to our loved ones. We lived in constant fear of the unknown."

Having grown up in sunny Southern California, I could barely imagine it. And yes, I took history classes, but I don't remember learning anything about this part of the world or what the people had to endure. Mr. Domas told me how he and his wife escaped in darkness one night, in a rowboat on the Baltic Sea. I didn't even know where that was.

I had so much respect for him. He was a brilliant engineer who worked tirelessly, and with such quiet but overwhelming gratitude.

When my husband Walt and I decided to get married, he asked Mr. Domas to be his best man at our wedding. He said yes, and came with his beautiful wife, Anna.

When Mr. Domas was almost 70, he would be required by the company to retire. Rockwell had a strict policy about retirement at a specific age. But Mr. Domas did not want to retire, he wanted to keep working. I never knew how Walt did it, but he finagled something so Mr. Domas could continue to work.

Four years after our wedding, my husband Walt died suddenly. It was a tragedy for me personally, and also for the many people who had worked for him.

Mr. Domas sent this kind memory to me and my children:

"Mr. Walter Ramelow managed the most advanced department of computer programmers and system analysts. He significantly contributed to the Rockwell International company. Mr. Walter Ramelow was a very kind and sensitive person. He was a real gentleman, we all loved him. I feel privileged I had a chance to work in his department."

I will never ever forget Mr. Domas; he showed a young woman how lucky she was to have freedom.

Thank you for this special gift, Mr. Domas.

COMPASSION THROUGH THE INTERNET, DAVE M.

I have "met" many people over the years via social media, mostly on Facebook.

Sometimes this happens by chatting through Facebook Messenger, or through comments on each other's postings.

One year I somehow became Facebook friends with Dave M., who lived a couple-hours' drive from Long Beach. Dave knew I had lost my husband long ago, and he shared that he, too, had lost his partner of many years. We chatted a lot about our experiences of loss.

I really treasured him. Dave was almost like a cheerleader to me—he always wrote nice comments about any community activities in which I was participating, and he would resonate with any feelings I shared. He was always supportive, and gave me reassurance when I needed it.

It was clear we understood each other, and we were "online friends" like this for a few years.

I utilized Facebook to let the community know what was happening in our neighborhoods, and sometimes about what was coming up in my restaurant. We participated in many events, from the Chocolate Festival to the summer events known as Stroll and Savor, to the annual Belmont Shore Christmas Parade.

There was one event that occurred annually in another part of Long Beach in which we had never participated—The Pride Parade.

The parade travels about a mile and a half down Ocean Blvd., right along the coast.

Anyone in the community can participate in the parade, and many of the members of the LGBTQ community were our frequent patrons at La Strada. So, in 2015, I decided to create my own parade entry representing my restaurant. My staff was excited to participate, and we got going on the planning.

I began posting on social media about the upcoming parade, and our plans to be in it for the first time. It was my custom to talk about whatever I was working on, whether it was personal or had to do with my business.

People in the community and loyal patrons rallied to support us. They enjoyed reading my updates and learning all about the effort it took to make something like this happen.

There is so much that needs to be done to create a parade entry and plan for the actual day:

- Ask staff members who would want to participate.
- Make sure all the other staffers are available to work at La Strada on that day.
- Fill out the paperwork.
- Cater for the 40 volunteers at their board meeting (because my paperwork was late).
- Order outfits for the girls and guys.
- Find a driver who will keep us at just the right speed.
- Wash the car.
- Order decorations for the car.
- Make a fun playlist of songs relevant to this audience.
- Have someone come over to install our sound system on my car.

All of this effort was just for our one little parade entry. But it was worth it. I posted frequently about all the "getting-ready" activities.

Dave followed along on all of my progress and frequently commented. He was part of the LGBTQ community and he was very touched that I was supporting it in this way.

Because he lived a two-hour drive away, Dave had never been to the Pride Parade. But Dave decided that this was the year he would finally attend.

The night before the parade, Dave messaged me he was coming for sure; I was excited to meet him.

But I didn't know how I would find him amongst the thousands of parade goers. And I actually didn't even know what he looked like, because he never posted photos, and his Facebook profile picture was a photo of a seagull.

"Dave," I wrote to him, "how will I find you? How will I know who you are?"

He told me, "Don't worry. I will find you."

The day of the parade came; everything was in place, and we waited way down Ocean Blvd. nearly at the end of the parade lineup.

It was finally our turn to begin the long walk down Ocean Blvd. I kept scanning the parade-goers wondering which one was Dave. But nobody stood out or was wildly waving to me.

About halfway through the parade route, I looked ahead of me. About 20 feet in front of me, a man had suddenly stepped out, and was staring at me with the kindest eyes.

I walked towards him, and before he even said, "Lisa, it's Dave." I knew it was him.

We hugged like long-lost friends. We were both in tears. Our support for each other as friends was palpable. We only had a few seconds at that moment, because I had to rejoin the parade and hurry to catch up with my group. But later that afternoon Dave stopped by my restaurant and we had a chance to talk.

Later, this is what Dave posted with a picture of me in the parade. He wrote:

This is one of the earliest FB Friends I met, Lisa Ramelow, and we have become such buddies sharing a lot, I so Love her!

Today we finally got to exchange the hugs we have been promising each other for Years. She is probably the biggest hearted private business entrepreneur in Long Beach. She is so involved in the community, giving ALL over the city. We are both looking for "Mr. Right," if you know where he is let us know (not the same guy, one for each of us, we do have a little bit of different tastes there LOL).

Let me tell you, whoever turns out to be Mr. Right for this wondrous lady is going to be one of the most fortunate guys on the face of this earth.

Lisa, I love ya kiddo.

God bless you Lisa and thank you for all your love and support.

I'm going to make this an annual event, our Ocean Blvd. hug in the Pride Parade.

Dave did come to the parade the next year. He also made the drive to come to my restaurant a couple times over the years. I always loved seeing him. He felt like a friend I could reach out to at any time, to ask for advice or support.

A few years later, Dave M. passed away; I never knew exactly what had happened because he did not openly share his life like I did. It was a friendship I truly missed, because even though he was far away and we did not see each other very often in person, we shared a bond. We had both lost our partners and we understood this pain.

We supported each other's life challenges. We rooted for each other. Yes, that was it. We both knew the other wanted the very best for us.

Thank you Dave, for always being in my corner. You were the best cheerleader ever.

MY STEP-DAUGHTER, ROBIN, AND HER GRAND-DAUGHTER, SOPHIE

I met Robin when she was 17.

I was then dating my future husband, Walt—he had three daughters from his previous marriage: Robin, Rene and Pam.

Robin was the oldest, and he was excited for us to meet each other. She was sweet and kind, and had such a maturity and grace about her, even as a teenager.

Because of the age difference between me and Walt, I was actually closer in age to Robin than I was to my husband, but she was always so supportive of us as a couple, right from the beginning.

Reflecting back, it must have been strange for her to be a teenage girl and meet a young woman in her 20s, who was about to marry her father, in his 40s.

But she didn't find it strange at all. Her loyalty to her father was so strong, her trust in him was so great. All she wanted was for him to be happy. She was warm and kind to me, so very accepting and only wished for our happiness.

Of all his daughters, Walt had such a special bond with Robin.

At our wedding, his daughters gave me a pink ribbon that said, "New Mommy"—I proudly pinned it to my wedding gown. They were all thrilled to see their father happy after their parents had divorced years earlier.

Robin herself married at age 18 to her childhood sweetheart. She had two children Kristin and Jason; Walt was so happy to be a grandfather.

I loved the kids, but being in my 20s I was a little uncomfortable being called "Grandma." Robin understood this and took no offense, and her kids just called me by my name.

They lived only 20 minutes away and we saw them often. At some point though, Robin and her young family decided to move to Oregon. They wanted a different lifestyle than what was offered in Southern California. Walt was not happy they were going, but did not express that to her because he would never have interfered in anyone's life choices.

The day came that they were all packed up and ready for the drive north. Saying goodbye was difficult, but off they went on the next part of their life's journey.

After our son Ryan was born, we made the drive up to their new home in Oregon to visit. While we were there, we had Ryan baptized in their local church. Walt wanted Robin to be Ryan's godmother. I understood and approved of his choice.

It was just a couple years later, when Walt died suddenly from a heart attack. My life was shattered.

Robin and her family drove down from Oregon the very next day. When she arrived at my home, her only concern was how I was doing, even though she was a young woman in her 20s, who had just lost her own father.

The many kindnesses she showed to me are detailed in my book, "A Kindness I will Never Forget."

I think Robin was the kindest person I have ever met in my whole life. She had a quiet special energy that made anyone who met her feel special, and appreciated, just by being in her unique presence.

Over the years, Robin's first marriage ended in divorce. She later met and married her husband Bill, and together they created a blended family with four children.

We kept close as best we could, but we were both raising our families and didn't talk as often as we used to. Still, I could call her at any time, and just hearing Robin's voice it was like no time had passed at all.

Robin's children were now grown and having kids of their own.

Her daughter, Kristin, had a 6-year-old daughter named Sophie— she had been born at a pivotal time in her mother's life when she was living in Montana. But after Sophie was born, Kristin had decided to return to her home town of Medford, Oregon to be close to her family once again.

Little Sophie captured the hearts of each and every member of her large extended family. She had this effect everywhere: even at her day-care, all the kids wanted to be around her.

Sophie was an enthusiastic little girl who embraced so much in life. She loved to dress up in princess dresses, and she could never get enough unicorns and sparkles. She had such a big heart for animals and had ducks, rabbits, guinea pigs, and more.

A special day for her was to go rock collecting with her grandparents, papa and nanny, followed by a visit to Black Bear diner to get chocolate chip pancakes.

She was just a joy to be around, and her teenage cousins enjoyed spending time with her, dressing her up and putting on makeup. And then Sophie would always strike a pose for pictures.

When she got excited, she had this high pitched, deafening scream and an infectious laugh. And then she loved to fall asleep while getting her feet rubbed.

Robin adored her granddaughter and they spent a great deal of time together, one of their favorite things was digging and planting in Robin's garden; they were just inseparable.

In September of 2021, I got a call from my other stepdaughter, Rene. Through tears she told me that Robin had drowned. I found it difficult to believe what I was hearing. But she had very few details, and was so upset she didn't want to stay on the phone.

The next day I learned more of the story. It was one of the saddest stories I have ever heard.

I only knew that somehow a huge wave had come unexpectedly out of nowhere, and capsized their boat. Robin and her granddaughter Sophie both perished under the water.

My children and I immediately made plans to go to Oregon.

When we arrived in Medford, we went immediately to Robin's home where her husband Bill was waiting to welcome us.

I was looking forward to asking Bill what exactly had happened, because it was so hard to understand how this accident could just happen so out of the blue. I knew he would probably want to talk about it—this pain was something I understood.

This was something I had learned after the loss of my husband. Many people will not ask you about what happened. They think it will upset you to talk about it. But I found the opposite to be true—it was all I wanted to talk about, how it happened, what it was like, about the great loss my children would suffer. It bothered me when people changed the subject as if that would somehow make me stop thinking about it. Nothing could make me stop thinking about it.

So, I greeted Bill warmly and we hugged for a long time, and then sat down. I asked him, "Do you feel like talking about what happened?"

He gave a resounding "yes" which did not surprise me. He seemed very grateful to be asked, and then told me the complete story, every last detail.

Robin and Bill had gone fishing at the same place for well over 30 years, a location where a river flowed out to the ocean. This was one of their favorite pastimes. On this particular outing, they were joined by their daughter Kristin and her boyfriend, Steve, and of course, little granddaughter, Sophie.

They had just started out for the day and were heading to their usual spot to fish. Robin and Sophie were in the interior cabin of their boat, where it was a bit warmer. And also, because Sophie loved to steer the boat.

Suddenly a very large wave rocked the boat. And then, with no warning, a second huge wave loomed in front of them. Bill later told me that it was the biggest wave he had ever seen, it was at least 20 feet high. All he could do was yell out to everyone, "Hold on!!"

It was what is known as a "rogue wave," and it capsized their fishing boat. It completely turned over in the water.

Bill, Kristin, and Steve had been up on deck, so when the wave hit, they were thrown off into the water. Even so, each one of them had to fight hard to resurface. Steve realized he was stuck underneath the front of the boat, but he was able to navigate swimming parallel to the surface, and then upwards. Bill also found his way to the surface. He could see Kristin struggling to keep her head above water, and he immediately swam towards her. He was able to slip the back of her shirt over the boat's now upturned rudder, to keep her head above water.

A nearby boat had seen the accident, and had called the coast guard right away, who were now speeding towards them.

As they approached, the three survivors were wildly waving their arms and screaming to direct the rescuers that there were still two people trapped below. Divers immediately entered the water to search for them, while the others were pulled onboard to safety.

The divers were able to bring both Robin and Sophie to the surface and onto the rescue boat.

My stepdaughter, Robin, was declared already deceased. Lifesaving measures were performed on little Sophie and she was airlifted to a hospital in a helicopter.

But despite all efforts, Sophie did not make it either.

The two of them had been wearing lifejackets, which ironically would have made it almost impossible for them to swim "down" and out from where they were trapped in the interior, to have escaped.

The news stations in the state of Oregon all carried the story of the grandmother and granddaughter who died together under the water's surface.

It was such an incredible loss for all who knew them, but mostly to Robin's daughter, Kristin, who lost her mother and her daughter on the very same day.

No one should have to endure that much loss. She took comfort in knowing her daughter had been in her mother's arms.

I honestly did not know how she could bear it.

These are the words she wrote one week after the accident:

"My sweet girl, my baby, you were the light in the dark always. Us against the world. I couldn't reach you; the water was so fast and my legs were trapped, I was tied down and I couldn't break free. I swam so hard to try and find you under the boat but I couldn't move, the waves kept pushing me under water and I couldn't find any air, there was nothing. It was just darkness until Papa grabbed my hand and helped me stay above water. I'm so sorry my sweet girl. I know Nana held you close until the very end. I know you went together.

I was outside the door when they tried to get you breathing again. I dropped to my knees and held my hands to the wall and begged anyone listening, please don't take my girl, please don't take her. Breathe baby, just one breath. It wasn't long before the doctor came to tell me what I had already heard through the wall. I ran to you so fast and held you tight. I kissed your forehead over and over and held your little hand. Mommie is so sorry baby. I was wrapped around you for hours until the coroner had to take you away.

I know you are in Heaven now with Aunt Sissy and Nana and that you are all dressed in beautiful designer dresses with glitter and sunflowers and the most perfect curls in your hair, exactly the way you like them. My whole heart is broken in ways that are immeasurable. I love you Sophie, I love you Momma. Please, please take care of each other. Mom, I know you held her with you, I know you fought so hard. We were all trapped and it's a miracle three of us survived. I would trade places with you in a heartbeat. I would give mine for yours in return. Losing the two of you is more than any of us can bear. You both are so loved. Our family will never be the same without you. I love you both with my whole entire heart."

ROBIN'S STORY

There is more about Robin, a story that is not my story at all, it's all about her. It is a story about loyalty and divine intervention. I am including it here because she was such a special human being who made a difference in so many other people's lives. And this story illustrates her loyalty to the father that raised her, and the great gift she gave to her birth father.

My husband, Walt, had good relationships with all three of his daughters, but with Robin it was as if they were two old souls who understood each other. Robin was not his daughter by blood; she had been one-year-old when he met her mother, and he just adored her. After marrying her mother, they had two more girls, Rene and Pam.

I once asked him what happened to Robin's "real" father.

Walt said Robin's parents were 17 or 18 when she was born, and had never married. They had tried raising her together, but her biological father was the oldest of seven children, and he was constantly pressured by his family to "come home" and help out his mother with his siblings.

Walt had begun dating Robin's mother, and they eventually got married. At first, they still saw Robin's biological father, but eventually they moved away and lost touch with him.

I met Robin when she was a teenager. She and Walt were so close and understood each other so well.

I once asked Robin if she would ever want to locate her biological father. "Oh no!" she answered right away. "I would never do that to Dad." She saw it as a huge sign of disrespect towards Walt. He had raised her, and he was 100 percent her dad.

It didn't matter to Robin that she was far taller than her sisters, and had dark brown eyes and hair, in contrast to their blondish hair and light eyes. To Robin, she was a Ramelow, through and through.

When Walt died and we had a viewing, she stood over him and calmly said, "Dad, thank you for always completely accepting me as your daughter. Thank you for accepting Kristin and Jason as your grandchildren."

Many years passed, and Robin was working in the medical industry. A colleague mentioned that she had a second job of reuniting adopted children with their birth parents. Robin mentioned her situation, and the colleague asked if she wanted her to try to find her biological father. Robin's immediate answer was "no."

Walt had now been gone over 20 years, but she was still steadfast in her loyalty to him. She had no interest in finding this other man. But one day, her curiosity got to her, and she called me and asked, "what do you think Dad would think if I looked for my biological father?"

She sounded nervous. I reassured her. "He wouldn't care at all, honey. He would be happy if that's what you wanted to do."

Robin gave her colleague the name she remembered being told was his name, and her birthplace. But that was all she knew about him, so the odds seemed low in finding him: there were no adoption records because Walt had never formally adopted her, and LA county had millions of people.

But, the very next day, her colleague walked up to her and handed her a piece of paper. "This is your father's phone number." Robin was stunned.

She held onto the paper for a few days, too afraid to make the call. Then, one afternoon, she got up the courage and dialed the number. A man answered. "Hello?"

"Hello," she said.

Then she took a deep breath. "I was wondering . . . if you remember, someone from long ago. Someone named Robin Ann." The phone went quiet for several seconds. And then, the man began to weep, uncontrollably. He could no longer speak, and handed the phone to his wife.

His name was Richard and he lived in Big Bear, CA with his wife, Joyce. He was the pastor at his small church; his health had recently taken a downturn, and he was worried. There was only one thing left that he wanted in his earthly life—to find his daughter, Robin, the only child he had ever had, and who he had not seen for over 50 years.

Now, in his 70s, he did not know of a way to search for her, he was never sure where she and her mother had moved. Every week, while leading his congregation in prayer, he requested all of them to please pray that somehow, before he died, he would find her.

So, on that day when his phone rang and he answered, and he heard the voice of the quiet woman asking if he remembered someone named Robin Ann, well, for him, it was just a miracle. His long-lost daughter was now calling him.

Robin made arrangements to go meet him in person in Big Bear. Her two sisters would join her in support at this reunion. After her trip, she called to tell me all about it.

He was tall, of course, and had deep brown eyes. She was mostly amazed to see that they had so many of the same mannerisms, and that their hands were the same. And they had the same temperament.

Richard expanded on Walt's explanation of what had happened. His relationship with Robin's mother had not lasted long, as they were so very young. Also, being the oldest of seven children and his father having died, his mother was always pressuring him to return home to help with his six younger siblings. He visited Robin as much as he could.

Then, Walt had entered the picture and married Robin's mother. At some point, the situation became untenable for Richard. He could see how much of a father Walt now was to Robin. He made the decision to back away and let her be raised by Walt. There was no formal or legal agreement, just an acknowledgement this was the best thing to do for Robin.

At some point, Walt moved his family to a different part of Los Angeles, and they lost touch.

Richard had never had any other children, and had made quite a sacrifice on her behalf letting her go to be raised by another man who could give her a better life.

I noted that this was a story about loyalty and divine intervention. Robin was so loyal to Walt, that she would never have gone looking for Richard. But, somehow, her coworker was put in her path who had the skills to find him in a sea of 20 million people. I would call that divine.

Richard lived another year, and Robin visited him as often as she could until he passed away. What an unexpected gift for both of them.

AGING PARENTS

ARDEN AND RITA, AKA, THE TWO CHARACTERS THAT CREATED ME

My mother, Rita, was born and raised in Philadelphia. Her father owned and operated The Press Bar. She was just 16 when her mother died, and her father was not sure how he could care for his children and still go to work every day. My mother insisted on keeping the family together, and began raising her 8-year-old brother herself, rather than have him go live with another relative.

My father, Arden, was a farm boy from Iowa, who learned the value of hard work from a very young age. He was up at dawn every morning to help his father in the fields, and to tend to the many animals. He also lost his mother when he was just a teenager.

It was difficult to run a farm without a partner, so at some point his father decided to remarry.

My father respected his father and understood his decision, but the situation was just too difficult for him; it felt like his mother was being replaced.

At age 17 he decided to leave home and join the Navy. But because he was not yet 18, his father would have to sign a consent form. He pleaded with his teary-eyed father to sign the form; his father reluctantly did so, and my father joined the Navy.

During his tour of duty in the Navy, my father ended up in the very city where my mother had been born and raised: Philadelphia. I believe by now he had turned 18.

And one night, he went to a dance club with his fellow servicemen, where all the pretty local girls always hung out. That night, my mother, now 17, went to this same dance club . . . hoping to meet a handsome sailor.

She found him.

They kept in touch while he was in the Navy, and when his service was finished, they decided to marry. My grandfather would do anything to make his only daughter happy, so he gave her the wedding of her dreams.

On September 6, 1952, they had a stunningly beautiful wedding, at St. Francis Xaiver Church in Philadelphia. She was 21, and he was 22.

From there, they moved to Ames, Iowa so he could acquire his Bachelor's degree in Electrical Engineering at Iowa State University. This was quite a change for my mother: she was 100% a city girl, and was now moving to the country. But, she adapted, and they had their first child there, my older sister.

After my father got his degree, he was offered an aerospace engineering job in California. This would be even further away from my mother's hometown and her family, so she was hesitant. But she agreed, with one stipulation—that she could go home to visit her family in Philadelphia every year.

And every year, she did just that. My mother went back east to see her family, and she took all of us kids with her.

AUNT SUZY'S PEOPLE

I was about 15 years old when my mother mentioned something very important to her:

"Lise" (my mom called me Lise, instead of Lisa), "I don't ever want to be a burden. If anything ever happens to me, make sure you pull my plug. And if there is no plug to pull, just wheel me to the end of the pier and dump me off—I don't want to be one of Aunt Suzy's people! Now promise me, Lise!"

I was her very serious, quiet child. She continued, "Of all my kids, I know you will be the one to make that happen."

"Yes Mom, I will," I promised. And I meant it. I didn't want her to be one of Aunt Suzy's people either.

Aunt Suzy was my great aunt. She and her sister, Julia (my grand-mother), had come to America from Czechoslovakia when they were 14 and 15 years old. It was in the 1920's. The two sisters married within one week of each other, and settled in houses across the street from one another on Green Street, in Philadelphia, Pennsylvania.

Over the years, Aunt Suzy acquired many of the row houses on one side of the entire city block, right in the middle of Philadelphia. I think she must have been rather wealthy at one point, but one would never know that by looking at her or spending time with her. She was short and roly-poly, was missing half her teeth, and always wore a housecoat-type dress.

Rather than retire and relax, Aunt Suzy filled her homes with the elderly, the infirm, those with Alzheimer's and dementia, and those with other undiagnosed illnesses. Sometimes Aunt Suzy would receive their pensions in order to take care of them, but even if she didn't, she would still take care of them. Money was never her motivation; she loved all of these people and cared for them as if they were her children.

My mother adored her Aunt Suzy. When we would go back east to see our cousins in New Jersey, we would always go visit Aunt Suzy too. My Uncle Bob (my mother's older brother) would drive us over to Green St. in Philadelphia in his big giant Cadillac.

But I didn't like going there very much; as a child I found it to be very scary.

I remember we visited her when I was 8 years old. Aunt Suzy stood on the front stoop in her housecoat to welcome us. She bent down to kiss us over and over again with her crooked smile, and spoke to us with her thick Slovakian accent.

We then went inside. From an 8-year-old's perspective, everything seemed odd. There were people wandering around everywhere; they seemed to be walking aimlessly through her house.

These were "Aunt Suzy's people."

Aunt Suzy hugged and kissed every one of them as they walked past. She never stopped smiling, and spoke words of love to them in Czech or in her broken English.

There was one lady with big round pink circles painted on her cheeks. She had no teeth and stood halfway up the stairs, holding a silver cup. She kept saying "Hellllo. Helllllllo. Helllllllo." over and over. She actually sort of sang it as she stared intently at me.

I held on tightly to my mother; this lady scared me. But my mother didn't even notice her; she was used to seeing all these people here, and she carried on her conversation with her beloved Aunt Suzy.

Even the dog, a Dalmatian, seemed different—he had a huge lump on his neck that didn't look quite right to me. I was afraid of the dog too. And, honestly, it didn't smell very good in there either. I kept trying to hold my breath, but it was pointless.

But I always remembered how happy my mother was to be there with her aunt. We all sat on the sofa, and my mother's face lit up while chatting with Aunt Suzy. And whenever Aunt Suzy got up to tend to one of her people, my mother stared at her aunt with so much love, kindness, and respect.

After that visit, Uncle Bob piled us all back into his Cadillac to take us back to Cherry Hill, NJ. We had barely left Green St. when we saw an older lady acting very inappropriately on the street. Uncle Bob said, "Uh-oh, that must be one of Aunt Suzy's people who got out by accident."

We respected Aunt Suzy for what she did, how she took care of all these elderly and infirmed people in her community. And we all understood what it meant to be one of her "people."

So . . . back when I was 15, I promised my mother that if she was terminally ill, or developed a disorder that affected her behavior, I would most certainly "pull her plug." I assured her that she would never be one of Aunt Suzy's people.

Somewhere around the time my mother turned 68, her memory started slipping—it was a very slow progression. Within a few years, she was diagnosed with Frontal Lobe Dementia, which is characterized by prominent changes in personality and behavior. In this type of dementia, the most affected areas are those that control conduct, judgment, empathy, and foresight, and it causes difficulty with producing or comprehending language.

There was really nothing to do to prevent her illness. There were medications to slow its progression, but they had untenable side effects. She would just have to live through this illness. And so, she did, with as much grace as possible.

But it was so incredibly sad that she had, indeed, become one of Aunt Suzy's people.

Over the many years that she was sick and did not speak, I used to hold her hand and tell her that I was sorry. "Mom, I am so sorry. I promised you when I was 15 that I would pull your plug. But there is no plug to pull. And I really can't dump you off the pier." She never really knew what I was saying, but she would smile and squeeze my hand with so much love. She didn't know who I was, but she knew I was someone who cared.

It was heartbreaking to watch her live in this body where she no longer had her mind, could not talk, and didn't even know who she (or I) was. I was sorry that she had become one of Aunt Suzy's people.

MY STUBBORN FATHER

It's not always easy recognizing when something is wrong with your loved ones, especially with your aging parents; it's strange to see them lose their mental acuity. The time comes when the roles are reversed, and they need care and protection from their children.

My mother Rita had always been a very lively, extroverted person. She loved to talk to everyone, and she was known to do outrageous things. In fact, every adjective that you could think of that is the opposite of "shy" applied to my mother. She was a total "character."

She was quite the storyteller, and it was not unusual for her stories to change with each telling—sometimes the endings were exaggerated, or the characters were now different people.

When I was 14, I listened as she told someone a familiar story. It was mostly correct, except she said it was about my Uncle Joe. I did my usual correction and said, "Mom, it was not Uncle Joe, it was Uncle Bob." I remember her looking at me and saying very kindly, "honey, does it really matter?"

Oh. It had never occurred to me that maybe it didn't matter, so I stopped doing that.

Also, we were used to her calling us all the wrong names—it was not unusual for her to hand me something and say, "Go give this to Lisa." I could usually figure out if she meant one of my two sisters. It was never a big deal.

So, my father's reaction to my mother's declining mental acuity was understandable.

Julie and I went to see him one day to talk to him about some of the things our mother was saying and doing. We thought these things went beyond her gregarious and outgoing personality. They were becoming beyond outrageous—they were becoming dangerous.

"No!" my father insisted. "She's just getting older, that's all." He didn't want to hear what we were saying, and he refused to listen or believe that anything at all could be wrong with her. He just could not get on board; he could not see it. He would not believe that our mother seemed "different."

By 2001, my mom was 70. She was still robust, eccentric, outgoing, and gregarious. She walked the entire length of 2nd St., in the Belmont Shore area of Long Beach, and then back to her home on Quincy Ave. She did that several times a day.

In spite of her good physical health, more and more things seemed different; something felt really off. My sister and I kept talking about it and we believed something was very wrong. We again went to our dad, and this time we asked our other two siblings to join us for the discussion.

All three of them disagreed with me and Julie. They said, "She's fine! She's always been like that! She's always been 'out there!'"

We just could not convince them that she should be evaluated.

One day, something happened that made it unmistakably clear her behavior had gone past simple "aging." My mom and I were in her car going to the Westminster mall; she drove. She never liked to take the freeway to nearby places; instead, she drove east on 2nd St., over both bridges, and continued as it turned into Westminster Blvd.

We approached the T-intersection at Studebaker Blvd.; the light had just turned red, and my mother slowed down and came to a stop in front of the crosswalk. But after about five seconds, she looked around as if she were at a stop sign, instead of a light, and started driving again, going right through the red light. "Mom," I said. "You can't do that. You can't just drive through a red light."

"Oh honey," she said ever so cheerfully, "I can do whatever the hell I want!" And she continued on her same route to the mall, right on Springdale, left on Bolsa. She had no comprehension of what she had just done. None.

It was true my mother was a rule-breaker. It was true she found ways to justify many of her actions. She did cross all the small streets as a pedestrian in Belmont Shore, even if the light was red, but almost everyone who lives there also does that.

But, never, ever, would she go through a red light while driving. This was different. This was new.

I called Julie when I got home and told her.

FORMIDABLE FOE

I told my sister about my mother driving through the red light. It was definitive to me. She agreed.

And she shared something that had happened for her as well, that she felt was just as definitive. It made her feel as determined as I was that our mother had some type of illness. This was not just "old age," or her being wacky.

That past Sunday morning, my mother had called my sister. "Jules!" she said happily. "I'm making your father his waffles. Do I put in water or milk?"

My sister couldn't believe it. Her heart sank. My mother had been making my father his waffles every Sunday morning for nearly 50 years. It was unfathomable that she would not know to add milk to the Bisquick recipe. Plus, it said so, right on the box. But at that point my mother could not read or follow simple directions.

There are many ways in which someone with Alzheimer's or dementia begin to show they are ill.

They "forget" how to cook and how to drive.

They lose their filter.

They make up excuses for all the apparent slip ups when someone has noticed. They don't believe that anything is really wrong with them.

My mother would say that her memory wasn't as good, and she would even get mad at herself. "My memory is a god-damned piece of shit!"*

------

* Note: my mother loved to say "god-damn" (her favorite adjective) and "piece-of-shit" (her favorite noun). They were like everyday words to her, that's just who she was.

She was angry about her memory, but she chalked it up to getting older. She became very clever at trying to hide what was happening. She made lots of excuses for things, or just claimed they never happened.

She wrote a lot of notes to herself too. One day I was in her bathroom and I noticed that all of her cosmetics and self-care items had black writing all over them. What was that all about? I picked up her shampoo and read what she had written using a black Sharpie: "Use this one first. Put on water. Then put on some of this. Then use the other one."

The conditioner had the same type of wording: "Use this one after the other one. Use water."

She was resourceful. She was fighting whatever was happening to her. But she was also trying her best to cover it up. I'm sure she must have been very scared about what was actually happening to her, although she showed no fear at all.

We went to see our father again, and our brother and other sister came as well. By this time, both of them had also had similar experiences with our mother that had now convinced them too.

Our father listened, but he didn't say much. He would not agree or disagree. He just looked mad. Really mad. We didn't know if he did not believe any of it, or he just didn't want to believe any of it.

And he absolutely did not want her to go to a doctor or be evaluated in any way. He was determined. He did not want her seen by any doctor or to have her condition checked out. He made it clear that he would not allow any of us to alter her life, not one bit. Not at all.

This was a huge problem. She had become a danger to herself and to others, and he was tying our hands to prevent us from keeping her safe. So now, in addition to trying to find out what was wrong with our mother, and doing what was necessary to try and help her, we now knew we were going to have to fight him on every single thing.

And we all knew, from our childhoods, that he was a formidable foe. This was not going to be easy.

MY MOTHER WAS DANGEROUS

Soon after this talk with my father, I was walking down 2nd St. with my mother, holding her hand. She suddenly turned right, and stepped into the crosswalk to cross 2nd St., trying to pull me along with her. But the light was red in this direction, and it was a four-lane street; the cars were going through the intersection on the green light, as they should.

But she didn't care.

Before I could pull her back, she dropped my hand and looked directly at the oncoming cars, wildly waving her arms in the air. Then she shouted, "Coming through!! Rita Boyd here, coming through!!" as she attempted to cross. She had a big smile on her face, and happily waved at the drivers who were now screeching on their brakes to avoid hitting her.

Oh my God!

I ran after her and grabbed her, nodding at the drivers and mouthing the words, "I am SO SORRY!! I pulled her back to the curb and said, "Mom, Mom! What are you doing?!"

We were now back safely on the curb, and she just laughed and said, "Yippee! Yippee Lise!! Let's go into this store, I love this store!"

It made no sense; there was no acknowledgement of what she had just done. It was as if it had never happened. And she definitely had no remorse, because she no longer knew what was OK, and what was not OK. She probably also had already forgotten that she had done it.

Also, this word "Yippee!" was one I had never heard her use before. I didn't remember her ever saying "Yippee!!," and it had now become a common word for her. And she frequently used it to avoid answering any question. "Mom, do you know what just happened?"

"Yippee!" would be her answer.

When my father got home I told him what happened. "She isn't safe anymore, Dad. She could have gotten hit by a car. Or one of those people could have gotten injured. We need to have somebody watch her."

My father looked as stern as I have ever seen him, and believe me, I had seen his scary, stern looks my entire life. "She's fine!!" he yelled.

He refused to budge. He did not want her freedom curtailed. He couldn't face that anything was wrong with her, his wife of over 60 years. His denial of the situation overtook his common sense and intelligence.

My sister had shown up when I called for assistance and she shared her thoughts as well with our father. But it did no good. He made it clear that if any of us tried to limit her freedom, he would change the locks on his house (we all had keys), and he would not let us see her. Ever.

He was resolute and now doubling down.

More and more things happened. My father told us he was keeping an eye on her, but she would climb out of windows. If he bolted the windows some way, she would find a screwdriver and remove the screws and climb out.

I frequently got calls at my restaurant. "Lisa, I saw your mom getting on a bus."

"Lisa, this is the Rubber Tree calling. Your mother is here and is insisting we make her keys. She thinks she is at Billing's Hardware." The Rubber Tree was an adult X-rated store, not a hardware store.

"Lisa, I just saw your mother on 2nd St. She is carrying her purse and she has her shoes on, but it looks like she is in her nightgown."

Thank goodness for the merchants and employees on 2nd St. They looked out for her and they called me when they thought she was in danger or in need of help.

My sisters and brother and I got together. We had to find a way to circumvent our father, for both their sakes.

We came up with a plan.

TIME TO TRICK HER

It was obvious my mother needed someone to look after her.

My sisters and I tried to spend as much time as we could with her, but it wasn't easy. We all had children and jobs. My Mom's older brother, our Uncle Bob, was a physician. He told us over and over, "Get caregivers for your mother. Don't feel like you have to spend every minute with her. Your mother would want you to look after her grandchildren. That is what she would want."

But my father wouldn't hear of it. He did NOT want her to have a caregiver; he did not want to curtail our mother's freedom in any way. So, we devised a plan to "trick" both of them. A plan that would not restrict our mom's freedom, and one that our dad would hopefully agree to. We hired a lady named Penney to be her secret caregiver.

My mother followed the same routine like clockwork. She went to her office every single day, even though she could no longer actually do any work. Her office was a very short walk from her home, upstairs in the tower of the Wells Fargo building at the western end of 2nd St.

We had met with Penney and filled her in on everything, and she was on board with the plan. Our hope was that once our father found out, he would be OK with it, because this was a way for our mother to (sort of) keep her freedom.

On the determined first day of our plan, we met Penney out in front of the Bank Building, and then walked upstairs to my mom's office. "Hi Mom! This is my friend Penney." my sister told her.

My mother jumped up and greeted Penney with a big smile and a huge hug. "Mom," we told her, "This is Penney's first time in Belmont Shore. Will you show her around?"

Bingo! It worked! My mother lit up. She grabbed her purse and put her arm around Penney. "Oh sweetheart, just wait until you see what I have to show you!" My mother would share Belmont Shore with anyone she could; she loved her community of 2nd St. so very much. We watched as our mother led Penney down the steps, and they started walking together down 2nd St. We were so relieved.

The two of them were out on 2nd St. for about four hours. My mother took Penney into all her favorite shops, and then they had lunch together at one of the little restaurants before returning to my mother's office. Penney sat quietly on the bench across from my mom's desk, telling her she was waiting for one of us to come back and pick her up.

At around 2PM my mother called. "Honey, your friend is still here."

"Oh, OK, Mom," I would say, "can she stay with you a little longer? I have to pick the kids up from school."

"Oh of course honey, take your time," my mother would answer. She would do anything for her grandchildren. And Penney would just sit in the office, supposedly waiting. That first day they were together for seven hours—we had kept her safe for at least part of the day.

The next day, we started it all over again. At 10AM we met with Penney at my mom's office, and walked upstairs. "Mom, remember my friend Penney? She can't remember all the things you showed her yesterday. Will you show her again?"

"Oh sweetheart, just wait until you see what I have to show you!" my mother would say again. She would hug Penney and grab her purse, and they would again head out to 2nd St.

By day three, Penney just showed up on her own and said, "Hi Rita! Remember me, Penney? I can't remember all the things you showed me on 2nd St." And then off they went.

Sometimes in the afternoon, my mom would call one of us and say, "Your friend is still here." And we would always answer, "Oh, thank you Mom for keeping my friend company! Can she stay there a little longer? I'm helping the kids with their homework right now."

Some variation of the same thing would be played out every day. Penney was a godsend. Our mother was safe for at least part of every day.

Our father didn't really like the setup, nor did he like Penney. But he didn't fight us on it because we had not curtailed her freedom as he requested—she was still doing the things she loved. But we continued to have one big problem: She was still driving!

"YIPPEE!"

I brought my father his dinner late one night, around 10PM, as I did several nights a week after closing up my restaurant. He never minded waiting that late to eat—he loved the food from La Strada and he especially enjoyed having some company.

I had to bring it up: "Dad, you can't let her drive anymore." I would say. "I don't want to take away her freedom!" That was always my father's answer. He wouldn't budge.

Oh dear.

Convincing our father that our mother really *was* sick, and that this really *was* necessary just made everything more difficult. He now had a new tactic he would use to make it clear what would happen if we did anything to affect our mom's driving: we would be disinherited.

He was determined. He just could not face that she was sick and getting sicker. And his stubbornness made everything so much more difficult. Absolutely everything.

So once again, the four of us siblings conspired, and came up with a new plan. We secretly had her turned into the DMV as a high-risk driver. We had someone else do it for us, just to lessen his wrath in case one of our names came back on the paperwork.

Finally, the paperwork came in the mail telling her that her license was to be taken away. Our father was livid! He threatened again to change the locks on his house and disinherit us if he found out one of us had turned her into the DMV. We convinced him that it must have been her doctor who had done it.

The DMV scheduled an appointment to have her evaluated. I explained to my mother that she would have to take a special test if she wanted to keep driving. She was a nervous wreck and asked me what she needed to study for the test. I got her a pamphlet from the DMV.

I spent the night before the appointment at my parents' house, so I could drive both of them to the appointment in the morning. That evening she attempted to study the DMV pamphlet. She tried over and over to read it and make sense of it. "Lise! Lise! Get in here!" she would call from her bedroom.

I went to her room. "What do you need Mom?"

"Lise, what do you know about railroad tracks?" I looked at where she pointed in the pamphlet. The first question on the practice test was about the distance you should keep between your vehicle and the rail-road tracks. "Mom, I don't know. I think 10 feet." I was just making up a number. I actually didn't know, and at this point it really didn't matter.

I returned to the guest room. Five minutes later, "Lise! Lise! Get in here!" I would return to her room.

"What do you know about railroad tracks?"

This went on for many hours until she fell asleep; it was a long night.

The next morning, I drove my parents to the special DMV office in El Segundo. They walked us to the examination area, and put my mom at a very small desk to take the test; my dad and I were directed to sit in chairs in the hallway.

They handed my mom the test and told her she could begin. She immediately poked her head out the doorway so she could see me. "Lise!" she whispered. "Get over here!" I got up and walked over.

"What do you know about this one?" she said as she pointed to the first question. The woman administering the test looked really mad. She stood up and said, "You're not allowed to help her!"

I walked over to the woman and whispered, "don't worry, she's not going to be able to pass it. She won't even be able to finish it. She won't get past question one." The woman nodded in understanding.

At some point the woman indicated that the test period was now over, and she took it from my mother. We were led to a small room where we sat opposite a very kind lady.

My father wasn't the type to show his emotions, but his own health had started to decline and his strength was diminishing, including the ability to hide how he felt. He was holding back tears. He knew what was coming. It had finally become clear to him that his wife was indeed quite ill.

"Good morning Mrs. Boyd," the nice lady smiled. "It seems we have a problem with your test. I need to tell you that you can't drive anymore."

My mother made the sign of the cross and said, "Sweetheart! You're a doll!"

"Mrs. Boyd, do you understand what I am telling you?"

"Yippee Honey!" she told the lady, smiling and laughing.

My father continued to cry silently. I stood up and thanked the nice lady. My mother had a huge smile and went over to hug her and thank her for being such a sweetheart.

"You're a doll!" she told her. "Yippee!"

"MY NAME IS RITA"

I know that many have experienced watching their aging parents lose their mental acuity. It is not always easy to recognize when something is wrong with them, and to properly care for them and protect them.

My mom had always been an extrovert. But by 2002, it was obvious something wasn't working right in her brain. There was no physical test for what she had, but an eight-hour psychological exam revealed she had Frontotemporal Lobe dementia. That part of her brain that told her what was, and wasn't appropriate, was slowly declining.

I have to give my mother a huge amount of credit for her determination and her drive to deny and hide what was happening to her. She could be really convincing. She knew how to cover up when she didn't recognize someone, she knew how to revise something she had said that wasn't right, she knew how to blame what was happening to her on other things.

Much later, we also found several journals where she wrote out these facts to study:

"My name is Rita."

"I have four children, Julie, Lisa, Fred, and Teresa."

"I have 11 grandchildren."

She tried valiantly to hold on to her faculties. I so admired her, and how she tried to fight that the physicality of her brain was deteriorating.

By 2007, my mother's dementia had caused her to decline significantly. She hadn't spoken in a couple of years. The changes in dementia happen gradually, sometimes you can't remember exactly when your loved one lost yet another skill, or another part of their life.

With speech, their vocabulary becomes smaller and smaller. They don't know very many words, or anyone's name, or even who they are. Eventually my mother stopped speaking altogether. She could only smile and nod when she saw us.

My mother would often sing these little old-time songs, and she did that often with all of her grandchildren.

On one of Bunkey's visits, my mother's dementia had progressed and she hadn't spoken in a few years. She didn't recognize anyone either, but she would smile and hug someone who she perceived had been important to her at one time. She always immediately hugged Bunkey and lit up with a smile.

"Hi Aunt Rita!" Bunkey would always say, and my mother would light up.

Bunkey knew how to play the piano, and on a visit to my sister's house she led my mother over to the piano bench and had her sit next to her. "Come on Aunt Rita, we're going to sing!" My mother obliged and sat next to her, even though she had no understanding of what Bunkey was saying or doing. My mother sat there with her blank look, and smiled and nodded like she always did. She had no understanding of where she was or of anything that was happening. We had gotten used to her being this way.

Bunkey began playing all the little songs my mother used to sing. "Remember this one, Aunt Rita?" My mother silently stared at her with a huge smile. She was so happy. She seemed to suddenly become more aware of what was happening around her.

It reminded me of a video I had seen of an older woman in Spain named Marta, who had been a prima ballerina. She was participating in a program that used music therapy to help those with dementia and Alzheimer's. As they played the music from "Swan Lake," Marta slowly sat up and began to move to the music. Her arms were beautiful and graceful as she recreated all the moves to each part of the song. The music had reached deep within her and touched her long ago memories.

I was now watching the same thing happen to my mother!

Bunkey began playing my mother's favorite songs, singing along loudly while she played. Suddenly, my mother started singing too! "I love you, a bushel and a peck! A bushel and a peck and a hug around the neck! A hug around the neck and a barrel and a heap! A barrel and a heap and I'm talking in my sleep about you! Yes about you!"

We were all stunned. I couldn't believe it! Hearing her sing was so startling; I hadn't realized how long it had been since I had heard the sound of my mother's voice.

And it wasn't just that she was singing—she included all the intonations and special parts of each song the way she had always done, including hand gestures like the ballerina Marta had remembered in the video. And my mom had the exact same look of joy and emotion on her face, as she sang out loud. It was so beautiful to see her so happy, seemingly free of fear and confusion, and so absolutely carefree.

I've never forgotten it.

MY MOTHER'S GENEROUS NATURE

My mother was so very generous in so many ways. She gave gifts to everyone, and hugs to people she passed on 2nd St. She always looked for a way to cheer someone up; being generous was a hallmark of who she was.

A prime example was her "Salt Water Taffy" extravaganza every year. In the summer she always returned to Philadelphia and New Jersey to visit her family. But before leaving she collected the addresses of everyone she knew, and I mean everyone: the clerk at Rite-Aid, the mail lady, the bank teller.

Once she got to the Boardwalk in Ocean City, she would send out over 30 boxes of salt water taffy, one to every person on her list.

There came a time around 2007 when she was deep in her dementia; I had finally accepted that I had become a stranger to her. She no longer spoke. She no longer said, "here's the thing" or "Yippee!"

She said nothing. She also seemed very sorrowful. When she walked up and down her beloved 2nd St. with her caregiver Martha, she looked down much of the time. Often they would stop into my restaurant in the afternoon, and would sit at the small table at the very front. My staff would bring her and Martha each a glass of water.

I was usually gone when they came by, but one day I was still there when they sat down. I pulled up a chair to join them. I put my hand on my mom's arm and lifted up her chin with my other hand to look at her face and see into her eyes.

"Hi Mom, it's me, Lisa, your #2 daughter!" There was no sign of recognition really, not even a smile. She stared intently at me with her brown eyes, looking into her #2 daughter's identical brown eyes, as if she was studying me.

I could see from inside her heart and mind that she wanted me to know she was trying. She knew, on some level, I was "somebody," somebody who meant something to her. She just kept staring at me.

Then, she looked down, and put her hand around the glass of water in front of her. She carefully lifted it up, and set it down in front of me. She then looked back up into my eyes, and slowly nodded, over and over, to let me know the glass of water was for me.

She was giving me a gift. It was all she had to give, but she wanted me to have it. I held her hand and nodded back to let her know I understood. She had lost almost every part of herself, and yet this sweet generous part of her spirit remained.

I took her hand and told her how sorry I was. She just stared at me with her eyes full of love.

WHEN OUR MOTHER DIED . . . THE LAST DAYS

"She has four-seven days once she stops eating and drinking." That's what the hospice nurse told me and my older sister.

My mother now had been ill with dementia for nearly 10 years. A neurologist described dementia as, "It's not just memory, it's not just movement, and it's not just behavior. It's a combination of all three, which makes it difficult to diagnose and difficult to treat." It's basically a terrible illness in which you lose all your memories, and slowly go backwards to almost being like a baby.

My Mom's hospice nurse had come to visit, and my sister had asked, "Are we talking weeks or days?" It was blunt of her, but I had been wondering the same thing. The nurse said "**not** weeks." That really upset me, which was surprising to me because I already knew we would be losing her soon.

Just the day before, she had done something unusual: she had opened her eyes and stared directly at me, and kept opening her mouth as if to speak. My sister was surprised and said she had not done that to her, or my niece, who had been there frequently as well. It looked like she was begging me, begging me to get her out of this life, in her condition of dementia. I told her it would be soon.

I thanked her for being so good to my children and helping me to raise them. I thanked her for all the special meals she made me when I was such a picky eater as a child.

I thanked her for the Snoopy bracelet she had bought me when I was nine. I had fallen in love with the bracelet when I saw it in a store, but my mom said we couldn't afford it. After that, for about two weeks, it seemed like we were eating a lot of macaroni and cheese for dinner, and my dad complained about the quality of the meat my mom was serving. I didn't know it then, but she had been saving up to buy me the bracelet.

Knowing it was not weeks, and instead probably a matter of days, I went to their home every day. My mom seemed to be staying stable, so a couple days later I made the decision to go ahead and participate in the Belmont Shore Christmas parade, and to walk in her honor.

A few days after that, it was Monday, and she stopped drinking anything, not even sips of water. We had been given special medicines to help her relax and ease any pain she might be having. My dad kept holding her hand and saying "Come on Munchkin, wake up." It broke my heart. My sister and I knew she would not be waking up.

We also knew we had to move into their house immediately. My father would not be able to administer her medicines by himself. I went home to pack. I put on the Snoopy bracelet, and rushed back to my parents' house.

My other sister, and my brother, could not be there as much because they had 9-5 jobs. They knew they would need to save their days off for the time coming up. Julie and I stayed in constant contact with them via texts and calls.

The next day, Tuesday, we realized we needed to give her the medicine every four hours, round the clock. We took turns, one of us slept in the other bedroom for four hours while the other stayed in my parent's room. We had moved a reclining chair into the room next to my mom's bed to sleep on, but I just couldn't get comfortable in it. So, one night, I crawled into the lower half of my mom's bed next to her and curled into a little ball. When my sister came in at 4AM to relieve me, she just started laughing when she saw me in my mom's bed like that.

On Wednesday, my dad suggested we call Dilday Mortuary, because he knew someone in the Lion's Club 30 years ago who owned it. Oh dear. The four of us had known that my dad would wait until the last minute. That is why we had already made all the arrangements (for both of them) nearly a year before; we wanted to be ready.

The hospice nurse came every day. Oxygen was delivered to make my mom more comfortable. I appreciated it when the nurse told me that normal breathing was 14-16 breaths per minute, and if that started increasing, we would know she was getting worse and we would need to increase her medicine.

For some reason, I was afraid to measure out the medicine; I don't know why, I had been a mother and an aunt for more than 20 years, and had given countless doses of medicine to children. But it scared me. So, my sister measured it out, and I took the task of trying to get my mom's mouth open so we could put it under her tongue. As time went on, it became impossible, and we would just shoot it alongside her cheek.

By Thursday her breaths became more and more rapid. I became obsessed with counting them every 30 minutes. I wanted to do *something*.

Thank God for my sister; she had thought of everything.

My mother had been wearing a pink nightgown I had bought for her at Target—it had fun monkeys all over it. It was perfect for her. But my sister did not think our mom would want to die in a monkey nightgown; she thought she might instead want to be in a pretty dress.

We went to her closet and picked out a soft dress that reminded us of Hawaii, one of my mom's favorite places. We put it on her, and brushed her hair as best we could. We brought over a CD player, and we put on my mom's favorites, like Frank Sinatra and Johnny Mathis.

I knew she especially loved the music from Phantom of the Opera, so I called Fingerprints Music, which was right down the street, and asked if they had it. They did, so I called my restaurant and asked the busboy to go buy it for me, and to bring it over. It was hard to hear "think of me, think of me softly, when the day is through . . ." which was one of her favorite songs.

We called St. Bartholomew, her local Catholic church, and asked for last rites. My dad looked at us strangely because he was not religious at all, and we explained to him it's what she would have wanted. Last Rites is one of the seven sacraments of the Catholic religion.

Father Birney arrived about noon. Thankfully my dad had been obsessed with getting a haircut and my niece had taken him out for a bit. I think it was better that it was just me and my sister. The ceremony was short, but beautiful. The Father administered it with such love, putting oil on her forehead and I think on her arms. I'm not sure. We were really crying now.

It started looking really bad around 2PM. We told our siblings to hurry; it wasn't looking good.

My mom and my children were particularly close. When my son was 15, my mom was deep into her dementia and she was very inappropriate in public places, so she could no longer attend church unaccompanied. My son showed up every Sunday, for nearly two years, at 9AM to walk her to the 9:30AM mass.

Later, when she lost most of her memory of people, and of her vocabulary, she would look at Ryan and say "Him! He's the one! He's the one!!" She still knew that he was important to her.

My son texted me that he would come the next day. "Honey," I told him, "I don't think she will be here then." He left his work immediately.

My sister sat quietly by my mom's head, stroking her hair. I sat cross-legged at the end of her bed. My dad sat on his hospital bed next to her. My other sister arrived and sat in a chair near her feet and started crying. She's not the emotional type, but she was closest to our mom out of all four of us, and now she couldn't hold it back any longer.

Then my brother came. He sat in the reclining chair by her side, he put his head down on the bed and he wept uncontrollably, telling her over and over what a beautiful mother she had been. He wasn't very close to my father but our mother was everything to him.

My older sister was kind and calm and offered her spot by our mom's head if anyone wanted it. None of us moved. She turned to our father and said, "We would all like to thank you for taking such beautiful care of our mother and keeping her here at home like she would have wanted." My dad doesn't like to publicly cry, but he just broke down.

My son texted at 4:15PM "Mom, I'm coming. Tell Grandma to wait for me."

Her breathing became fast now. The nurse told us that when she started gasping we would know it was near the end. It was helpful to me to have all of this information. My sister now gave her the meds every 15 minutes until at one point we decided we could just stop with those. And my brother, very distraught, said "can we just turn off this oxygen thing now?" It was so very loud. So, we did.

My sister suggested we say the Lord's Prayer. We all did. Then she started the Hail Mary. I was the only one who joined in; I don't think my younger brother and sister could remember it; their catechism days ended long before mine.

Then we decided to sing the Lord's Prayer, just the way she loved it. It was a great suggestion because my mom had a hand-written will in which she requested all of her grandchildren to sing it at her funeral. She had taught it to them more than fifteen years before.

We started to sing. My brother just sobbed. All the words were all choked up with all of us crying. She would stop breathing for a few seconds then would start again. She did that through the whole song.

"For thine is the kingdom, the power, and the glory for-ev-errrrr . . . more . . ."

Right after, she stopped and let go. It was beautiful for her. I think she heard us. I think she was at peace.

We all sat there for several minutes, crying. One by one we each left the room to call waiting loved ones.

My son had not made it there yet and kept texting me "???" asking for a status. I just wrote back "see you when you get here." I didn't want to tell him she hadn't been able to wait for him.

I called my daughter who was 400 miles away at college readying for finals. "Honey, Grandma died." We cried together.

Soon after, my son arrived. He could already tell. He walked straight in and sat quietly in the chair next to her. I don't think he liked seeing her like that and only stayed in the room for about five minutes. He went upstairs to join his grandfather in his office to help him write an email to waiting family members. His calmness worried me.

People started showing up. My sister, of course, had remembered to call hospice and a wonderful man named Martin came. He waited 30 minutes before calling the mortuary to give us a little more time with our mom.

It bothered my younger sister greatly that our mother would be lying in a morgue somewhere. That didn't bother my brother at all, he felt our mother's spirit was now gone and what happened to her body did not disturb him.

The two mortuary men showed up in their dark suits. What a weird job to have to be on call for; to go pick up dead people. They were very nice and respectful.

I had been in the kitchen talking to someone, so when I returned to my mom's room, I saw they had covered her head with a sheet. I got terribly upset; I had missed the explanation from Martin that that was going to happen, and apparently he noted that it upset some people.

One of my sisters took me out of the room to explain it to me. I don't know why it was so disturbing. We see that all the time on TV. But I just didn't like her covered up; I almost said, "She won't be able to breathe under there."

Then they put her in a body bag which was a very difficult thing to see. They took her out on a gurney. My father asked "Who will look after her tonight?" It was a sad question. We walked her out and watched them take her away.

I don't remember much of the night after that. I know I went home and tried to sleep. My mother finally got her wish, to be freed from her horrible condition.

But as much as I wanted her out of that, I had no idea what it would feel like to lose my Mommy.

THE MOTHER PLANT

After years of drought, we were finally getting a lot of rain in Southern California. I felt so grateful. Plus, rain gives me a soothing feeling, and it also waters all my plants, a chore I am notoriously bad at doing.

I had purchased this bougainvillea about 10 years before; it had a few blooms on it when I bought it, and I loved the variegated pink colors. It was gorgeous. I added a stone angel I had received as a gift from my mother and put it in my backyard. Over the next couple months, it lost all its flowers, and looked completely dead. It was my fault; I had stopped watering it.

This was when my mother was coming to the end of her illness and on hospice care in her home. My sister and I had hastily moved into our parents' home and took turns sleeping and staying up all night to provide her and my father with everything they needed.

On the night my mother passed, I returned home and, in a fog, I did a litany of household chores, including watering every plant I owned. Most of them appeared to be dead. I was up late into the night trying to catch up and revive everything.

Four days later on the morning of my mother's funeral, I went out my back door to go to my laundry area. I suddenly stopped short. I couldn't believe it.

There it was, in the morning sun—one tiny beautiful pink bloom on the bougainvillea plant.

I felt like my mother wanted me to know that she was finally at peace. There was no truer sign to me than that tiny pink flower. After that day, I called that plant the "mother plant."

MY MOTHER, RITA

I didn't have the relationship that some people do with their mother, where they are like best friends. We were very different from each other, but she tried her hardest to understand this quiet, shy daughter that she had created. Looking back, I always felt how much my mother loved me.

She did struggle to understand me; she thrived on communicating with other people. Everywhere we went, she would stop to talk to anyone and everyone. She tried to include me, but being shy, I didn't know what to say to anyone. "Why did we have to stop and talk to every person?" I always thought.

Sometimes she would tell me "You're too much like your father!" And she didn't mean it in a good way. I asked a lot of questions. She would tell me to try to "go with the flow" but I didn't know how to do that. I required a lot of explanation, too much for her natural state of creative and crazy energy, her wonderful way of looking at the world and just enjoying it.

But I felt her love by the actions she took. As a child I hadn't realized she understood my need for quiet time, but she actually had. She would let me frequently go visit our elderly neighbor, Miriam, who was like a grandmother to me and patiently answered all of my questions. She had wonderful coloring books and perfect crayons and would let me color inside all the lines. I needed that time at Miriam's before returning to our loud and noisy household.

My mother made allowances for me in other ways as well. As a picky eater I wanted everything to be boring and bland. She took the time to make me very plain meals alongside cooking for the whole family every evening. Today's books on child rearing tell you not to do this, but she did. And I am so very grateful she had. It made me feel very taken care of and loved.

One time in elementary school, I came home and told my mother about a project we had been assigned six weeks before. Each student had been designated a plant that we were supposed to grow and bring into the class after the six weeks. I told my mother about the project the night before it was due.

I explained that I needed to grow a potato by the next day. I think I just told her matter-of-factly, and she took it that exact same way, matter-of-factly. OK, we need to grow a potato in one day.

I don't really remember how, but I do know that on that next day, I walked into my classroom with my report on potatoes, and some sort of plant that was (or maybe wasn't) a potato plant. I never forgot that she did that for me.

I must have been so frustrating for her, because yes, I acted too much like my father. But in the end, I was her daughter too. I am her only child with her brown eyes. And I walk just like my mother— she walked so fast everywhere, all the time, it was hard to keep up with her. I am the exact same way; I walk super-fast, even if I am not in a hurry.

And most of all, I share her sensitive, emotional heart. We did have rough times. She did not accept some of my life choices. But she eventually came around, which I know wasn't easy for her. She was the very best grandmother; she gave my children such unconditional love.

The last two weeks of her life she slept, except for one moment. One day, as my mom lay in bed, I held her hand. She suddenly opened her eyes, and it looked as if she was trying to speak. The hospice nurse noticed it too and said, "She's trying to tell you something. Talk to her."

I turned and looked at my mother. I felt like she was asking me for reassurance. So, I began listing each member of our family, one by one, using the nicknames that she called each person. I told her what they were doing, and let her know they were in a good place.

"'The Big Little Boy' is an accountant now. 'Miss Claire! Miss Claire!' is dating a wonderful man. 'Hannah Joyful' is finishing up college soon." I went through them all, one by one. She nodded along as I spoke. After I finished with her last grandchild, she nodded again, and then closed her eyes. She didn't open them again, and died five days later.

I saw into my mother's soul that day. I never knew why it was me she gave this blessing to; the daughter she didn't understand, but loved so very much.

MY FATHER, ARDEN

My father was proud of his four children. But he was a tough taskmaster.

He and my mother did not have polite conversations. Their conversational style was "yelling." They were always hollering at each other, and they liked it that way. But it was rough for us as kids.

We were all scared of our father, and we feared "getting in trouble." We learned to avoid the living room when he came home from work. He worked such long hours at Rockwell International, and worked on the Apollo programs, which led to the first man landing on the moon. It must have exhausted him.

The teenage years were even tougher, as explained in an earlier chapter.

Our mother had always told us, over and over, "stick together, the four of you, even if it is against me and your father. Stick together!" And we always had over the years, many many times, saving each other from some very stern consequences.

Years and years later, I remembered watching an old home movie of us roller skating and riding bikes down our street on Daphne Ave. Four little blonde heads, smiling and playing. My Dad watched the movies with a big smile and said, "I had the best-looking kids on the block! And the smartest ones too."

I really wanted to say to him, "Then why weren't you happy with who we were?" But I didn't say that.

Even though our dad was so very smart, he could never accept his, or our mother's, mortality.

As our mother got more and more sick, we knew we needed to do some planning. My sisters and brother and I decided to do it ourselves without telling our father. We picked a good cemetery, set up a meeting with the funeral director and made all the arrangements. We knew we could never bring it up to him because it would make him angry.

In fact, at the burial of our mother's ashes, the four of us stood there alongside our father watching the proceedings. The grave was REALLY deep, and there was a ladder to go down to the bottom to put in this little urn that contained her ashes. Our father looked down at the hole, and then slowly turned to look at us, very confused, and said very seriously and sternly, "That is a really big place for one person."

We all gasped and held our breath. We grasped each other's hands and exchanged glances. Suddenly we were no longer four grownups over age 50; we were the four Boyd kids worried about *getting into trouble* with our strong German father. If we told him that he would be going in there later, that it was a double grave, he would probably have shunned us for the rest of his life.

Somehow, I mustered the nerve to say, "Dad, that's how they do it these days." He stared at me intently, with the same look I remembered from our childhood—stern and like he was ready to explode. But I was his logical, factual daughter, so he just said "oh" and turned back to the proceedings.

We looked at each other and collectively breathed a sigh of relief. For us, we had just dodged a bullet. Our father would never have been able to forgive us for *planning* in advance for his mortality. He would have considered it to be disloyal and disrespectful of who he was as a person. He needed to believe that he was immortal, so we let him have that.

At some point my father was diagnosed with Parkinson's disease. In fact, he was diagnosed SIX times. He just could not believe he had it, and he made my sister accompany him to six different doctors "just to be sure."

"Parkinson's disease is a brain disorder that causes unintended or uncontrollable movements, such as shaking, stiffness, and difficulty with balance and coordination. As the disease progresses, people may have difficulty walking and talking."

My father didn't have the most common symptom of this illness—arm tremors when the arms are lifted. But he did have trouble walking and maintaining his balance. His writing became illegible, and it was difficult to understand what he was saying after the disease affected his vocal cords.

He had a difficult time accepting his illness, just as he had been about our mother's dementia. He didn't want to be contained in his house, he didn't want to stop driving, and he didn't want any type of caregiver around. But at some point this was unavoidable. He had to have a caregiver.

Another common complication of Parkinson's, down the road, is dementia. Oh no, here we would go again. As he became more ill, he became more emotional, and more reflective. It was during this time that he had summoned me over to his house to tell me he thought he had been too hard on us as children.

As difficult as Parkinson's Disease had been for him, having this illness did give him (and me) this added blessing of sharing what had never been spoken about in almost 50 years. The illness softened him to the point where he could feel and express his emotions, and we were able to share that special moment of understanding and forgiveness that provided both of us with healing and closure.

In January of 2013, my father contracted pneumonia, and we took him to the Emergency Room at Long Beach Community Hospital. After five nights he was well enough to transfer to a long-term care facility, in another part of Long Beach. He only lived three more months and never did return home after that.

But a strange thing happened on the day he died. Because of my insomnia I'm never awake early and usually drift back to sleep around 4AM. However, on this particular Monday morning, I was awake at 6:30AM and my phone rang. Normally I wouldn't bother answering it, but something told me I should.

"Hello?" I said.

It was an emergency room doctor from St. Mary's Hospital in Long Beach. My father had gone into some sort of cardiac distress and his care facility had called an ambulance. The doctor explained that they had resuscitated him twice, and they needed me to get to the hospital as fast as I could.

I threw on some clothes and jumped in my car. I made it in about 12 minutes. As I walked up to the open emergency room doors, a nurse greeted me and asked, "Are you Lisa?"

"Yes, I am."

"Follow me." She took me directly to my father's room. He was still alive, but not conscious.

The doctor asked if I was his medical power of attorney. "Yes, I am," I said. "He asked me to do it when I was 15 years old." The doctor explained why he needed me there so quickly. By law, they had to continue to revive my father each time his heart was failing, unless they were given permission, by him or his power of attorney, to let him go and not to do any intervention-type procedures. The doctor was happy I was there so I could give him permission to stop administering life-prolonging procedures.

"Ohhhhhh," I said. "I am so sorry. I can't give you that. You will have to keep on reviving him no matter what. He always made me promise that I would make sure everything was done to keep him alive. He always said he wanted to live until he was 100."

They sort of stared at me. "I'm sorry." I repeated again.

I stood near my father as the room went quiet, except for my father's heartbeat on the monitor. I took his hand and bent down to whisper to him. "I love you Dad. Thank you for being a good father. Thank you for teaching me to be a hard worker. Most of all, thank you for loving Ryan and Hannah as your own children." I stood back up and looked at him. I knew it was his time. And I knew he didn't want to let go.

It wasn't long after that that my father "coded" again and went into cardiac arrest. The team got busy putting the paddles on him, and giving him every resuscitation effort as I had requested on his behalf. I quickly turned around as they started the procedures.

I fiddled with my mother's engagement ring that I had been wearing on the 3rd finger of my left hand since she had died. I even made the sign of the cross, hoping to reach my mother. And then I prayed directly to her. "Mom, please take him. Take him now. Even if he survives this, he will have no quality of life left. Please Mom."

The hospital personnel followed all of their procedures, but this time he did not come back. He was gone. I turned back around and tears ran down my face. "Bye Daddy. It's better this way than if you lived to be a 100. You're with Mom now. I love you."

It had been a miracle that I had answered the phone, and I felt blessed to have been there with him and hold his hand while he passed. It would have killed me if he had died alone without any of us there. And I think he would have been happy it was me.

Years later, my sister and I went to the cemetery, and it didn't take us long to find the place where our parents were buried—we stared down at the gravestone.

My sister said, "I think we all did a great job in caring for them."

I nodded in agreement.

We really, really did. All four of us.

We stuck together, the way our mother always told us to do.

DESTINATIONS

I'M A QUIRKY TRAVELER

I think I may be a bit of a different traveler than most people.

I usually seek out concerts or "oddities," to decide where I am going. I have no interest in the things many other people want to see. For example, I would never go to the Louvre in Paris, or the Sistine Chapel in Rome.

In fact, I rarely have any interest in any museum at all; I purposely stay out of museums. I don't understand art, and I don't feel any sort of serenity by looking at it. I usually feel frustrated, and am thinking, "why is that so famous?" So, art museums are not for me.

I feel the same way about most of history, especially ancient history.

I once went to an anthropology museum in Mexico City that my nephew raved about, and I was bored to tears. I walked through one of the nine buildings and I was done; I had no interest in looking further. They had rocks on display that were millions-of-years old, but I looked at them and thought, "those look like the rocks in my backyard." I just could not look at any more bones or rocks or artifacts.

But there is one historical period in which I am very interested, World War II.

When I was in 11th grade, there was a new curriculum in our US History class that our teacher had to follow. It was very interactive, and each part of our history took way longer to teach than in previous years. It seemed we started the year off learning about the Mayflower, and never made it past the year 1900, and then the school year was almost over. Our teacher seemed disappointed that he had run out of time to teach us some things about the current century we were in, so in the last few weeks, he played many movies for us of the atrocities of World War II.

I remember sitting there in class being so shocked, as images appeared of what had happened in the concentration camps in Europe during those years. It was so atrocious, that it seemed to me it must have happened centuries before, way before "modern" times. But I knew that didn't make sense, because there were no movie cameras in the 1700s or 1800s.

Our teacher explained it was in the early 1940s, and I was shocked to learn this happened just 30 years earlier.

I'm not sure how, at the age of 16, I had never heard of World War II, but I knew absolutely nothing about it. I was not an avid reader, and my family never discussed history or any deep subjects like war.

I knew my father had been in the Korean War, because he complained often about a skin condition he had gotten while he was there. Sometimes he would fill a bucket with warm water and add bleach, and then he would soak his hands in it for hours. It was the only thing that gave him any relief from the itching. And believe me, it was not a good idea to ask him anything about that war, or any war.

After that experience in 11th grade history class, I became fascinated with the history of World War II, and I read many books on it.

I knew that once I was no longer running my restaurant, that I wanted to travel to some of these places where World War II took place. I decided not to wait until I no longer had my restaurant business before beginning my journeys. You see, The Rolling Stones were going on a tour through Europe; this would be a perfect opportunity for me. I had frequently traveled to different cities to go see concerts, and I knew I would make these concerts a part of my trip.

I had never left my business for more than seven days in the previous 25 years, but I went ahead and planned a 16-day trip to Europe. I hadn't been there since I was in my early 20s, in over 40 years!

And I was nervous. Most of the time when I had traveled alone in the past, it had gone well. But there was one time when I traveled to Chicago to see the group, Jethro Tull. The day after the concert I was supposed to fly to a different city to see another concert. But when I woke up that next morning, I felt terribly lonesome. And all alone. And so lonely.

And I felt like a loser, "why didn't I ever remarry?" I thought. "What a loser I am, here all by myself." I did go to the airport that day, but I got on the first flight I could find to get me back home.

This is why I was nervous. I did not want to be so far away from home, all the way in Europe, and then suddenly decide I needed to come home because I was lonely. So, I put in some contingency plans.

I decided I would attend two of the concerts. I always meet wonderful people at these shows, and I would definitely not feel alone. I looked at the tour schedule and the various cities in which the band would be playing. I saw they would be in Prague, of the Czech Republic, and then in Warsaw, Poland, four days later.

I then studied a map. Just about halfway in between, and a little bit south was Slovakia, where my maternal grandmother had lived until she was 15 and had traveled to the United States. I remembered the story my Uncle Bob had told me about finding his mother's small town once the cold war had ended in 1989. I always thought it was a fascinating story.

Some of those relatives in Slovakia were now my friends on Facebook. We sent messages to each other on holidays, and they were super nice and always wished me well. I took a chance and wrote to one of them, Maria, and asked if I could come visit their town for two days. I figured I could do that on the four days in-between the two shows.

Maria wrote back with an emphatic "yes!" They would love for me to visit, and invited me to stay with them. I was really excited about that! Now I had two concerts, and a family visit, to give me time with others, and ward off any loneliness.

I also wanted to visit Paris and Rome, and decided to put those at the beginning of the trip when I would be so excited to be there, and would probably be OK being by myself.

On this European trip, I used the services of a travel agent. There were so many details to nail down, and some were easy. For instance, I always want a beautiful view out of my hotel room window. Looking out over a city makes me feel very peaceful.

But some things were more difficult to pin down. At times the travel agent seemed to get rather frustrated with me when he would suggest many things to me, and I had no interest in any of them. For instance, he called one day and he listed several things for me to see in Rome.

"Lisa, how about the Sistine Chapel?"

"No, I don't need to see that."

"How about the Colosseum?"

"No, that sounds boring to me."

"How about a cooking class to learn to make pasta?"

"Oh, hell no! I've been in an Italian restaurant for 20 years watching chefs make pasta. I have no desire to cook when I am on a vacation!"

"Well, what do you want to do in Rome, then??" he asked, sounding out of patience.

He ended up booking a local "photo shoot" for me, where the photographer took pictures of me in front of various landmarks in Rome. I wore several pretty dresses and brought along some 1940s-era hats.

He also booked for me a Vespa tour of the city, riding (and holding onto) my guide, Eduardo—I loved it! On my own I also attended mass at the Vatican, and I found that moving. I wore a beautiful dress there too, along with a stylish hat and white gloves.

And in Paris, rather than going to the Louvre, he booked a tour for me where I rode in the sidecar of a motorcycle with my guide. It was fantastic as we drove around the Arche de Triomphe, weaving in and out of 10 lanes of traffic.

As for domestic travel, there was a time when I wanted to travel to each and every state. I had been to 38 states at that time, so I needed to visit the remaining 12. During those three-four years I think I traveled enough to narrow it down to 45, with just five more to go.

Many times, on my state trips, I did find things I wanted to see or do, like Mount Rushmore in South Dakota. That was actually a museum I really enjoyed, as it explained all the engineering that went into creating the monument.

I also frequently checked the website, Atlas Obscura, to find oddities and weird attractions I might like. I found a walking suspension bridge in Maine, and a weird outside art display of 38 filing cabinets in Vermont.

But there were some states where nothing appealed to me at all. For those states, I would dress up in clothes that inspire me from that state, for instance, in Wyoming I wore a prairie dress. I realize no one else is dressed like me, but I don't care. I bring my tripod and take pictures of myself in front of famous or weird places.

See? I don't think anybody else really travels to dress up and take pictures of themselves!!

I will begin this chapter with my stories about going to Europe, most specifically about my experience in Slovakia.

And I will finish the chapter out, with some stories about states I have visited here in the U.S.

UNCLE BOB AND SLOVAKIA

I planned to visit Slovakia in between the two concerts I was attending in Prague and Warsaw.

I had always been fascinated by an experience my Uncle Bob had in 1990 when, on a whim, he decided to depart from the travel schedule he was on, and take a chance to find the small town in Slovakia where his mother had been from.

My Uncle Bob had been very close to his mother, and her early death from cancer was what motivated him to go to medical school and become a physician.

His memories of his mother were strong, and he always dreamed of going to Czechoslovakia and finding the small village she had talked about. But it was never possible due to the political climate.

After the Cold War ended, Czechoslovakia split into the Czech Republic and the Slovak Republic. Prior to that, people could not move freely between countries—now it was possible to visit.

My Uncle Bob and my Aunt Doris were traveling in Europe, and were staying in the city of Prague, located in the Czech Republic. He knew he wasn't far from the Slovakian border, and it was now possible to cross. He looked at a map and determined it would be about a 6–7-hour drive to get to his mother's tiny village called Sunava.

He hired a driver and a translator to take him to the little town his mother always talked about; it had now been over 50 years since his mother had died. He had no idea what to expect. He brought along a treasured photo of his mother's that pictured a small church in the town.

Upon arrival in the tiny village of Sunava, he was surprised to find it pristine and idyllic. He located the church from the photo he carried, and went in and talked to the priest there. He gave him his name and his mother's maiden name, and explained that he was looking for any kind of family that might still be in the village. It had been a long time. The priest asked him to walk with him to a nearby house.

The priest knocked on the door of the small house. When a man answered the door, the priest explained (through the translator) why they were there. The man listened intently, nodding his head.

He looked very serious, and told them to wait a moment, he would be right back, and he left them on the doorstep for a few moments. Then he returned with an old trunk, and he opened it up to show to my Uncle Bob.

Inside the trunk were hundreds of old photos. There were photos of my mother as a little girl, of Uncle Bob and Uncle Joe, her brothers, as little boys. In addition to all the photos, there were many handwritten letters.

It turned out my grandmother had been sending the photos back home to her family in Slovakia for all those many years until she died.

My Uncle Bob realized he was now standing in front of his first cousin, Ondrej. He had found them. They warmly embraced as they now both understood they were first cousins.

Ondrej had kept the photos of his cousins in America that he had never met. He never imagined he would ever know any of them. It was unbelievable that one of them was now standing on his doorstep, the "doctor in America."

Ondrej took Uncle Bob to the house where his mother was born, and then to the small cemetery where many of his relatives were buried. They went to the homes of many other relatives, who were very excited to meet one of their family members from America, one of the little boys in all of those photos.

They were all so hospitable, and Uncle Bob felt it was the experience of a lifetime.

So, on this trip I was taking to Europe, I thought it would be fascinating to have this experience in Slovakia. I had connected with some of my Slovakian relatives via social media, and they were excited to have me come visit.

I admit I did not know what to expect about the Slovak Republic. I had heard a lot about Prague and the Czech Republic, but nothing about Slovakia.

One of my nephews, Jeff, had made the trip there when he was in his 20s while on a sojourn with friends. I decided to check in with him and ask about his travel experiences.

"Aunt Lisa," he said. "There will be three families that you will visit. You will not have to do anything; they will take care of you. They are very nice and accommodating. They will take you to the church and the cemetery. They start feeding you and giving you vodka at 7AM."

Jeff clearly loved the vodka part. He continued, "there is a sweet lady who makes a lot of cakes and cries when you mention Grandma. I think her son is a glass blower." This was getting more interesting by the minute.

"They own the land where everyone was born. The father will play the accordion. And they also have traditional clothing if you want to try it on."

"Yes, yes! I do!" I remembered the picture of my mother dressed up and sitting at a spinning wheel—I wanted to do that!

The day after the Rolling Stones concert, I was picked up by a driver that would take me the seven hours to the little town of Sunava, population ~ 1900.

It was a long, but beautiful, drive through the countryside. I was so excited when I saw the "Sunava" sign indicating we were entering the town.

We went directly to the home of my 2nd cousin Maria, who would be hosting me during my two-day stay. They greeted me warmly: Maria, her husband Jan, and their adorable little boy Tadeas. They were so welcoming and kind. Jan spoke excellent English because he had worked in Scotland for a few years.

Later, Maria's parents, Ondrej and Anna, arrived. They were dressed in the traditional garments of their village. They brought with them their grandchildren, Radka and Ondrej, also dressed in village garb— they were carrying welcoming baskets of bread with salt, and cookies.

Her father brought his accordion and they played and sang a welcome song for me. I was so honored. We sat and talked for hours.

My grandmother had been one of eight children; three died when they were babies. Three left for America, and two remained in Slovakia.

The next day I went to visit many homes. I had never seen such wonderful hospitality. At each house I visited, there was a beautiful table set with homemade soups, cheeses, baked goods, and everything and anything you could think of.

My grandmother had left for America when she was 15, because there was very little opportunity for her in her village. The family knew a priest who lived in Philadelphia, and they felt she would have a better future there. She left home with her sister Suzanna, and traveled across Poland to get to the coast to sail to America.

Apparently my grandmother was closest to her brother Jan, whose family members I was now meeting. They wrote frequently to each other.

I was told many stories and shown many photos, some I hadn't seen before. The most special had my grandmother's writing on the back. One photo was of her family and she wrote, "we have three children, the girl, Rita, is very nice and will be 15 in April." That was my mother.

Upon learning my grandmother had died, her brother Jan tried to make contact with her family in America but was unsuccessful.

I talked to his daughter, Anna; she said her father talked about his sister frequently and wondered about her children. All of Jan's children knew how important she had been to him; that is why they had always kept all of the letters and photos she had sent.

Anna said the saddest thing for her was that her father died one year before my Uncle Bob came to find them. She said he would have been overcome with joy at this reunion, to meet his sister's oldest son, his nephew.

That evening, we attended an evening Mass with many family members (the town is basically 100% Catholic). The church was the one in the photo that my Uncle Bob had brought with him when he first came looking for his family.

I sat with my mother's first cousin, Maria, who held tightly onto me. The service was so beautiful to hear. There seemed to be about 10 altar boys, they were so sweet; they all looked like children of long ago with their short haircuts and stick-out ears.

It was absolutely so special to be in this tiny church, listening to the singing in another language—I felt like I had been transported back in time to the 1940s.

All of the other children attending sat together in the first several rows, and they spoke in unison at times during the Mass. The Slovakian language is so beautiful.

After Mass, we went to the adjoining cemetery—family is very important in Slovakia. They treasure all the mementos and memories of those who have come before them. The graves are taken care of and respected. Ondrej very kindly brought along a bag of photos and held each one up at each grave so I could tell who was who, and who was buried where.

I tried very hard to follow along, but it was a little bit difficult because there are so many Marias, Annas, Jans, and Ondrejs. Everyone is named after everyone else. There are a lot of Josefs too. I understood most of it.

They also took me to an old home still belonging to the family—it held several old possessions, including a cradle that my grandmother used to play with.

We spent the remainder of the evening at the home of my mother's first cousin Ondrej, and his wife Anna. They made me a delicious cauliflower soup and so many other good things.

They gave me beautiful gifts: a book of their village, a flag keychain, Czechoslovakian vodka, and another special drink that came with four small drinking glasses. Also, an oven mitt with pictures of sites in their country. I treasured all of these gifts.

The life they lead is very different from what I know; everyone knows everyone else in their town, and they greet everyone they pass. They are such a respectful and gracious people.

And even the nights in Slovakia were an unusual experience as well.

At 4AM the sun came up.

At 5AM the sheep started baaaa-ing.

At 6AM some church bells started ringing.

At 7AM a rooster began crowing. I wondered why he didn't crow at 4AM when the sun came up, but I never did find out.

What struck me most about Slovakia is that I felt like I was visiting a foreign land out of a fairy tale. I cannot explain just how much the entire visit meant to me, meeting so many family members, who extended such warm greetings to me. The love and hospitality they showed was so pure and from the heart.

It was hard to say goodbye; I know I will be going back.

I NEVER THOUGHT OF GOING TO POLAND

After my two-day visit in Slovakia, I was heading to Warsaw, Poland.

Poland was never on my list of must-see places to visit. But since I was going to Warsaw for my second Rolling Stones concert of this trip, I would indeed be traveling through the country.

After my visit in Slovakia, I had a driver pick me up and take me to Krakow. I was going to spend one night there before heading to Warsaw for the concert the next day.

Because I was always so interested in the history of World War II, I decided that on my way to Krakow, I would stop to see the memorial at Auschwitz. It doesn't sound quite right to say I was "excited" to go there, but I wanted to feel a part of history, a connection to all those souls who perished there.

The driver came to pick me up at my family's home. Once we made it to Auschwitz, I joined an English-speaking tour. My guide was named Karolina, and she grew up in the adjacent town of Oswiecim.

The Germans had given the camp the name of Auschwitz. She made it clear that it was improper, and even offensive, to refer to it as a "Polish Concentration Camp"—it was a German Concentration Camp on Polish land. I had been to the Holocaust Museum in Los Angeles and it was very moving. But seeing Auschwitz, an actual part of history, was an entirely different experience. There was a reverence you felt from the moment you entered this sacred space, as if you could feel the lost souls all around you.

We walked through the barracks, and then to Birkenau, about two km down the road. What struck me most was how it felt to take the long walk on the gravel road along the train tracks, past the dividing station, where prisoners were selected to live or die upon arrival.

World War II history came alive for me that day.

After leaving Auschwitz, my driver picked me up and we drove through the countryside of Poland toward Krakow. It reminded me of driving up to Big Bear, CA, with many turns and little towns, although the colors of the buildings were much brighter—many orange and bright yellow houses.

We came to a small town and stopped at a little restaurant. They spoke no English so my driver helped me order. Most menu items were some sort of meat dish, which I don't care for, so I ordered a bowl of tomato soup. The soup was sort of creamy and it had rice in it. It was so delicious.

I felt like I had eaten this soup before, and then, I had a sudden epiphany. Ohhhhhh! My mother used to make us soup just like this!!

I think she probably just used a can of Campbell's Tomato soup as a base, but rather than follow the directions to add one can of water, she always added milk. So, it was creamier. And then she separately made rice, and added it to the soup. When neighborhood kids came over and my mother made the soup for lunch, all of them loved it and said they wished their mothers made it that way.

I learned later that this soup was a staple in this part of the world. So, my grandmother must have made tomato soup like this for my mother, the Polish way. And my mother prepared it for us, in just this same way, creamy smooth, and with rice added in. I think it was one of the loveliest meals of my trip.

And that evening, when I lay down to sleep, such a reverence came over me. How lucky was I to have met long-ago family members, to see real life history, and to feel like I was experiencing a homeland I never knew I really had—it was so incredibly heartwarming.

I discovered more on those few days than my heart could ever have imagined.

I LOVED POLAND

I left Krakow early on Sunday and took the train to Warsaw. Much of the countryside reminded me of Iowa—it was very flat in this part of the country.

The Rolling Stones concert was that evening and I had a great time.

The day after the concert, I had a guide coming for me at 9AM. This was going to be difficult, because I had stayed up until 5AM hanging out with the new friends I had met the night before at the concert. We had all returned to my room after the show, and devoured the bottle of special vodka my relatives had given to me as a send-off.

Before I had left on the trip, I re-watched "The Pianist" which is set in Warsaw, and illustrates much about life in the Warsaw ghetto. I booked a tour more focused on the World War II history of the city. I was ready for my guide after just three hours of sleep. Her name was Joanna and she was the perfect guide for me.

Joanna was excited to tell me all about her city. She had an interesting perspective because she was born in 1980 and grew up during the communist era, so she was old enough to understand what it was like with the fall of communism. Also, her father, now 82, had always voiced his political views to her. He was not happy with communism, and let her know the propaganda that was being forced upon her in the schools.

When we met up, I was wearing a black dress and red shoes. Normally that is not something that I would wear, but I wanted to get a black and white photo that would look more like something from the 1940s—in that case it wouldn't matter what color the shoes actually were (they were Mary-Janes and looked 40s-ish).

She greeted me speaking in English, but with a thick accent, "Oh! You are a Rolling Stones girl!" as she knew I had gone to the concert the night before. I think she was also referring to my red shoes, as red is the main color of the band's logo.

We walked and drove around the city. She brought along an old book of photos and would hold up a photo of what an area used to look like, compared to what it looked like now. We walked to the area where the Warsaw ghetto began. In 1944, Hitler was so angry with the Poles for fighting back, that he ordered the entire city be blown up, building by building. Only 15% of it had remained.

We went by a memorial to Pope John Paul II. He was the first Polish pope and this was monumental for the Polish people as their country is predominantly Catholic. The communists reluctantly allowed him to come back to visit Poland during his tenure as Pope, and he used carefully worded expressions in his speeches to poke at the communists and encourage his fellow countrymen not to give up hope.

The Polish flag was flying in front of many buildings. It is simple, being half white and half red. The white stands for their proud independence, and the red stands for all the blood that has been spilled to achieve that independence.

After hearing about their rich and deep history, I felt a little silly asking Joanna to take my picture with my hat and gloves. But she was delighted to do it, and took me to different places where she thought it would work best. She was happy that I had been so interested to learn about her city and her country.

When it was time to say goodbye, I asked to be dropped off at a restaurant. She had pointed out many good ones, especially a pizza one, but I opted for the one with her native dumplings. She was beaming with pride.

I loved Warsaw. I loved Poland. I never knew I would. But I did.

NORMANDY—IT WAS SO INCREDIBLE

I returned to Europe for a shorter time the following year. I visited London to see my daughter where she was spending a semester for Law School.

But I also went to Paris for a few days, because I wanted to take the day trip to Normandy, where the infamous D-Day occurred on June 6, 1944, the Allied Invasion during World War II.

I knew going to Normandy from Paris would be quite a commitment of time—the train ride is more than 2 ½ hours each way, so I was up at 5AM and on my way to the train station.

I was excited that upon arrival, I would be experiencing the tour in a unique way—in a 1943 Willy Jeep driven by a knowledgeable (and handsome) paratrooper, Hubert, who was from the Netherlands.

This tour was quite different from the standard bus tour which just goes to a hill over the beach and on to a museum. But traveling by Jeep allowed me to go down all of these little roads that the troops had actually walked to achieve their mission on June 6, 1944. We traveled down tiny road after tiny road, seeing little churches with bullet holes and bloodstains, and farmhouses that were made into aid stations.

Hubert said he attended the commemoration ceremonies of D-Day every year. Along the way, he met many of the veterans and learned their stories.

He shared those stories as he drove me around. He would hold up pictures from war times next to the buildings as they stood today.

He told me about two of those veterans, Robert Wright and Kenneth Moore of the 101st Airborne Division. They were both conscientious objectors, but wanted to do their part so they joined as Paratrooping medics. They were part of a group who parachuted in at 1:30AM that morning ahead of the infiltration by sea.

They found a church nearby and declared it an aid station. There were injured men everywhere. They decided their mission was to save lives, all lives, and so they took in both German and American soldiers. Every soldier was required to leave his weapon outside. Without enough space for 80 men to lie on the floor, the soldiers sat side by side in the church pews. At one point a German officer barged in with a gun ready to shoot, but when he saw Germans among the patients and was told aid was given to all soldiers there, he changed his mind and departed. All of the 80 patients lived.

Hubert and I went inside, and he showed me all the bullet holes that remained in the church.

He told me how he later met a lady who told him that she was 12 years old at the time of the invasion. After the troops had moved on from the church, she and her mother went over to clean it. But try as they could, they could not remove all of the bloodstains—they were still visible on many of the pews as Hubert and I peeked inside.

Hubert documented this story and had a memorial built to honor these two medics and what had taken place at this church.

Years later, when Robert Wright was dying, Hubert talked to him on the phone and asked if there was anything that he could do for him. Robert kept saying, "I want to jump with you." But Hubert knew that wasn't possible because the former Paratrooper medic was now very old and ill.

Hubert asked to speak to the man's son, who explained that his father wanted to be cremated, and then have Hubert make a jump with his ashes. That was what he meant by, "I want to jump with you."

Hubert did exactly that after Robert died, and his ashes are now interred at the church.

There were many other stories like this, too many to mention. Hubert's love of Normandy and preserving the memories of what happened in those few days in 1944, has made a huge difference in the lives of the heroes that landed there. And it was the experience of a lifetime for me.

Hubert got me safely back on the train after dusk, and I made it back to Paris later that evening.

I once again had that feeling of reverence, of going back in time and imagining what it must have been like for all the soldiers who lost their lives there.

These trips to Europe were incredibly memorable for me. I mixed together deep historical and meaningful visits of World War II memorials, along with fun and silly things, like my Vespa ride through Rome, and the motorcycle sidecar ride through the small streets of Paris.

I felt eternally grateful.

HELLO BISON AND BUFFALO!

I had decided I would try to visit all 50 states. I think I had been to about 38 states when I made this decision.

I don't count going through an airport as having visited that particular state. I believe one has to "walk on the soil and breathe in the air" before saying they have been there. At least, that is the standard I hold for myself.

I love traveling to other places to see concerts, so that was one opportunity I would use quite often to visit various cities around the country. While there, I would take the time to see and visit important things in those particular cities or states.

But if there weren't any concerts happening in which I was interested, l would instead look for things and attractions in these states that I might enjoy.

South Dakota was a state on my list to which I had never been, and it didn't have any large concert venues. So, I decided to travel there with my sister, to see the national monument, Mount Rushmore.

We signed up for a day-long tour through the Black Hills that would take us to Mount Rushmore and its museum, and also to the Crazy Horse Monument.

I was excited about these two portions of the tour.

The third part of the tour I was a little worried about—the "Wildlife Loop through Custer Park" portion of the tour, for several hours.

I had called and asked the tour operator exactly what we would be seeing and he said, "Well, ma'am, have you ever been to the Black Hills? There's a lot to see. Believe me, I'm not going to drive you around and just show you a tree." OK.

We both felt seeing one or two buffalo would be interesting. The tour website also discussed prairie dogs, and how we would not be rushed as we gazed at the wildlife.

Hmmmm. Seeing lots of prairie dogs had never been at the top of my list. But oh well, we would go with the flow.

First up was Mount Rushmore—it did not disappoint.

We learned the idea for building a monument came from a local historian. He noted many people from the eastern states were driving straight through South Dakota to get to Yellowstone in Wyoming. None of the tourists were stopping and actually staying in South Dakota, so their tourist dollars were not spent there. It seemed a good opportunity to add tourism to the state's economy, by creating something people would want to come see.

I found this fascinating to be the reason for a monument to be built.

A prized sculptor was hired, and he came up with the idea of a large scale sculpture with the presidents, once he saw the mountain. Construction began in 1927 and was completed in 1941. It was not finished exactly as planned; World War II got in the way as well as several other factors. Miraculously, no one died in the creation of the monument.

I thought it was stunning to look at—it boggles the mind how they knew exactly where to put dynamite and blow up just the right part to make it look the way it does. There was a short movie in the museum explaining how they had extrapolated the measurements and used plumb lines and other measuring devices. It is an engineering marvel and I thoroughly enjoyed all of the exhibits (and I am not a museum person, so this was rare for me). It appealed to my engineering brain.

Also, I know this was touristy, but they supposedly had Thomas Jefferson's special vanilla ice cream recipe on display. They said if you ordered the vanilla, it would be the exact same recipe as Thomas Jefferson's, made to the exact same specifications.

Of course, I went right in and ordered it, and yes it was probably just Thrifty ice cream hahaha but still, it was good, and I said a silent thank you to Mr. Jefferson for his recipe.

I bought a pair of Mount Rushmore socks at the gift shop, and on we went to the Crazy Horse Monument.

Our guide had told us the two most asked questions about Crazy Horse are "When will it be finished?" and "Why is it taking so long?" He said it would not be finished in his lifetime (he was about my age). It is taking so long because there is one family in charge of creating it.

The Crazy Horse monument is even bigger than Mount Rushmore. The face is completed and you can see where the horse head and arm will eventually be. We took a quick bus ride to the base of the mountain. As soon as we were all boarded, the driver asked if anyone had any questions. Someone said, "When will it be finished?"

"It should be completed by next Friday," he said. I loved him. He then went on to explain the actual timeline of probably 40 years.

He also pointed out these animals that he called "whistling pigs" and said we would probably see one named Steve while we were out.

We did. I really don't know what kind of animal Steve really was. But it was definitely worth the time to get that close to the sculpture.

Now it was time for the wildlife loop! As our guide drove us around, we learned that bison and buffalo are the exact same thing.

Also, once an older male finds that he can no longer win in a fight against a younger buffalo, he goes off and stays by himself, or hangs with other older buffalo dudes. It kind of reminded me of those groups of older guys hanging out in the early mornings in front of coffee shops on 2nd St. in Belmont Shore, slowly drinking their coffee. I'm glad they have friends, but I wondered if they feel like they are being put out to pasture too.

Back to buffalo: When I look at a buffalo, I think "Wow a buffalo." But then I'm done. I think how boring it must be to be a buffalo—you just stand there all day and eat grass and then lay down. Then you get up and do it all again the next day. What a life.

So . . . we saw a buffalo, and then another, and then some groups of buffalos. OK. Hi Buffalo. I took some pictures.

Our guides kept pointing out buffalo after buffalo. I began to find it more interesting to observe the guides, and wondered how someone becomes so fascinated with buffalo. Every buffalo they spotted required another stop.

It occurred to me that these men were probably more interested in looking at buffalo than they would be at looking at dancers in a strip club.

One of them was also really into birds, bluebirds in particular, and he kept stopping over and over searching for birds and pointing here and there. I did actually see a bird that I thought was pretty, but I said quietly to myself, "Hi bird, you are pretty, but please stay here in South Dakota and do not come to Long Beach, 90803. Thank you bird." (Birds always woke me up too early after working late at my restaurant. I didn't like them).

We also saw some donkeys called the "begging burros", and then some antelopes and some deer, but I don't think I ever saw a prairie dog. At one point the guide glanced at us in the back seat and said, "I think you ladies are ready for Happy Hour."

So, the wildlife portion was a bit too long for me, but there were some fascinating tunnels we passed through that were designed to frame Mount Rushmore as you exited them. The engineering and creativity were so impressive to me.

My sister and I discussed later why we are the way we are about wildlife and why we find it so boring. Was it where we grew up, or how we were raised, or is it just in our DNA? We don't know.

But we said goodbye to South Dakota; we thought it was interesting, educational, and fun! And goodbye to all the buffalo!!

THE FARM, IN IOWA

Usually when you plan a trip, you have certain expectations about what you want to visit, and how you will feel after the experience. But the most memorable are the adventures you take that offer up twists and turns you could never have imagined or thought possible.

That was our experience in 2017 when visiting our father's birthplace, "the farm," in Iowa.

Our whole life, we always called where our father grew up, "the farm," just like how we would say that our mother was going "back east" (to Philadelphia).

I always wanted to go back to the farm one day and see if it was how I remembered it. I had only been there twice as a kid; I think the last time I was about 9 years old. Both times we took the train out from California.

I remembered riding the ponies and feeding the chickens. And my father put on overalls as soon as he was awake, and was gone all day with his father helping him out in the fields.

These memories had really stayed with me. I wanted to smell the hay, and see the cornfields again. And I wanted to feel the spirit of all who had lived there.

The farm held a special place for my father. He adored his parents and said only wonderful things about them; he held a very deep reverence for them. He had worked hard his whole life, and didn't mind helping his father before and after school.

But, also, the farm represented difficult memories for him. His mother had died when he was 14. He, and one of his sisters, still living at home, tried to fill her shoes. But being a farmer is tough without having a female counterpart, so his father remarried. My father then left for the Navy when he was 17. He said it was the only time he had seen his father cry, except for the time when his mother died.

My sister and I decided we would make this part of our next trip. After all, true to our concert-going travels, Paul McCartney was playing in Des Moines, so if anything, we would have a great musical experience.

Before leaving, I spoke to my Aunt Kathryn on the phone—she was my father's younger sister, and then 85. She told me many stories about my grandparents. And my brother had recommended that we get in touch with our cousin, Donna. "You will love her," he said. "She was so helpful and nice when I was there."

I emailed Donna, and she responded right away. She was happy we were coming and explained that she lived about 45 minutes from downtown Des Moines. We shared what we could remember about the past. She said she would take us out to the farm and then to the old-time cemetery. Donna was raised in Iowa and knew more of the relatives, and had spent a lot of time with our grandfather.

I told Donna I would like to get a picture on a horse or on a tractor. Donna said she would work on that . . . AND, she added she remembered a farm nearby that had a lot of heavy equipment, and she doubted that any farmer would mind showing off his equipment to us.

I packed a farm type dress with me, even though it was pretty dowdy—I always like to dress for where I am going (sometimes I do go way overboard). But I thought maybe I could pose in it while holding a basket of eggs or something. I began to think of this as a fairly light-hearted adventure after all.

We arrived late one evening, and my sister's luggage didn't make it, so we decided to stop at a grocery store for some things she needed.

We had so much fun in this store! It was an experience in itself. We couldn't believe it—we walked in and right up in front, there were rows and rows and rows of Angel Food cakes!

I never really liked Angel Food cake, but my father loved it. My mother was always making Angel Food cakes when we were little—she had a special pan for them, and when it came out of the oven, she would flip it upside down and balance it on three soup cans, so it could cool down. I remember kids coming to my house, pointing at the inverted, cooling cake, and asking, "what's that?"

And I never saw anyone else's mother making Angel Food cakes either. So, I didn't know why my mother was always making them for my father. Well, now I knew! Angel Food cakes are a big deal in Iowa!

We were also fascinated with what they called the "Salad aisle." In California, a "Salad aisle" would consist of plenty of leafy greens, and organic healthy things to go with them.

But, a "Salad aisle" in Iowa was quite different. It was shelf after shelf of Jell-O "salads," and things loaded with whipped cream or mayonnaise. The only green thing we saw in that aisle was something labeled "Watergate Salad" which was about as far away from a salad as you could get: "pistachio-flavored instant pudding mix, canned pineapple, mini marshmallows, nuts, and whipped topping."

Jell-O was a big deal in Iowa too. All of these "creations" reminded me of the Jell-O salads my mother was also always making for my father, another nod to his upbringing, along with the Angel Food Cakes.

I had a greater appreciation of my mother after that visit to the Iowan grocery store. She had obviously learned to make all of these things that were so important to my father, even though she had been a city girl from Philadelphia. And I remembered the year my mother talked about when they had lived in Iowa so my father could finish his degree. She said she had stepped out of a car and into a mud puddle wearing very non-farm-like shoes. Still, she shrugged it off as being a positive experience.

I had expected this trip to be filled with memories of my father. But on that first night, I went to sleep thinking about my mother's fearless spirit, as a young bride, to live somewhere so different from her upbringing, and away from her family. And to learn so many things to make her new husband so happy. That's what all the Angel Food cakes had been about.

We headed off to our hotel, and had a surprise waiting for us, thanks to our cousin, Donna.

THE BARBIE DOLL

I think we all have moments in our lives where, upon later reflection, we realize that maybe we could have handled something differently than how we actually did. And this holds true even if it was a situation that occurred when we were just 5 years old. Maybe we wonder if we hurt another person's feelings. Those moments can sometimes stay with us, and we wonder if the other person involved remembers what happened in the same way that we do.

We were excited to see our cousin Donna—her mother was our father's older sister. We hadn't seen her in 50 years! Even though we always went back east to visit my mom's family, we didn't travel to see my father's family as often. I don't think it was as important to him once his father had died.

But Donna had been at the farm when we visited as kids, and one time her family had come to California for Christmas.

My brother had shared with me a story Donna had told him about something she felt bad about, that had happened when we were children.

It was during her family's only visit to California that one Christmas: my sister, Teresa, and Donna were about the same age, five or six. Donna remembered that Teresa had two Barbie dolls, and Donna did not have any Barbies at all. My mother made Teresa give up one of her Barbies and give it to Donna. Teresa cried and cried, and didn't take it very well. Donna felt so bad for her, but she was so thrilled to finally have her own Barbie doll that she decided to try not to think about it. But she had always remembered.

I relayed the story to Teresa and she laughed; she had absolutely no memory of it whatsoever. And she didn't know how Donna could remember it either.

In my email exchanges with Donna, I told her that Teresa had no memory of the Barbie incident and there were no hard feelings. We laughed about it.

Donna asked me what hotel we would be staying at—I let her know and told her we would be in late on a Thursday evening and would be in touch with her the following Friday.

That Thursday in July, after a day of two flights and our exciting adventure at the local grocery store (with all of the Angel Food cakes and weird salads), we finally made it to the hotel. The desk clerk checked us in and told us to enjoy our stay.

We walked into our room, found the light switch, and turned it on. Right in front of us, on a counter, was the most exquisite, 50s-style, Barbie doll I have ever seen. Next to her was a note that said, "Welcome to Iowa."

After 50 years, Donna wanted to make things right.

What a wonderful cousin.

THE CORN FIELDS

The day came for us to go to the farm. Little did we know we were about to find far more than what we were looking for; it was way beyond remembering the farm house from when I visited as a little girl.

Donna was waiting for us in the lobby of our hotel the next morning. My sister thanked her profusely for the Barbie doll we had found in our room the evening before.

We headed out to the small town of Creston in southwest Iowa. There was an appliance store owned by a man around our age named Gayle Bruckenheimer. I had heard my father say this last name many times, always with affection. He loved and respected the Bruckenheimer family.

We learned that he now owned our grandfather's farm; he had purchased it in the '60s, after our grandfather had died. Gayle explained that our grandfather had been like a grandfather to him.

Gayle told us many stories about growing up in that area, and then sent us on our way—he said we could wander wherever we wanted to on the property.

As we approached the farm on a small dirt road, I felt a sense of giddy excitement. It was a hilly drive, and we would go up and down the small hills, each time looking for the farm in the distance.

Then there it was!

Donna pulled over on the road so I could take a picture of it from far away. We then drove the rest of the way there, pulled up and parked. It seemed very quiet all around us. We got out of the car, and Teresa and Donna walked toward the house, chatting away.

But I headed in a different direction, up a hill toward some old buildings. There was just something pulling me in that direction. There was a hill in front of me, and I suddenly started running like an excited little girl to see what was beyond the top of the hill. I was not disappointed.

Once I reached the top and looked down, there they were: rows and rows and rows of corn, as far as I could see. it was just so beautiful and breathtaking. It looked like it went on forever, and like something out of a fairy tale. I remembered it from before, and I could imagine my grandfather out there working in those fields.

I walked back to the farm house. We had brought with us pictures of our grandmother sitting, and standing, on the stoop with her children. My sister and I sat on the stoop in the same spot. Then we stood where she posed with her children and took pictures of our own.

After that, we walked over to the side of the house where our father had sat on his pony, probably 80 years before. We had a picture of that with us as well, and could see right where he had been as a little boy.

The air was very hot and stagnant, but we didn't care. We walked back up the slight hill and over to where I had been standing before, and all three of us quietly looked out at the rows and rows of corn. It was eerily quiet and still.

Then, suddenly, from seemingly out of nowhere, a strong breeze came through and rustled all of the corn stalks that lay before us.

It felt magical and surreal. My sister said, "It's Arden (our dad). He's here." She was right, it did feel that way.

At some point the neighboring farmer, Tony, had walked over from his farm down the road—he was Gayle's brother. He told us about growing up there and what farm life meant to him. Then he casually mentioned he still had our grandfather's tractor! His father had bought it years ago, and he had never let it go. He said we could come over and see it.

We headed into his huge barn and spotted the bright green tractor. Tony even helped us up so we could sit on it. That was so special for us. I had wanted to take a picture sitting on any tractor, but never in my wildest dreams did I think I would be sitting on my grandfather's actual tractor.

Our experience on that day in Iowa was nothing like we expected. Listening to the memories the men told of our grandfather, made him come alive as we stood and looked out at the acres of cornfields below us. And as we were riveted as we were hoisted up to sit on his special tractor.

And our father was everywhere while we were there, in a good way. My sister and I both felt his presence. And he no longer felt scary to me any more.

This is where he had come from, the house where he was born in an upstairs bedroom, the fields where he had worked so very hard every day as a little boy, the place where he had watched his mother die when he was only fourteen. Growing up on this very farm had shaped him into who he was, into who he became as an adult.

I thought back to how my father had only spoken about his own father with absolute reverence and pure love. He hadn't resented him at all, even after all that hard work and the strong discipline. He accepted his father completely for who he had been, and it was as if forgiveness was not even necessary. On that day, I knew I had done the right thing when my father had died; I could honor his memory with reverence and love.

Feeling his presence that day, especially when the strong breeze came through and rustled all the corn stalks, felt like he was telling me he was grateful I now really understood him. Grateful I now knew why he had been who he was.

We walked quietly back to the car. And I kept thinking, who would think that, in Iowa, we would find all these magical feelings?

DOGS

I WAS NOT A DOG PERSON

We did not have pets growing up—my father had been raised on a farm and he had no interest in taking care of any more animals. And he didn't think animals belonged in the house. We knew better than to even bring the subject up, because he also thought anyone who had a pet was a "less credible" person. I know that is extreme, but he drew hard lines like that on most subjects.

I was also allergic to so many things, dogs and cats included, so I rarely hung around any animals or pets. Even if we went to visit someone's home who had a pet, I couldn't get near it, or pet it, or I would end up having an asthma attack.

But it went beyond the allergies. Dogs terrified me. If I encountered a dog outside, I immediately ran, which often made the dog chase after me. I found dogs to be scary.

Fast forward to when I had children. My son was about 10 years old, and like many children that age, he longed for a dog. He talked about it constantly and just kept asking me if we could get one. Like me, my daughter was allergic to everything, and also not a dog person—she had many of the same fears I did.

My son persisted. I found it hard to say no to him because he was such a good kid. He got straight A's, he had many friends, and he was kind. We negotiated, and I made it clear he would have to be the one to take care of the dog; he agreed wholeheartedly.

We went to a local pet store and immediately fell in love with a mixed-breed puppy there. With his blond fur, he looked to be part Labrador Retriever. We purchased the puppy and brought him home. Ryan named him "Kenny." I had no idea why he chose this name; he wouldn't say exactly how he thought of it. But Kenny it was.

My lack of knowledge about dogs and/or puppies was actually immense, even astounding—I knew nothing about taking care of a pet. I had absolutely no clue what I had just signed up for. The first few days, Ryan did absolutely everything. If the dog whimpered, he was there. Several times each night, Ryan got up to take Kenny outside.

By day three, and with very little sleep, Ryan was absolutely exhausted. He came to my room where I worked at my desk, tears running down his face. "Mom. I'm sorry. I just can't do it. I'm so tired Mom, I don't know what to do. I'm sorry Mom."

My heart broke for him. His face was bright red and he was falling apart. I told him to lie in my bed and rest, and I would take care of the dog. In less than a minute, Ryan fell asleep.

Full of energy, Kenny constantly wanted to play. I had purchased a crate, as was recommended by many dog owners I knew, but he cried whenever I put him in there. Ryan and I were both out of our league as to what to do. We hired a trainer named Jackie, who came over and showed us a few things to give Kenny structure and keep him happier.

A few weeks later, things were better with the dog, but then my sister left her two kids with me to go away for a couple days. I now had a household of four kids, plus the neighbor boy who was always over, and Kenny too.

One afternoon I returned from the market and pulled into my driveway with my groceries. It had rained all day, but had finally stopped.

Adam, a contractor friend of mine, was waiting out front by his truck for me to discuss a project we were working on. Ryan came out to unload the groceries, and Kenny followed. More than once, Ryan said, "Mom, Kenny is outside. Make sure he's OK."

Clueless, I stood by the edge of the street and continued chatting with Adam. Kenny was nowhere near me, so I wasn't worried he would run into the street. Suddenly I heard the horrific sound of something in mortal pain and anguish, along with accompanying fierce grunts and barking. Adam and I ran to the side gate of the neighbor's house near my driveway, where the sounds were coming from.

Kenny had wandered over there to bark through the gate at the two large 150-pound Akitas living on the other side. Because of the rain, the ground was soft. Those big dogs had clawed at the mud under the gate and created a tunnel; Kenny slid down into it, and the dogs had grabbed him and pulled him through to their side. And they were now mauling him to death.

I ran screaming to the lady's front door and pounded on it over and over again telling her that her dogs were attacking my dog. I was a basket-case. I felt completely helpless. I could hear the puppy crying as it was being mauled. She immediately understood, and closed her front door, and I could hear her running through her house and out into her backyard. I heard her screaming at her dogs to let go of the puppy.

I ran back to the side gate. I could even hear her hitting her dogs trying to get them to stop and let go of Kenny. By this time, all the kids had come running out of my house when they heard the commotion; they were all crying, especially Ryan.

Adam had turned on my hose and sprayed it over the fence onto the dogs, attempting to break up the fighting. The lady was finally able to wrestle Kenny away from her two dogs. She gently handed him up and over the gate to Adam. He put him in a towel he had grabbed from his truck. It was clear that Kenny had already died. Those dogs had killed him.

A neighbor volunteered to take him to a vet nearby to be sure. He also let us know that the vet would take care of the dog's body. Ryan was beyond devastated. All five kids at my house were now crying uncontrollably.

Everything seemed to have happened so fast. I was very angry at myself for not listening when Ryan had said more than once, "Mom, Kenny's outside." I had only been worried about him getting hit by a car, and he had been far away from the street so I wasn't concerned. Never in my wildest imagination did I understand that those dogs barking on the other side of the fence would actually kill a puppy. And it never occurred to me that he could slide right under and they would grab him. And it wasn't just that the poor dog had died. It was also the pain of hearing him helplessly cry, and the awful feeling of not being able to do anything except stand on the other side of the gate and hear it all happen.

We all went inside and waited for the neighbor to come back from the vet. He did, and he confirmed that Kenny had not made it. Sadness filled my home. Ryan cried for hours and hours. For him it felt like an even bigger loss—Kenny was his first dog. He had worked so hard to take care of him; he had tried to incorporate all of the trainer's suggestions. He had pushed himself beyond exhaustion to be a good dog owner and do all the right things. And he adored Kenny.

And while Ryan could never remember the experience of losing his father, he kept asking, "Mom, is this how it was when Dad died?" through his tears. Of course, they were different experiences, but for a 10-year-old boy to go through this loss, was very traumatic. I think I just said over and over again how sad and devastating it is to lose something, or someone, we love so dearly.

When all the kids went to bed that night, I barely slept at all. I felt like I had failed as a mother. I felt like I had let my son down. It was just horrible.

A few days later I still had a houseful of sad kids. I needed to get them out of the house, so I took them to our local shopping area. We stopped at Target for some household things, and we all got popcorn too. We needed something at Rite-aid, so we walked over to that part of the mall, but it did concern me as I knew that store was very close to the pet store. The last thing I wanted to do was to "remind" the kids of what had happened.

But after Rite-aid, one of them suggested we all go to the pet store. I honestly don't remember which kid suggested it, but I do remember we had a consensus and they all wanted to go in—if anything, they liked seeing all the fish in the tanks, and sometimes there were iguanas or hamsters they liked to watch running through their cages. The pet store didn't regularly have a supply of puppies, so that made the decision easier.

We went in and there in the front of the store sat an adorable little blond puppy. The kids ran over to him and gushed over how cute he was. He had an entirely different body shape than Kenny, and seemed to have a very different temperament as well. I'm not sure if this is an attribute for a puppy, but he just seemed very "laid-back" and relaxed.

The kids fell in love with him immediately. "Please Mom! Can we get him?" Ryan looked at me with pleading eyes and desperation on his face. "Please Mom! Please!"

The other kids joined in with their pleas. With my heart still overloaded with guilt over Kenny's death, I said yes.

Sigh. We brought the new puppy home, and Kyle became a new member of the family. How could I say no?

KYLE WAYNE

All the kids were ecstatic we had gotten another puppy. Ryan named him "Kyle." "Kyle? Why did you name him that, Ryan?" I asked. Ryan would always tell me he just "thought of" these names, but I discovered years later that he was naming the dogs after the characters on the TV show "South Park." I don't think he wanted me to know he had been watching that show.

I couldn't believe I was now a dog owner again so quickly. I still did not consider myself a "dog person" because I had thought of Kenny as Ryan's dog, and I had never formed that bond I had seen people have with their dogs. I did not feel this attachment with Kyle either, because I had adopted him into our home to appease my horrible guilt over Kenny's death. It wasn't that I didn't like him, I was just exhausted, and he seemed like an extra responsibility to me. I had never experienced the love of a pet, and the only reason I agreed to get him was to make my son happy.

The next day the kids were off to school, and there I was alone in my kitchen with Kyle. He was tall for a puppy and had on a new red collar and leash. We didn't want him wearing the blue leash and collar that had been Kenny's—we thought it was bad luck. I washed dishes while I talked out loud to this new little puppy.

"Well, don't worry, I am not going to let anything happen to you. And I will even help take care of you. But I'm warning you, I'm not a 'dog-person' so I have no idea what I'm doing." I swear, on that first morning, Kyle and I had a mind meld. Because he was so mellow, he didn't require much. I could put him in his kennel and he would sleep. Ryan would take care of him when he came home from school. He was a far easier dog than Kenny had been, and didn't require the same amount of attention.

It wasn't long after that a friend visited with his neighbor who lived about two blocks away. His name was Ross, and he absolutely loved dogs and he had a Great Dane named Kilo. Ross immediately took to Kyle, and stopped over several more times to play with him. One day he asked if he could take him to his house to play with Kilo. I said yes, and from that day forward, Kilo and Kyle became best friends.

Ross was a cabinet maker who worked out of his garage to build cupboards and cabinets. Kilo was relentless in trying to get his attention during the day, so Ross wanted to have another dog over to keep Kilo occupied while he worked. It turned into a perfect arrangement for me, Ross, and for the dogs! Every afternoon when I picked up Kyle, Ross would tell me to bring him back over the next day. And so it went.

Every morning I made my kids their school lunches. Then they all piled into the car—all three of them—Ryan, Hannah, and Kyle.

I drove to the elementary school and dropped off my kids, then I drove over to Ross' house. I left the engine running as Kyle bounded out of the passenger side of the car while I opened up Ross' gate for him to run inside. As I returned to my car, I would hear Ross' delighted voice welcoming Kyle. "Hey Kyle!! Hey Buddy!!'" I would drive off and start my day.

After school it was a similar routine: pick up the kids from elementary school, then swing by Ross' to pick up Kyle. Ross insisted that having Kyle over was helpful to him, so he didn't want me to pay him or compensate him in any way. But I thought of the perfect thing!

Ross was a bachelor, and definitely not much of a cook from what he had said. Each week, I had three meals prepared in to-go containers before I left work on Friday. There was always Spaghetti and Meatballs and Lasagna, his two favorites. Then I would throw in one other dish, usually Lobster Ravioli. I packed them all up with some of our famous bread.

When I got to Ross' house in the afternoon, sometimes he would be off installing cabinets. His door was never locked (because he had a Great Dane, after all) so I would walk in and put the food directly into his refrigerator. Sometimes Ross would not realize I had brought the food over, so we came up with a system. I would always pass by his office, and take something off his desk and place it on his office chair, whether it be a pen or pencil, or a stack of post-it notes. That way Ross knew immediately when he got home if there was some delicious Italian food waiting for him in his fridge. This system worked out great for both of us.

One day my kids were watching a movie called, "Jury Duty." A character in the movie was named Carl, Carl Wayne. His friend kept calling out his name with a strong Southern accent. It sounded more like "Kyle Wayne," so we added onto Kyle's name and dubbed him "Kyle Wayne."

Kyle Wayne felt like a "shared dog." Because of all the love and attention Ross gave to him all day long, he was exhausted by the time I picked him up at the end of each day. When we got home, I would feed him, and then he would pass out for the night. I made sure he had everything he needed.

Kilo and Kyle were best friends for 8 years until 2006. That year I moved to the Belmont Shore area of Long Beach to be closer to my business and my aging parents. It would no longer be convenient for me to take Kyle over to see Kilo every day. Ryan went off to college, and Kyle was now "my dog."

But still, he didn't feel like "my dog," he felt more like Ross' dog who slept over at my house.

THE POLKA DOT DOG

I still did not feel like a "dog person." I didn't have that strong bond with Kyle I saw with other owners and their pets. I don't know why it never developed for us. I can only surmise that he spent so much time at Ross' house, that he seemed more like Ross' dog. He only came to my house to eat and sleep.

Even though I did not feel I had that special connection that I saw with other pets and their owners, I still took very good care of him. I spent most days during the day time at home working on paperwork for the restaurant, and Kyle always rested at my feet. And I hired a guy to pick him up twice a week so he could hang out with other dogs.

Every night after work, I brought him home some meatballs or chicken from La Strada. He especially loved any leftover lobster bisque—I would pour that over his dry food and he adored it. I know some people say never give "people food" to dogs, but Kyle loved everything from La Strada, and it didn't hurt his life span at all—he lived until he was almost 16 years old.

A few years into living at my new house, we had a good routine going. I spent the day at home with him. And he slept during the evenings when I was at work.

One day in 2010, I woke up feeling very depressed and not sure why. It happened to be St. Patrick's Day. This holiday held little meaning for me because I wasn't Irish and I would never eat Corned Beef and Cabbage—that dish looked so awful to me. My restaurant was always slow on this particular day, because everyone was patronizing Irish pubs and restaurants. I always highlighted all of our "green" dishes, such as Penne al Pesto, just to make it more fun.

I had to force myself to do my usual chores and paperwork. But as I went about my normal day, I suddenly had a thought. I don't remember at all why this idea popped into my mind, but I decided it would be fun to somehow paint or dye Kyle and make him into a green dog for the holiday.

Of course, I would want to do it safely, and not actually use paint, but I wondered if there was something else that would do the trick. I looked it up on the Internet. Food coloring. Green food coloring was the way to go. Perfect! I went to the closest grocery store and bought two packages of food coloring—I wasn't sure how much I would need.

I found an empty spray bottle, filled it with water, and added the green dye. I spread out an old blanket outside, and started spraying Kyle with the solution and then brushing it into his fur. Kyle loved all this attention and all this brushing; he had no idea he was slowly being turned green. After he was completely green everywhere, I put on his leash and we headed up to walk on 2nd St., the business corridor of my community.

He was a hit! Everyone loved seeing a green dog. One lady yelled at me that I harmed him by putting "chemicals" on him, but she was drinking a green beer, and I noted to her I had used the same "chemical" that was used to turn her beer green. Later in the evening, we went on another walk and passed by some inebriated young men. One just stopped and stared at Kyle. "Wow," he said. "I'm so drunk I think that dog looks green." It was a fun night.

I left Kyle green for about a week, and then had to hose him down in the shower—the color came off easily.

The next holiday coming up was Easter. I thought it would be fun to again dye Kyle another color, but Easter isn't known for any specific color, mostly just pastels. Suddenly I had another great idea! Polka dots! Polka dots in Easter colors.

Using cardstock, I made a template by cutting out a circle. I put the template on Kyle, and then brushed various colors into each circle. I now had a polka dot dog! I again walked him on 2nd St. Everywhere we went, children would stop to pet the polka-dotted dog. Besides being a fun thing for me, Kyle adored getting all the extra attention.

Every October I entered Kyle in the local dog-costume parade, and my niece Marissa would walk with me and Kyle in whatever coordinated outfits I had created. One year I ordered dresses that represented the game, "Twister"—they were covered in symmetrical rows of red, blue, yellow, and green circles. Marissa and I were going to wear them with glossy red boots. I painted those same colors on Kyle, and I painted his feet, and half-way up his legs, with red to match our boots. We were a big hit!

I then created a theme every year.. One year we did a patriotic theme and I dressed as the Statue of Liberty, Marissa wore an all-American outfit, and we painted a flag on Kyle. Another year I wore a Gumby dress, and Kyle came along dyed orange to resemble Pokey. He always loved all the extra attention.

After Kyle died in 2014, I decided I would never again get another dog. I didn't want to be responsible for taking care of anything anymore. I had raised my kids and looked after my elderly parents. I took care of all my customers and the young people working for me. And I had taken care of Kyle.

I knew I would never, ever, get another dog again; that was not part of my future.

But . . . then . . . What happened?

LOVING YOUR BOYFRIEND'S DOG MORE THAN YOU LOVE HIM

My daughter, Hannah, had warmed up to Kyle, but she was similar to me, and had not really become a "dog person" either. In 2019, she lived about an hour's drive away from Long Beach where she attended law school. She began dating a man who owned a gray Frenchie, named Pepe.

Hannah did not like Pepe. She didn't like it when the boyfriend brought his dog over. She would send me text messages: "Ugh! He brought the dog over again. It smells weird."

"Ew, the dog was in my bed and laying near my pillow."

"I don't know why he puts the dog on the bed."

Then, sometimes, he would leave the dog at her apartment while he went to class. Her text messages began to change: "He left Pepe here while he went to class. It hasn't been too bad. I felt lonely and Pepe kept me company."

A few weeks later, I started getting this type of message: "Darn, he took Pepe back home with him. I wish he would just leave him here with me." And then, "I miss Pepe so much!" It seemed my daughter had fallen in love with the dog. In fact, more in love with the dog, than with the boyfriend.

They eventually broke up, and I don't think Hannah really missed the boyfriend at all. But she definitely missed the dog. And so began her love for dogs. And mostly, her love of Frenchie's. She began following several Instagram accounts that featured Frenchie's, with their goofy and fun antics.

Within a year I got this text: "Mom, I'm going to get a dog." I couldn't believe it. But I was so happy at her excitement.

Soon, a new litter of Frenchie's had been born, and were featured on one of those Instagram accounts. She looked at the account every day, to see which puppies had been adopted, and which ones were left behind. She hadn't been sure yet if she was totally ready to adopt a dog.

But day after day, on the Instagram account she was following, the same little black Frenchie was passed over, and finally, all of his brothers and sisters had been adopted. He was the only one left. Every day after, another photo of him was posted with the caption, "I hope I find my furever home soon!" By the third or fourth day of no one coming for him, she could no longer bear it.

"Mom, I made up my mind. I'm going to go get that little black dog."

"Are you sure honey?"

"Yes, Mom, I'm sure."

And . . . she did.

MY GRANDDOG

A few days later, I drove to Santa Monica to meet her new puppy. I had to admit he was very cute. And she was so very proud. And having a dog to care for suited her very well—it was a good responsibility for her to have. And she just adored him; that was very clear.

I had a friend whose daughter also had a dog. My friend referred to her daughter's dog as her "Granddog." I thought that was sort of dumb and ridiculous. It was a dog, after all, and not a human. It wasn't really a "grand" anything. But I jokingly began to call Hannah's puppy "my Granddog," and then . . . guess what?

Karma got me. The name stuck. Now all I could call him was "Granddog!"

It didn't help that Hannah was taking forever to decide on a name for him. Finally, she settled on a name: Finley. I decided to look up what the name, "Finley," meant. I could not stop laughing when I read the definition: Finley means "a fair-haired child, usually of Scottish descent." And here he was, "a dark-haired child, of French-descent."

Hannah always did things in her own unusual and quirky way. And he actually did look like a "Finley," but I just couldn't call him Finley. Because from the first day forward, he was "Granddog" to me. That was it.

LETTERS FROM FINLEY

The time came when Hannah asked me to watch Finley for an entire weekend. Of course, I said, yes! I watched him very carefully; I didn't want anything to happen to him.

After the first day, I decided to send my daughter a report on how it was going via text message. But it suddenly clicked in my mind to write the message as if Finley was writing it directly to her. As I wrote it out, I felt like I could hear his voice in my head. I sent this message to Hannah:

Dear Mommy,

I hope you are having fun.

I went on four walks today and got to see the Bay and 2nd St. This is a pretty nice place.

Grandma ate something with a spoon and she wouldn't let me have any of it.

Then Grandma forgot she had to go somewhere so she left me in my pen for a little bit. She said she was sorry about 100 times. I let her know it was OK by licking her face when she came home.

OK, I have to go get ready for bed now. I love you!

Love, Finley

The next day I sent:

Dear Mommy,

Today I played Hide and Seek with Grandma. I was only hiding a few seconds, but she sounded so nervous I came out of my hiding place. Geeeez. Good thing you left me here to take care of her while you're gone.

It's not that I'm not missing you, but I'm OK if you leave me with Grandma again.

I was really worried I had the wrong kind of Grandma, but today she really came through with the treats and presents.

BTW, Grandma never stops talking. I'm trying to get used to it, but I don't know how you could stand it for 18 years.

Your loving son, Finley

And then I just kept going:

Good morning Mommy,

Grandma and I were on a walk earlier and went past the orange ball place. Grandma took two of them out of my mouth. She then checked my mouth about 25 more times, and said we will go a different way next time.

Grandma keeps calling me Kyle by accident. She told me all about him and how he ate meatballs and lobster bisque. She says I can't have that because "Times are different now" whatever that means. I was really starting to think this Kyle had a way better life than I do. But then she rambled on about how she painted him green and put him in polka dots. Wow, what a sad life he must have had.

Grandma put me in my pen while she was eating. That's OK, I will look for crumbs later.

She keeps calling me her new roommate.

But I'll be nice to her, because I'm a respectful grandson.

OK Mom, I'm doing the best job I can to take care of her.

I love you!

Love, Finley

"A LAB/SHEPHERD/MYSTERY MIX"

One night I went to a local eatery for dinner; I decided to sit at the bar which I didn't usually do. I met a man named Bob. He told me his dog had died a year before and he said he was thinking of getting another one.

He added, "I think I am a better human when I have a dog." I thought that was an interesting observation.

I had been watching Hannah take care of Finley for almost a year now, and I had admired her love for him. And I had grown very attached to him myself. I really enjoyed having Finley visit. I decided to throw the idea of "maybe" getting a dog out into the universe, and see what happened; I always believe in "signs."

A friend said, "if you're meant to get a dog, your dog will find you."

I went to the Long Beach animal shelter one day and a nice volunteer walked me around. I didn't feel connected to any of the dogs there, and I left feeling bad for all of them. It was the beginning of the new year, and I mentioned the dog idea on Facebook as part of my list of New Year's intentions: "Maybe I'll get a dog this year."

A Facebook friend, Lisa A., posted a photo of six puppies that had been found in a box in Tijuana, Mexico—their mother had died after being hit by a car. The puppies were being fostered by a couple that rescues pregnant dogs and finds homes for all the puppies.

I drove to the home of foster parents, Marsha and Don; they had a green tarp spread out on their living room floor, and the puppies were running all over everywhere. They had no idea what breed they were—they called them a Lab/Shepherd/Mystery mix. Don said, "they're like Heinz 57 sauce—who knows what's in there!"

All six of them had the exact same body shape and size. But they were all different colors: two looked like German Shepherds, one was white, one was medium brown with a black patch around its eye, and there were two that were "your basic tan." I sat on the floor learning all about dog rescue from Marsha and Don, while I interacted with the puppies.

I didn't want either of the darker ones because I wanted a dog that looked very different from Finley. They suggested the brown pup; they said she was very photogenic. Oh, that would be perfect for me! With all my storytelling and picture-taking, it would be great to have a dog that liked that sort of thing. I scooped her up and tried to get to know her, but she had no interest in me and just kept running away.

One of the tan ones came over and was sweet, but she was SO yippy-yappy. I didn't want a dog that never stopped barking. Marsha pointed to the other tan one and said, "she never stops playing with that same toy. She loves it. And that is a real sign of intelligence." I liked that.

I went over and picked her up. She seemed just right. I took a picture of her and she didn't seem to like it, but I figured that must all be in my head because how would a dog know I was taking a picture, right? I told Marsha and Don that I would probably take her, but I needed a day to think about it. It seemed to be happening way too fast for me. Maybe I wasn't ready, or maybe I wasn't sure.

I drove home and could not stop thinking about her. After only an hour had passed, I knew. My dog had found me. I called Marsha and Don and told them I would take her.

A couple days later, I drove to La Habra and picked her up; I put her in a laundry basket lined with a pink blanket for the drive home. And I named her Gracie. Gracie Mae.

She was my very best New Year's intention.

SURVIVING A PUPPY

To say I was not prepared for a puppy was an understatement—I had envisioned "looking into getting a dog" maybe in the summer. But there she was! The lack of sleep was expected, and I adjusted to it faster than I thought, but I did have a raging headache every morning—it was nothing that my friend "Excedrin" could not remedy. One time I did want to take her back, but I thought that was actually really good that it was just the one time.

I couldn't have done it without Hannah—she had immediately ordered all this stuff I would need, and had it delivered to my house. I would have been lost without her. And she gave me tip after tip of what worked with Finley. I also watched some training videos—some were helpful. But one lady with seven dogs illustrated how she was training her new puppy, and her dog acted perfectly. I wanted to find the videos on "training a puppy, that acted like a puppy."

But we did make some progress. At first if I left the room, she panicked, so I had to take her everywhere. It must have been an adjustment to be away from her siblings and her foster parents. But over time, she had learned to trust me, and knew I would always come back. So, we established quite a routine, and I was determined she was here to stay.

Over the first week, I lost two pounds. Why? Because she was so glued to me that it wasn't even fun to eat. This was an unexpected bonus.

I thought we had made it through the hard part. Boy, was I wrong!

It turns out, this journey had barely begun.

SCABIES, ANYONE?

After a month or so, I finally adjusted to having a puppy around. But my skin was breaking out everywhere. My whole body became incredibly itchy. I thought it was probably an allergic reaction, as I have had many of those in my lifetime. But during the night it became so intense that I actually ran a bristle brush over my entire body—everywhere!

I looked on the Internet at every possible rash and nothing looked like what I had. I knew it couldn't have anything to do with Gracie, because I had had her for five weeks, and this had only been going on for a week. Finally, I could no longer bear it, and went to the doctor. She took one look, and I said it was worse at night. She stopped me right there. "You have Scabies."

What??

"You most likely got it from your new puppy."

"But I've had her for five weeks. She was terribly itchy when I got her, but they treated her and she's fine."

My doctor pointed at her computer screen, and I read: "For someone getting scabies for the first time, the symptoms do not appear until four to six weeks after exposure." Oh. And I'd had her for five weeks.

Holy crap!

Having Scabies is like having lice. I had to wash every blanket, towel, pillow, couch cushion, every fabric and fiber in my home. Everything needed to be vacuumed. I even used my clothes steamer across my mattress and sofa to kill any bugs or eggs with the heat. I took Gracie to the vet, and they gave her a shot of Ivermectin, which would stop her from getting Scabies again (I could now pass it back to her).

After all of that, I took a shower and applied an entire tube of this medicated cream over my whole body. It said not to miss the soles of your feet or your entire scalp. And that's exactly what I did. I didn't want even one of these ugly creatures to continue to live on me!

The next morning, all the bedding needed to be washed again. The good news: the mites are killed by the medicine. The bad/disgusting/gross news: even though the bugs are dead, it's their "waste" under the skin that causes the itching. So that had to continue for one-two weeks until my skin eliminated their "waste."

It was bad enough knowing I had creepy-crawlies living all over me. But the idea of all this crap in my skin made me want to throw up. I know there is a reason for all creatures, but I cannot figure out the reason for this disgusting thing called Scabies.

After 15 loads of laundry, moving all the sofa cushions to the garage (all the mites die in three days), spraying an entire can of Lysol on the base of the sofa, and throwing out the area rug in my dining room, I was on the road to recovery. I'm so lucky to have a house with extra rooms, because I moved into Hannah's room while mine sat empty for three days with everything completely washed (just to be sure).

Gracie kept looking at me, seemingly confused, as we went in and out of the laundry room for days. She seemed to be saying, "Why are we doing everything differently now?"

I must have said to her twenty times, "Because, sweetheart, you brought me a disease from Mexico."

But then I always added, "But that's OK, you didn't mean to."

I still loved my little Gracie!

FINALLY, SOME TIME

You would think I would have all the time in the world after retiring, but that's not the case when there is a puppy involved. Those first few weeks I had carried Gracie all over the house because she seemed so scared. And then the scabies situation took about two weeks for the "cure" to take effect.

The lack of uninterrupted time had affected my ability to write, and that depressed me. It's so important to me to feel like a productive human, and writing makes me feel that way.

When I had my restaurant, La Strada, I used to sit at the very back table until way past 11PM, with the door locked and the lights off. The only sound was the constant hum of the refrigerators. I would write for hours, editing a story to get it just right. Then I would head home and search for just the perfect picture to go with it. I did the same late-night story-telling when I traveled. Each day I looked forward to returning to the peace and quiet of my hotel room to write about the day's events.

But everything had been different since Gracie arrived. There were no long periods of uninterrupted time. I had to check on her frequently to make sure she was not into some kind of mischief. I had a friend who suggested, "she's a dog, put her in the backyard, she'll be fine." I couldn't do that. She would eat everything, and I didn't know which plants were poisonous. And a few times she had gotten into the laundry room and made a meal out of socks and underwear. I didn't want to have an emergency vet visit.

I tried to put her in her crate twice a day, but I used that time for errands and appointments. But writing stories? It became almost impossible for me.

I heard about a training program, but I just kept thinking, "I should be able to figure this training stuff out myself." But really, I was horrible at it. I watched videos, but nothing seemed to work the way it did with the dogs on YouTube.

It finally dawned on me, "Hmmmm, I didn't homeschool my kids. Why do I think I can train a dog?" So, I put her in a puppy school, and I was so grateful I could do this. The trainer at the school reassured me she was one of the sweetest dogs he had ever met, which I was so happy to hear since I had been worried that maybe she wasn't.

I was so excited to finally have some time to myself. It was peaceful just to eat lunch without her staring at me. And I could finally get back to my passion of writing. But just a few weeks into puppy school, Gracie developed a very contagious virus. Even though it was harmless, I had to take her out of the school. She was back with me all day again. I had mixed emotions. It's not that I didn't love her, but I had been downsizing my life in a way that there were fewer things I needed to take care of.

After a few weeks when she was well, I felt conflicted about sending her back to the school. I had enjoyed her being gone for a few hours a couple days a week, but I was having trouble following the training methods of the school. The main trainer was a lot like Cesar Milan (the Dog Whisperer) on his TV Show. He would make those "Tch! Tch!" sounds to correct her behavior. And I was supposed to do that as well, but I just couldn't. I felt like a military leader when I tried.

I decided to just keep her at home and have a positive attitude that I could make it all work; I was determined I now had a handle on everything.

I didn't.

STOP BARKING!

After about three months, out of the blue, Gracie began this incessant barking. A friend asked me, "Why do you care if she barks? Dogs are supposed to bark." But it never stopped. In the front yard, Gracie barked at nearly everyone, in a horrible way, thrusting towards them like an attack dog. Everyone told me she was being protective, but she just seemed mean to me.

When she was in my living room with my big picture window, she barked at almost everyone walking by. In the backyard, she barked at things going on in the alley outside my property gate. When taking a walk, I had to avoid all other people and animals because I didn't know if she would lunge at them.

So, I couldn't sit in my front yard or my backyard, or on my sofa in my living room, or take my dog on a pleasant walk. I could accept many things: scabies, potty training/waking up all night, chewed up sandals, cost of training, etc. But this new incessant barking? No.

I startle very easily; sudden noises make me jump and disrupt my nervous system. And her barking sparked fear in me—the same fear I had as a child. I had been afraid of all pets: cats, dogs, lizards, probably even my brother's turtles.

So, Gracie's constant sudden barking startled me all day and made me a wreck. And I worried she was becoming a mean attack dog. I constantly felt frustrated and like I didn't do things the right way with her. Someone told me she was even more scared than I was. I felt confused and like I was completely failing her, and myself.

Remember that man I'd had dinner with a few months before? The one who said, "I was a better human when I had a dog." I was finding I felt like a lesser human when having a dog, and I began to wonder if maybe I was not equipped to do this.

I loved her most in the mornings and the evenings because she was calm and sweet. But was that enough? No matter how cute she was, I felt like I was losing my sanity. Everyone told me it would get better in two years.

Two years??

I didn't think I could make it that long. And honestly, I didn't think I had the right skills to do it. And I missed my writing. I felt like my writing was what made me a better human being. Not a dog.

Now what?

I'M NOT AN ALPHA

I never had an alpha-type of personality, where I was the leader in a group of friends or colleagues. I was forced into an alpha role at 33 when I became the head of my household, raising my children by myself. I did feel confident being in charge at my restaurant, La Strada, although there were definitely things that were really difficult for me to handle.

But I didn't know what to do with this new continual barking problem with Gracie, and I was afraid she would turn into a mean, jumpy dog. I can't stand dogs like that, and owners who think it's OK to let their dog jump all over you.

Everything I read said I needed to become her leader, be stricter, be more routine, make her know I was in charge. But instead, I became completely overwhelmed and scared; there was no room in my brain or my psyche, to somehow suddenly become an "alpha."

The training school had been OK, but I needed an individualized approach. I hired a different trainer, named Tiara. She arrived and I asked her to first be my therapist. She was more than happy to do that, and even said it was part of her job. She sat right down and listened. She let me know I was not alone in having difficulty in dealing with a puppy: 35% of dogs do not grow up in the first homes in which they start. Many people struggle with the early part of dog ownership, but no one likes to talk about it.

Tiara let me know it was OK for me to be me. It was OK to take my time. I wasn't the only one. I immediately felt relieved. She never put down anybody else's way of training, but she let me see a different way. I didn't have to close my drapes so my dog wouldn't see people going by. I didn't have to sit in a more dominant place on my sofa. I didn't need to talk to my dog less.

I could still be me, and she could still be a wonderful dog. What a relief!

After an hour together, Tiara said, "She is not aggressive at all. She is fearful. And she is nervous. And, she is 10 times more nervous because she knows you're nervous." Tiara noted that Gracie had been with me three months, and that is when puppies realize they are home to stay. They get protective and are unsure what to do when someone new approaches their home. They start barking out of fear, and look to their owner for guidance.

This helped me so much. I'm a person who handles things and situations better if there is some sort of logic involved. I know that isn't always possible, but it's better for me when things make sense. And this made sense. Gracie wasn't mean at all. And what I described as her, "lunging," was her being completely fearful.

Tiara gave me practical tips and actions I could take for situations when there was no hope of me "changing my energy." Everything we did together seemed to work, and I felt hopeful and peaceful again.

This one-on-one training worked better for me than the training in a group setting. I began to have more confidence. But I never could have imagined owning a dog would be this much of a roller coaster ride.

THE BEST MEDICINE: NURSE GRACIE

Another person had told me, when you are really sick, you will appreciate having a dog with you.

About four months after I got Gracie, I started to feel more worn out than normal. My throat hurt a little bit. My daughter, Hannah, said, "Mom, you should take a Covid test."

"But I don't have a fever—that's one of the main symptoms. And I can breathe just fine."

"Mom, just take the test anyway. I have one; I'll bring it over."

Hannah brought me the test and I took it.

"See? I don't have it." I didn't see any lines at all.

"Mom. Look again. The line is very faint but it's still there. You're positive."

"Where? What line? You mean I had the cataracts fixed in both my eyes and I still can't see a little line?"

"Mom!"

Then I saw it. "Oh, that? You can barely see it." My god, I must be so annoying.

So yes. I was on a new unplanned adventure of Covid. The lethargy was no fun—there was no way I could walk my 10,000 steps a day. I could barely do anything at all; I was so very tired, just completely exhausted. I lay on my couch most of every day. I was so grateful to have pain meds for my sore throat.

Through it all, Gracie never left my side. For the next five days I laid on my couch, barely moving. Gracie got right up to snuggle next to me, almost the entire time. And she didn't bark at anyone going by. All of her attention was focused on me. I recovered, and I realized something really wonderful happened while I was sick.

I finally fell totally in love with my dog. I knew for certain she was now here to stay.

THE LISA-METHOD

Remember when someone told me, "It gets easier when they turn two?" When Gracie turned two, our life together had gotten better. I had gotten even more training—some of it worked for me, but some of it I just could not do.

This is what I learned: There is really strict dog training, there is no dog training at all, and then there is something in the middle. I chose the middle; I created the Lisa-method. It would not be considered ideal by most dog trainers. But I have come to accept this fact.

I know professional trainers are there to help you learn what is best for the dog, so the dog will have better behavior. This will give the dog confidence, and the understanding their owner has control and authority. This is what they want and need, it's what they crave and is their natural way of being.

Dogs like to follow a leader. They like to have a schedule. They like to know what is expected of them. I understood all of this. But I learned I cannot possibly do everything that is best for my dog. I had to do some things that were best for me. I tried to fit into the mold of what the trainers suggested. But I was so unhappy to the point that it no longer became fulfilling to own a dog.

So, I implemented a modified version for me and Gracie. We have somewhat of a schedule: we go to bed and get up at the same time usually every day. And after we get up, and she goes out in the yard, we return to my room where I do some writing. All the experts say I should do a minimum 20-minute walk every morning. I don't want to do a walk then; I love my dog, but that is when I do my best writing.

We do go on an hour and a half walk later in the day. And no, it is not at the same time every day as I was told would be best for her. Because it isn't best for me.

And most trainers say your dog needs to quietly greet you when you return—it's not good for them to get amped up and excited when you come home to them. But . . . why would I want to train a dog to show no excitement? I made the decision that I want my dog to be happy to see me. I let her be excited for a minute or two when I return.

It was also suggested I should not talk to her as much as I do—she doesn't understand what I am saying anyway. Well, so what if she understands or not? I like talking to her. It's part of who I am. So, I continue to do that too.

Choosing to do things the way they work for me, has made me more confident and relaxed, so Gracie is now less nervous. Sometimes I do feel a little guilty for not following the advice of all the dog "experts"— maybe if I followed all of their rules she would be an even happier, more fulfilled dog. But I would be an unhappy, and unfulfilled, dog owner.

Sometimes I will tell her, "Sweetheart, I know I'm not doing everything right. But I'm here for you as you are for me. You're stuck with me. And even if I get it wrong, look at it this way: you could have lived your life as a street dog in Mexico where you were born. But you're now here with me, an imperfect dog owner. I think we're OK."

Does she know what I'm saying? Of course not. Does it matter? Of course not.

And, remember that very first day I met her, when she seemed annoyed that I took her picture? And I thought what I saw was all in my head, because how could she possibly know what I was doing? Well, she never changed. She still looks away every time I try to get a picture of her. She doesn't like it. But I make her pose anyway. It's OK. We have an arrangement. She knows. She knows I have to do the Lisa-method.

Remember what I said at the beginning of this book? There's a difference between "normal" and "average."

"Average" is just how most people might do things. But, you are still "normal" even if you do things a bit differently.

I am happiest doing "Lisa normal."

I am happiest being me.

TURNING INTO AN "OLD LADY" (WHAT I LIKE TO CALL IT)

I VOWED TO BE A COMPLIANT ADULT

We learn so much from our parents, don't we? Even if it is not the intended lesson.

Neither of my parents were good at accepting their aging. "Dad, let me get you a cane. I think it will really help you."

"I don't want a goddamn cane!"

Months later, "Dad, why don't you let me get you a walker?"

"I don't want a goddamn walker!"

And when he could no longer drive his old beat-up stick-shift truck, we bought him a brand new automatic one. We loaded up a bunch of the grandkids in the back, and drove up his street, honking as we pulled up to the curb in front of his house. He opened his front door and stood there on the porch while the grandkids waved and yelled, "Surprise, Grandpa!!"

He stared sternly for a few moments and then walked back in, slamming the door behind him. "I don't want a goddamn new truck!"

We have so many stories in our family about how difficult my parents were in dealing with getting older; the stories now seem rather humorous, even though that wasn't true at the time.

My mother had been even more difficult. She had early onset dementia, and it was hard to tell what was wrong at first. And she also fought all our efforts to help her as her condition worsened. And my father made that situation difficult as well.

My mother reached a point of having very little quality of life. She didn't know who anyone was, she didn't speak, or appear to understand anything. And I often wondered if she was afraid deep down inside. I remember telling both my kids, "when I get like Grandma, put me away somewhere." My son famously said, "Don't worry Mom. We will put you somewhere BEFORE you get like Grandma."

I loved it.

Fast forward to more recently. When I visit Hannah in Santa Monica, I take her dog, Finley, on a walk, and I always go past this assisted living facility. One day I said laughingly to her, "honey, if I ever end up like Grandma, you could put me in that place around the corner."

"Uh, Mom," she said. "Don't get mad, but I've already thought of that." Then she added cheerfully, "Finley and I could come visit you every day!" I loved that too.

I vowed to be the most compliant old person ever (I would try!) And I have my parents to thank for this amazing gift.

DR. HANDSOME

In my late 50s, I started noticing I wasn't as strong as I used to be, even for very small tasks.

For instance, I could not unscrew the bottom of my blender to clean it properly.

I tried everything to unscrew it—I used one of those little rubber things, I tried a towel . . . I even took out a hammer and tapped the ridges on the bottom, until I decided that was probably not a very good idea. I felt so old and feeble.

The outside of my house was being painted, so I went out and asked the painter if he could unscrew the blender. I was secretly hoping he wouldn't be able to get it off either; then I could pretend that nothing was really wrong with my arm.

He paused for a second and then simply unscrewed it. No problem.

I had already heard from others that I probably had a torn rotator cuff. But I just kept avoiding doing anything about it. My cousin Patty, a nurse, told me to get it fixed as soon as possible. She explained that if I didn't, I would start using my arm less and less and the muscles that aren't torn will atrophy over time. Ugh. I knew she was right.

It felt weird to me to be so weak because I was always a really strong girl. Not athletic, but strong. When I was a young teen at Rogers Junior High School, we had to do all these things in gym class to get the presidential fitness award.

There was always an arm test; one year it was pull-ups. You only had to do ONE pull-up, but most of the girls could not do even one! I could do a zillion. The next year they changed it to the "bent-arm-hang." You were lifted up into a pull-up position, they let go, and you had to hang there for some allotted amount of time, maybe 20 seconds. Almost every girl would just fall off! I couldn't believe it; I could hang there all day.

Now I wondered if I could even hang there for one second.

One day, my arm would no longer bend how I needed it to and I couldn't zip my dress. I thought about asking the mailman to zip it for me—he usually came to my house around 4PM which was just the time when I would be getting ready for work. But then I was worried he would start coming by at other times to see what else needed zipping (or unzipping).

The pain continued getting worse and worse and I could barely lift anything, I couldn't carry anything heavy, and I had to maneuver this way and that to avoid more pain. I said, "OW!" about a hundred times a day.

I finally made an appointment with an orthopedic surgeon. The day came. I sat in the little room and waited for the doctor. There was a quick knock, then the door opened and the doctor came in.

Wow! He was really attractive, and close to my age. Suddenly my arm didn't hurt so much.

Dr. Handsome (his new name) examined my arm and asked some questions. He predicted it was indeed a torn rotator cuff, which is actually a shoulder injury that involves the muscles that connect your arm to your shoulder. I still continued to call it my "arm problem." He gave me paperwork to get an MRI so he could see what was going on inside my shoulder.

A couple weeks later I returned to Dr. Handsome's office with my test results. I wore a pretty dress and heels, of course. I sat down and crossed my legs.

Dr. Handsome walked in and was even more handsome than on the last visit. He didn't wear a white lab coat; he was dressed in a nice suit with a crisp shirt. I'm sure he did that because he knew I was coming in—I love men in suits!

He explained I had two major tears, plus a bicep tear that were pretty serious. He said this injury is caused by frequent overhead movements, like a pitcher would make. He asked me if I had been playing tennis lately. I could barely keep from laughing. I had no interest in tennis, nor was I pitching any balls.

So, he asked if I had been doing anything else that was an overhead swinging motion. No, I hadn't done anything with an overhead swinging motion.

How about a repetitive motion for an extended period of time? Well, I told him, I had recently bleached the white grout on my bathroom floor. I would apply bleach and cleanser and scrub all the cracks over and over. I had probably scrubbed it for two full hours.

He seemed surprised at my answer, as he suddenly looked away from the screen, stared directly at me with his gorgeous smile, and said, "Well, you must have the cleanest floor in the world."

I smiled, and batted my eyelashes at him. I was probably the first person he had met who had torn their rotator cuff from cleaning, and not from sports. I'm sure he was impressed. He explained that 20% of the population my age have this same injury, and most live with it without any problem. But the surgery was recommended if you were in pain.

I explained my difficulty in zipping and unzipping my dress. I demonstrated by turning to show him the back of my dress, and how I just could not reach the zipper to get it unzipped. This had absolutely no effect on Dr. Handsome, which surprised me.

Because my pain had gotten worse, I agreed to get the surgery. But I had a major trip coming up, so he gave me a cortisone shot in my shoulder to help with the pain until I returned. It worked.

A few weeks later, I made it home from my travels and went for my pre-op appointment with Dr. Handsome. This time I wore a red dress, and a little higher heel. This was not a foot injury, after all.

Dr. Handsome asked how my trip had been. "Great," I said, "I got to meet family I didn't know before, and I saw the Rolling Stones, twice."

"Twice!" he exclaimed. "I've seen them once, at Desert Trip a couple years ago."

Wait, what, WHAT???

Dr. Handsome went to Desert Trip? And was a Rolling Stones fan? I had hit the jackpot. I thought he would be more of the golfer type . . . I was thrilled he was a music fan.

I resisted pulling out my phone and showing him all of my awesome concert videos. I didn't want Dr. Handsome to think I was weird or anything.

I sat poised in my chair with my legs crossed, showing off my pretty high heels while we discussed the surgery. My mind began to wander and I wondered if the surgical gowns would be available in one of my best colors. Hopefully blue or a shade of green. I had recently worn a paper gown for a completely different doctor, and I thought the navy-blue color of that gown really accentuated my best features.

Dr. Handsome turned toward his computer screen to study the images of my torn muscles—they looked like large fluffy balls of white cotton candy. I did find it a bit disconcerting that he seemed more interested in my MRI photos than he did in my red dress and heels. *This could be a problem in our relationship,* I remember thinking at the time.

I tried to look interested as he explained "arthroscopy" and "debridement." Whatever you say, doctor.

I was not looking forward to the surgery because every single person told me it was horrible, awful, the worst pain ever, blah, blah, blah. But the day came. And I lucked out—the surgical gown was a gorgeous blue and I really did look quite fabulous in it. Dr. Handsome came over in his scrubs to say hello before I was given the anesthesia. His scrubs were also a shade of blue, and I kept thinking what a cute couple we made. I could only hope he would be able to concentrate on the procedure once I was put under.

The surgery was successful and I was now in the recovery room. The nurse there explained how after surgery I should begin eating some simple foods like yogurt or soup.

My brother, Fred, was there to drive me home. As we headed out, he told me he had gone to a donut store while I was having the procedure. Now all I could think about was donuts. "You want to go get a donut, don't you?" he laughed.

"Of course!" I said. And off we went to the donut store. I had no interest in soup or yogurt.

I was very lucky. I did not find this surgery or this experience to be as difficult as everyone had said it would be. But also, I had done everything that was suggested to make it smoother: icing it, pain meds, even a special recliner I rented for a month to help with sleep.

But a week after surgery I could not stay in my house for another moment. I decided I would go into work for a bit, just to see how things were going. It took me a long time to get ready because I only had the use of my left hand. My right arm was safely in its sling. But I got ready and put on a pretty dress and shoes, and walked the half mile to work. I only lasted 45 minutes before feeling woozy; I had to be driven home by an employee.

The next day was my post-op appointment with Dr. Handsome. He was happy to hear I was already off the pain meds, and he began to give me his speech of directions by rote. He probably has to do this all the time: "Wear your sling in social situations, you can take it off if you are sitting on the couch, but wear it if you are doing housework just to remind yourself not to move your arm in the wrong direction . . ."

As I listened, it suddenly became apparent to me I was just another shoulder to Dr. Handsome. He didn't even mention how lovely I had looked in my hospital gown, or how nice I now looked in my sling. He continued to be way more interested, and even excited, to reiterate to me what he discovered once he was doing the surgery—about my "full tear" in my rotator cuff, and how my bicep tendon was actually "exploded." He lit up while talking about it.

I had to accept it. Dr. Handsome was clearly way more turned on by my shredded muscles than anything else. I decided that maybe our relationship was one-sided.

Goodbye Dr. Handsome. It was good while it lasted.

ARTHRITIS, UGH!

I was in a state of denial.

My big toe had been bothering me for more than a year at that point. It was the upper joint, and I figured it was not a big deal. It was just one toe.

Even though it was mostly just "annoying," I figured maybe I could get it fixed. I had my shoulder (rotator cuff) repaired by Dr. Handsome. So why not do the toe too, right?

A nurse practitioner had once told me, "It's because you wear high heels. You should stop wearing them."

Hahaha, OK, do you really think I'm listening to you? I was not a high heel wearer my whole life, but I certainly had been since around age 45 (after my pole-dancing classes).

So, I mentioned it to Christine, the physician's assistant I had seen for years. "It doesn't really hurt when I'm just sitting here. It only hurts if I bend my toe in any way."

"Hmmmm . . . How would you feel about getting an x-ray?" she said, with a nervous look on her face. You could . . . possibly . . . have arthritis, and then, well, if you had the x-ray, you would know."

"Oh. Ok. Well, is that another 'old-age' thing? Everyone gets it, right?"

"No, not everyone. And you may need to take certain steps to address it."

"OK, let's do the x-ray."

I didn't mind an x-ray; and I wasn't even thinking about what the "certain steps" could be. I headed off to the x-ray room with Gilbert. He posed my foot this way and that. He commented on how beautifully done my nails were—they were an exquisite purple on that particular day. Gilbert told me that all of the x-rays were digital, and they would be ready in a matter of minutes, so I would get the results right away.

He walked me back to the examining room to wait for Christine. So . . . I waited.

The door opened, and she walked in. She looked so serious it seemed like she was about to give me a cancer diagnosis. "I looked at your x-rays," she paused. "You do have a 'more than significant' indication of the beginning of arthritis."

She looked at me with sad eyes. "I can give you a recommendation for a podiatrist, in case you want to get some inserts . . ." She braced herself.

Inserts?? Inserts??? INSERTS???? My head began to spin. "Inserts??" I said, "A podiatrist, to get inserts?"

I was not even sure what an "insert" was, but it sounded like it would only go with the ugliest shoe imaginable. Definitely not some beautiful sleek and sexy red high heel with a pointy toe and a spiky heel. I imagined an "insert" would look like something to put into a nurse's shoe.

I must have looked horrified. She said, "I had to mention it." OK.

I gathered up my purse and sweater and basically ran out of the room. "Bye Christine!! Thank you!!!" I yelled over my shoulder.

Inserts. No. No one was going to make me into an old lady. Not yet. I was just not ready.

I WAS A FRAUD AT THE PODIATRIST'S OFFICE

I made an appointment with a podiatrist, just to ask his thoughts on my arthritic toe. And I sort of went into his office, well, in a "fraudulent" way. I wore sneakers.

I had had arthritis in my big toe for a few years now. I felt blessed that it didn't get in my way very often—I could still walk and travel, and it only hurt when it was pulled or bent a certain way.

But it had seemed like my arthritis had been "spreading." I know that is not the right word, because arthritis doesn't exactly "spread," but it did appear to be creeping up, and over, on my foot.

BTW, arthritis happens when the cartilage between your bones wears away—cartilage is there to keep everything running smoothly. But once it's gone, your bones are rubbing against each other, and all the nerves nearby are not happy about it.

So, regarding my fraudulent behavior: I arrived at my appointment in a dress . . . and these little pink sneakers. I didn't want to get in trouble with the doctor.

I know the fashion rules have been changing, and they always show ladies wearing dresses with white sneakers. They have even renamed the white sneakers, calling them "trainers." I think that's dumb—what are you "training" for?

I just don't think it looks pretty, or feminine either, to wear sneakers with a dress (just my opinion). So, I NEVER wear sneakers, unless I am on some kind of hike.

I always wear pretty wedge-type sandals, usually with a 3-inch heel, and sparkly straps across the top. I knew this would not be acceptable to a podiatrist who I was seeing for arthritis. Hence the reason for the sneakers.

I was led into the examining room. I sat in the chair with my feet prominently displayed in the little pink sneakers. The doctor came in, and I took them off—after all, they were for appearances only—I wanted to get an "A" in "arthritis."

The doctor gently moved my toe very slightly. I wasn't expecting what he said: "You have almost no range of motion, it is very advanced." What??

Advanced?? Usually being "advanced" would be a good thing, right? But I knew it wasn't in this case.

He listed my three options:

1. Let the bones naturally fuse together and over time the pain will go away.
2. If it's too painful to wait, have surgery to fuse the bones now. But this would mean I could never stand on my tip-toes again, because my toe would never again bend at that joint. (I didn't want to give up my "tippy-toes!")
3. Have a joint replacement.

He would not do number 3 because replacements only last 15 years, and he thought I was too young for that.

"If I do nothing and let the bones fuse together on their own, how long will that take?" I asked.

"Oh, not long," he said. "Probably only about five years."

"Five years?!!? That's not a long time?" Well, to him it wasn't, and that's what he thought I should do. Wait it out.

He said, "once the bones fuse, you can still do everything." He added, with a huge smile, "even wear a 2 or 3-inch heel!"

Ugh. I guess he thought that would thrill me—apparently he had never attended the Belmont Shore Christmas Parade and watched me walking in my 5–6" parade heels!!

He suggested I get this specific brand of shoe, Hokas, basically an ugly sneaker, so I decided I would get them for long walks, where almost no one would see me. He also explained there is this anti-inflammatory medicine you can take when you might need it, like when you go on a trip where you will be walking a lot.

I got the medicine. The Christmas parade was only three weeks away. I decided I would take it that day, just in case. Because come hell or high water, I would be walking the entire parade route . . . and I would not be caught dead in a 2 or 3-inch heel during a parade.

I have standards.

But what about all of my beautiful high heels? Initially I gave a few pairs away. I then put a few favorite pairs on a shelf as part of a display—they were both red satin, and covered with rhinestones; I had worn them in Christmas parades. They do illustrate an important part of my past after all.

And all the other pairs? Oh yes, yes, yes, I still wear some of my other high heels if they are just perfect with a particular outfit. But it's rare now.

Oh, and "inserts?" I never got them. I'm still not even sure what those even look like.

BILL M. CAME TO MY RESCUE

I had closed my restaurant business, La Strada, after 27 years. It was a planned closure—I thought it was time to move on to a new chapter in my life.

I was so happy I did not have to go to work every night, or deal with plumbing issues or employee problems.

But a few weeks later, I just didn't feel quite right. I didn't miss all the problems in my business: plumbing issues, customer complaints, staff issues, equipment malfunctions, etc.

I thought I would wake up and feel absolutely glorious every single day, but in thinking that, it had now become the problem. I expected every day to be some magical, memorable experience, something extra special like the way you feel when you have a "day off." Because now, every day was a "day off."

But every day just ended up feeling "flat" overall. Let me explain.

I usually woke up in good spirits. I followed my routine of making coffee and catching up on emails, and then doing some housework. I continued my usual pattern of just hanging around in my nightgown all day, like I always had. But then 4PM would roll around; that was the time when I got ready for work: I would do my hair and makeup, then put on a nice dress or sometimes something more casual. And I would head out to work about 5PM.

But now 4PM would arrive, and I would think, "what's the point?" So, I started to just stay in my nightgown.

It didn't take very many days of doing this that I knew I was on the wrong path. So, I began a new routine. After my morning coffee I got dressed, not in anything fancy, but always some nice leggings and a cute top. And I did my hair and threw on some makeup. This did feel better—at least I was more presentable if someone happened to come to the door, like the UPS man.

I had a long list of projects I wanted to start, but I could somehow never get going on any of those. They all felt "too big" and I didn't know where to start. For instance, I have eight boxes of pictures I want to sort and put into folders. But I was always worried that if I began that project and made piles all over a table, it would feel overwhelming and like a big mess. And then I knew I would scoop it all up one night and throw it back in the box. So why even start?

I also wanted to write this book. But where would I begin? Should I print out every story I have ever written? I wasn't sure, I couldn't figure out how to begin. So, I never really started on anything at all—my projects just sat there waiting for me to get inspired. But I could never get there.

Every evening at 5PM or so, I was glad I didn't have to deal with anything difficult, but then the night would seem eerily quiet. It felt like something was missing, but what could be missing? I knew I had made the right decision in closing my business, so what was wrong? Why didn't I feel great, every single day?

I was always happy to go to bed, knowing I would feel more "normal" in the morning, because the mornings were the same as they were before I closed my business.

As I described it, I felt this feeling of "flatness," as if something was wrong, but nothing at all had gone wrong. I just couldn't identify what that feeling was at first. I later came to understand that it came from "not doing anything to help anyone" that day.

I didn't realize that each and every evening when I returned home from work, whether it had been a good night or a difficult one, I had accomplished something. I had helped somebody; I had improved someone's life in some small way, even if I just chatted with them for a few moments, or brought them a new shaker of Parmesan cheese.

A dear family friend, Bill M., came to my rescue. His daughter, Megan, had reached out to me asking how I was doing. I told her the truth.

"Not very well," I answered. "I don't know what's wrong with me. I should be happy, but I can't find joy anywhere. I don't feel 'right', or like doing anything at all. It's not that I don't have enough to do—I just can't do it."

She told me that her father experiences this malaise every year after tax season. He is an accountant, and works long hard hours for months, and then when April 15th hits, he always feels out-of-sorts and grumpy. He has learned to never plan anything for two weeks after tax-time, because he can't mentally shake it—she said he described it as more of a "physical adjustment."

I asked if I could call her dad—she said yes, and sent me his number. Bill answered cheerfully; I think he was expecting me. I described what was happening with me.

He said, "well, you just summed it up perfectly. This is exactly how I feel every year, 'flat.'" He went on to talk about adrenaline.

"Just think about all that adrenaline running through your body for the last few months. Even if you stayed home one evening, and left the kids running the restaurant, YOU were still running the restaurant. And all you needed to do to get another hit of adrenaline, was just to 'think' of your restaurant."

"OK," I said. "But I knew this was coming and I was excited about doing whatever I wanted to do."

"Sure. But it's like having a baby. You don't know what it's like until you actually do it." Well . . . that is definitely true!

He continued, "You'll get there. Your body needs to even out. And how are you with change?"

"Not very good at all."

"Well, sweetheart, I was pretty sure of that, but didn't want to say it until you did. That's another part of this—you know, 27 years is a long time."

"Also," he said, "be nicer to yourself. Don't forget that you're beautiful, capable, intelligent, and successful. This is a rebirth."

I thanked him over and over, and told him that he should be a psychologist. He credited his age and wisdom. I texted his daughter and told her that her dad was a genius. Bill gave me back a piece of myself that night.

STILL CAN'T GET "RETIREMENT"

I was grateful to Bill M., the accountant who helped me out a few weeks after I closed my business.

He thought I was going through a normal adjustment time of several "super-adrenaline months," and needed to adjust to learning how to survive without that.

In typical "Lisa-fashion," I made note of the "two weeks" he said it took him to adjust, and put a big circle on my calendar, exactly two weeks after the date I spoke to him. In my mind, that was the day I would magically be all better.

Hmmmmm. That didn't happen. I still didn't feel right. Soon it was months after I had closed my business.

My old friend Matt, and his wife Kris, invited me to stop over for a drink up the street. We chatted and I explained the general malaise I continued to feel, as if I am somehow lost. He said, "I've seen this many times. This is normal considering the change in your life." (He is a local practicing psychologist.)

He explained that what makes up peoples' identities is their spouse, their family, their job, and maybe a serious interest they have, like a certain sport. If any one of those are disrupted, your life balance becomes skewed (this is my understanding, and not his exact words).

"For you," he said, "You lost your husband long ago, and your kids are grown. So, La Strada was a huge part of your identity."

"Well, I know," I said. And then I started all of my "Buts."

"But I didn't like my job anymore."

"But I knew this was coming."

"But I chose this."

"But I like being at home and getting caught up on projects."

He looked at me and said, "It doesn't matter. YOU were effectively La Strada. It was YOU. Now it's not there. A piece of you is missing and you feel it everywhere. You need time to readjust. Give yourself that gift." He added that he had seen people take a year to adjust after leaving their jobs.

A year????

Ugh, I did not like hearing that. At this point I decided I would really rather be friends with Bill the accountant, than with Matt.

"I could have told you a long time ago, that you were not cut out for retirement." I can't stand when people are right and I didn't see it. So now what?

Believe me, Matt offered plenty of hope, and many ideas. I realized I needed to stop catching up on these little things around the house, and start being more focused on my "reinvention" as Bill M. called it.

I started writing more and more. And I kept my eye out for new adventures, and ways to celebrate life.

Very slowly, and without me really noticing it, this feeling of flatness and being lost, started to go away.

MY MEDICARE BIRTHDAY

Milestone birthdays can be difficult; some are harder than others.

For my 21st Birthday—I didn't mind (or care about) turning 21 at all. I did not drink at that time, or want to, so it really didn't mean anything significant to me.

My 30th Birthday—I was blissfully happy, newly pregnant, with a just-starting-to-show belly. I couldn't wait to be a mother.

40th Birthday—I was content. My kids were 7 and 9, and these were great times for me as a mother. We flew to Seattle to surprise my oldest and dearest friend, Michele, at her surprise party (our birthdays are two days apart).

50th Birthday—Ugh. I really struggled with this one. Who wants to be 50??? But I talked to a friend who was older than me, Candy W., she was 52 at the time. She told me, "Don't worry. Once you get to the other side, it will all be OK."

She was right.

Once the day came, and I turned 50, it was all just fine. Life returned to normal.

And just like turning 50, turning 60 was so hard for me too, I can't remember why. That year I decided to throw myself a party. Why not? But the whole theme of my party that year was about how I didn't want anyone to know how old I was.

I even put it on the invitation: "Shhhhhh! Don't tell anyone how old I am!!

But now, I was approaching my 65th birthday. I had been thinking about it a lot, and wondered if I should do anything special to celebrate.

Of course, turning 65 meant it was time for Medicare. That sounded like such an "old people thing." But turning 65 was even more significant for me. Because of my mother.

I remember, so clearly, my mother's surprise 65th birthday party— we held it at my restaurant, La Strada. We had enlarged a beautiful photo of her, from when she was 16 years old; we had it on display. She and I stood there together, very quietly, looking at the photo.

I remember she was trying to be so nonchalant, as she stared at the image of her 16-year-old self. But soon her eyes filled with tears, and she said wistfully, "I still feel exactly like that, like her. I still think I'm 'her' . . . I'm still 16, I'm still her."

She didn't quite know how to explain what it was like to be 65, and yet still feel like you were 16 years old. It was a soft, quiet moment of recognition and realization.

I never forgot that look on my mother's face. Especially, because only a couple years later, her long road of dementia would begin. And this illness would take away the real "her."

But on that night, of her 65th birthday, she was still healthy, and she actually WAS still "her," still my mother. I wondered if the same thing might happen to me. What if I began on the road to dementia in only two more years? It became clearer to me, more than ever that it was so important to celebrate every moment I could.

So . . . I decided to celebrate my 65th birthday in a big way, the same way my mother did—full of life and looking forward. She had no idea how sick she would become, and I knew I didn't know my own future either. I celebrated with my wrinkly, veiny hands, that look exactly like my dad's, and threw myself a block party.

I called it my "Medicare Birthday Party." The very first thing I did was to hire a Rolling Stones tribute band called Jumping Jack Flash, to perform in my front yard. I had seen them many times, and the members of the band are local guys in Long Beach.

There were so many other things I needed to do to make it all happen. In order to invite the whole block, I needed to get a permit to have my entire block closed for two hours. And I needed to get 60% of the residents to sign off that they were OK with the block closure. I went from house to house knocking on doors and collecting signatures.

I had to rent the signage and blockades to be put up at each end of the block, and I needed to pick up all those signs and blockades the day before, and return them the day after. Then I made a flyer, and invited everyone I knew, and all the neighbors on my block.

I had food catered from a local Mediterranean restaurant, and plenty of drinks of all kinds. I even made my own sheet cake, the kind I always made for the Customer Appreciation parties I had held at my restaurant every year, a buttery yellow cake with decadent buttercream frosting. And I topped the cake with a custom "edible image" of a giant Medicare card with my name on it.

I wore my Rolling Stones mini-dress, along with my red-hot sparkly boots. It was just perfect. And it was the right thing to do.

Because . . . "Time waits for no one."—Mick Jagger, Keith Richards

MY "FLAWLESS" SKIN

When I look at my arms, I see old wrinkled, freckled skin, and I have the same deep-veined hands of my father.

Growing up in sunny Southern California, it's a given that it is a good idea to get what is called a "full body scan" by a dermatologist. There is no machinery or equipment involved, the doctor simply puts on special super-magnifying glasses, and "scans" your skin from head to toe to look for any abnormalities.

This skin check is to make sure all that "fun-in-the-sun" we had as youngsters has not morphed into something more dangerous (skin cancer).

In my hometown of Long Beach, almost everyone went to see the same doctor, the renowned dermatologist, Dr. Kane. It was an easy appointment every year, as she is a super kind lady, and I was always in and out of there pretty quickly after she stared at my face and arms, and everywhere else, wearing those big bug glasses.

"See you next time!" she would say.

I never needed anything on my skin tested or "burned off" or treated in any other way. I had seen several people in my age group post pictures on social media of how they had had biopsies or other procedures done where larger portions of their skin were removed and the areas were all stitched up. Their motivation in posting these photos was always to warn others about too much sun exposure.

At some point, Dr. Kane retired. I decided to stay at her office, and see one of her associates. That appointment had gone quickly, just like they always had. And while the doctor was nice, after I left I did not remember his name or what he looked like.

When a year passed I returned for my next scan. They scheduled me with the same doctor I'd had the year before. The doctor walked in, and said "I remember you!" I found that strange because he had only met me for about 10 minutes and that was an entire year before.

So, I asked, "How can you possibly remember me from a year ago?"

He answered, "I don't remember names, but I remember faces. And what I REALLY remember is skin. And I completely remember YOUR skin." I was flabbergasted as to what was memorable about my skin. Especially since I didn't remember him at all.

"Oh," he said, "I remember you so well because your skin is practically 'flawless.'" OK, now I REALLY liked this doctor! He didn't see my old wrinkles and freckles, and the deep-veined hands I inherited from my father. He was seeing something that was unusual for a person my age.

Because I was always an "indoor person," I have almost zero skin issues. I had some bad sunburns as a kid, but I only "laid out" to get a tan a few times, and did not spend copious amounts of time outdoors. This really paid off for me.

I was now beaming at this doctor—what a great guy! He then looked at my legs and said, "your legs are perfect, just beautiful." OK . . . I know he was only referring to my lack of skin issues/spots/cancer. But, still!

Any man who tells you your legs are beautiful, while you are standing there in a paper gown . . . Well, he might just be the next doctor I fall in love with.

I walked out of that office feeling like I had just won a beauty contest. Thank you doctor. I can return next month if you'd like, no need to wait a whole year.

WHAT IS A CATARACT ANYWAY??

I had promised my children that I would be a very compliant older adult. After everything my siblings and I had to experience with our parents' difficulty accepting their aging, I knew I wanted my children to have a better experience.

But I wasn't expecting to suddenly begin encountering all these different "old people" things. But now here I was, and it was beginning to happen.

When I was in my early 60s, I had a brand-new experience—I went to the eye doctor.

I was always blessed with wonderful eyesight. I don't know if it was perfect, but I never needed glasses. Once I was in my 40s, I slowly started moving small print further and further away from my face in order to read it. Then, one day, that no longer worked.

I bought some inexpensive reading glasses at the drugstore. Those worked just fine for many years.

But there came a time when I was driving to Palm Springs at night, and I was alarmed at how blurry my vision had suddenly seemed to become, especially in one eye. What was going on?

I made an appointment with an eye specialist immediately. I did this not only because I had been scared while driving, but because of my vow to be a graciously aging adult.

I arrived at the doctor's office and completed the paperwork. One thing I really liked about this doctor's office was that you didn't have to get on the scale!

They put me through a lot of tests, and put tons of potions in my eye, but nothing really hurt. The doctor came in and he did a quick exam. He was fairly gruff, and to the point. But that was fine, as long as he was an expert at eyeballs.

And he was actually very attractive, but I certainly didn't need to fall in love with every doctor, like I had with Dr. Handsome, who fixed my rotator cuff. The doctor sat back and said the words: "You have cataracts. In both eyes."

He began to explain and give me the benefits of cataract surgery. But I politely stopped him and said, "I will take the first available surgery appointment you have."

My father had cataracts, and he had refused the surgery. He had to be almost completely blind before he would even consider it. This was an easy decision for me. I did not want to be difficult like my father had been.

Back to the eye doctor . . . I repeated, "I will take the first available appointment you have." I think he was surprised. More than likely he had to try to talk people into this surgery. I could only guess he came across many fearful (or stubborn) patients.

While I was there, I also learned a lot more about cataracts—I honestly did not even know what they were—I only knew they developed as you got older.

So, what is a "cataract?"

It is a blurring of the fluid in the lens of your eye, and it usually develops very slowly. Mine happened very quickly. During the surgery, they remove the fluid and put in a new artificial lens.

I went to my pre-op appointment and learned something exciting—I could get a "corrective lens." I had absolutely NO idea that was even possible. It was exciting to think I might not need reading glasses anymore! I had grown quite used to them over the years, and they were sprinkled throughout my house, and in my car. I usually had several pairs in the bag I took to work every evening. And, if I forgot them, I would just look in our Lost and Found and use a pair of reading glasses someone else had left behind.

I signed the paperwork, and read the preop and postop instructions. I laughed when I read this one instruction: "You can do simple exercises like walking or yoga, but strenuous exercises or headstands must be avoided." What? Who was doing a headstand after they got surgery??

The day arrived for my surgical procedure. I arrived at the surgery center and everyone was so very nice and accommodating. They asked when I had last eaten and I answered "8AM," just as I had been instructed. I had even put a post-it note on my refrigerator to remind me in the morning; it said, "DON'T EAT!!!" because I was nervous I would forget!

But then the nurse asked WHAT I ate. Really? Why? "I had oatmeal and a protein bar." She wrote that down. I continued, "And, you will probably think this is weird, but I also had Brussel sprouts." Both of the nurses started laughing, and said they had NEVER had anyone say they had eaten Brussel sprouts before 8AM. Of course, I had to explain that I eat two cups of them every day because they are an easy-to-microwave, low-calorie vegetable, and I wanted to get them out of the way. They wrote it down.

When another nurse came over, they told her, "She had oatmeal and a protein bar before 8AM, but you will never guess what else she had for breakfast!" I was glad I could add some levity to their day.

When I met with the anesthesiologist, I told him I wasn't nervous or anxious, but that I am a very fidgety person . . . My daughter can barely watch TV sitting next to me. The doctor ordered me a Valium. I'll take it!

With this procedure, you are awake, but "comfortable." They need you to be able to do what the doctor tells you to do during the operation. During the procedure, I couldn't feel anything, but he did tell me more than once to stare at the three bright dots. He also had to remind me many times to keep still (even with the Valium).

After that I went to the recovery room and I didn't have to stay very long before they discharged me. My sister Julie came to pick me up. She greeted me with, "Hello Arden Junior!" We both laughed.

Arden was our father's name, and her reference was probably due to two things: one, the giant black sunglasses I had on, and two, the very strong resemblance that she and I both have to our father, especially when we look serious, pale, and are not smiling. And that's probably how I looked as I got into her car.

I had been determined to go get a donut afterwards, but I changed my mind and ordered take-out from Super Mex.

Everything was blurry, but that was to be expected. My dog, Gracie, was thrilled to see me, and was attached to me all night.

The post-op directions said not to wash your hair or face for a week, but I didn't plan on following that instruction. But at least I was able to keep myself from doing a headstand!!

Very soon after that when I was at a follow-up appointment for the surgery, I signed up to have a second cataract surgery on my other eye. It was not as bad as the first one, but cataracts will never get better on their own, so I decided to get it done as soon as possible.

My experience the second time was not as smooth as the first; I had a different anesthesiologist. During the procedure I could feel them "prop" my eye open. It didn't hurt, but it startled me and I jumped somewhat. The doctor took quick note, and asked why I had jerked in that way. I said, "this feels different than last time."

They immediately upped my medication. I was glad I had spoken up. It was soon over; I was out in no time and eating my graham crackers in the recovery room. My sister picked me up for the second time, and we again went to Super Mex for my cheese enchiladas.

When I got home, my son called. I chatted with him as I was walking around my house. I walked into my kitchen and said, "Oh My God!"

"What Mom? What is it?" he asked. He thought something was wrong.

"Oh nothing, honey! I just can't believe how bright my kitchen is! I always thought it was dimly lit! But it looks like 20 light bulbs have been added." I looked around in awe. "Wow, it's so beautiful in here," I thought, and my kitchen was not really that beautiful. But, after cataract surgery, everything in life looks brighter, crisper, and just all around prettier.

The next day I went back for the required post-op appointment. I sat quietly in the little room waiting for the doctor; he was running a little late. I wondered if I should apologize for sort of flinching during the procedure; I remembered it seemed like he reprimanded me a bit. But I wasn't sure if I was remembering correctly, because my brain was foggy with the anesthesia.

Finally, the doctor came in. He said hello and studied the computer screen. Then he turned to me. "You were an excellent patient. You did great."

"Oh," I said, "I wasn't sure." I was about to continue, when he said, "I want you to know that it is my job to protect you, and make sure you are safe. Sometimes I use a stern voice to make sure you aren't moving when I need you to be still. I only have a millimeter or two that I am working in." Then he repeated, "You were a perfect patient."

Ok. I felt good after that. I always want to get an A+ in everything. And . . . any man saying he is protecting me, makes me swoon. I floated out of there on air. Are you single, doctor?

EPILOGUE

I hope you have enjoyed this small glimpse into my life.

I continue to live and write my stories in Belmont Shore, a community that is part of Long Beach, California. My dog, Gracie, is usually by my side.

Part of my writing now consists of a series called "Block by Block" which details the businesses in our corridor, one block at a time.

I also keep busy with any and all activities put on by our local business association, The Belmont Shore Business Association, which represents the businesses on our beloved 2nd St. I attend, and write about, any new businesses opening their doors on our street, or celebrating a noteworthy milestone.

I also write as a volunteer for various Long Beach organizations. I tell the stories of the Scholars chosen to receive Scholarships from a prominent community group. And I joyfully volunteer for a program that helps young women who have achieved sobriety, go to college. I love telling their stories as well.

I am so happy to have discovered the gift of "writing stories"—it brings me so much joy. Please keep in touch!

You can reach me at LisaRamelowAuthor@gmail.com.

Or follow along on my stories on Facebook: https://www.facebook.com/akindnessiwillneverforget/

Or Instagram: https://www.instagram.com/lisaramelow/

Thank you kindly for reading along.

Much love to you, Lisa

ACKNOWLEDGEMENT

This book exists because of the help and support of one person.

In 2004, I owned and operated my restaurant, La Strada. On a quiet afternoon, a young lady, quite statuesque, walked in wearing a lovely pale blue suit. She had an elegance about her, even though she was quite young. She seemed to have a quiet confidence.

I don't remember the interview or what I asked her. But I hired her on the spot simply because of her energy. There was just something about her. She told me much later that she had been completely uncomfortable and unsure about looking for a job on 2nd St. But I had made her feel welcome and that she belonged.

She became a favorite of both staff and patrons. Her name was unusual; it was Umoh.

I was embarrassed at how many times I had to ask her how to pronounce her name. She graciously said I could call her by her middle name, Anne, but I didn't want to do that—it felt dishonoring in a way, as she was clearly proud of her heritage. Her father was Nigerian and her mother was American, so she had a Nigerian first name and an American middle name.

Umoh had this special skill I had never seen before in any of my staff. She said "goodbye" to everyone.

I had never before seen anyone so intent on bidding farewell to each person leaving the restaurant, be it a customer or another staff member. It didn't matter whether they had been dining at one of her tables or not. She seemed to have a sixth sense of anyone heading to the door, and would slowly pause and turn, and cheerfully call out, "Bye! See you again!" or something like that.

I found it strange at first; I wasn't sure why she thought that was important to do, although she was clearly doing it because it came from her heart.

And then one day, I came across a list of "The Top 20 Things Important to Restaurant Diners." Most items on the list were things I thought were obvious like "good food" and "good service."

But I was rather shocked when I saw #4 was: "Say Goodbye to everyone. It is the last interaction with that customer and will wrap up the entire experience."

What??? And it was #4 in importance? I had never realized the importance of doing this. And yet Umoh did it so naturally. She loved thanking people and wishing them well as they departed.

Fast forward many years, and many experiences. Because of social media, I can now keep up with my past staff members. I always enjoy seeing they have married or had children. I realize some of them are in their 40s or even 50s, and yet they are still in their 20s to me.

I have watched Umoh's journey of how she created a business for herself, helping women create and complete projects that were important to them. She did this not only by giving them guidance and support, but also with marketing help and business advice. And she included a spiritual element over all of it.

This is what I needed. I had written over 2,000 stories and wanted to figure out a way to put them all together in a book, in a way that made sense.

And there was something else that made Umoh perfect for my endeavor: She "knew" me. She understood who I was as a person. And

Umoh had worked for me, she had watched my kids grow up, and had known both of my parents.

In the ensuing years she had followed my stories on social media, and remembered many of them because she had actually been there when they were happening. So, I reached out to Umoh to avail myself of her unique talent.

And now . . . this book, *Misadventures in My High Heels*, is here. And I could not have found a way to put it together without Umoh's love, kindness, and support. Oh, and her cheerleading—Umoh is a great cheerleader for your soul.

Thank you from the bottom of my heart, beautiful Umoh.